HANDBOOK OF APPLICABLE MATHEMATICS

MATHEMATICAL METHODS
IN
SOCIAL SCIENCE

HANDBOOK OF APPLICABLE MATHEMATICS

Chief Editor: Walter Ledermann

Editorial Board: Robert F. Churchhouse
Harvey Cohn
Peter Hilton
Emlyn Lloyd
Steven Vajda

Assistant Editor: Carol Jenkins

Volume I: ALGEBRA
Edited by Walter Ledermann, *University of Sussex*
and Steven Vajda, *University of Sussex*

Volume II: PROBABILITY
Emlyn Lloyd, *University of Lancaster*

Volume III: NUMERICAL METHODS
Edited by Robert F. Churchhouse, *University College Cardiff*

Volume IV: ANALYSIS
Edited by Walter Ledermann, *University of Sussex*
and Steven Vajda, *University of Sussex*

Volume V: GEOMETRY AND COMBINATORICS
Edited by Walter Ledermann, *University of Sussex*
and Steven Vajda, *University of Sussex*

Volume VI: STATISTICS
Edited by Emlyn Lloyd, *University of Lancaster*

MATHEMATICAL METHODS IN SOCIAL SCIENCE
David J. Bartholomew, London School of Economics and
Political Science

HANDBOOK OF APPLICABLE MATHEMATICS
Chief Editor: Walter Ledermann

MATHEMATICAL METHODS

IN

SOCIAL SCIENCE

DAVID J. BARTHOLOMEW

Department of Statistical and Mathematical Sciences
London School of Economics and Political Science

A Wiley–Interscience Publication

JOHN WILEY & SONS
Chichester – New York – Brisbane – Toronto

British Library Cataloguing in Publication Data:

Bartholomew, David John
    Mathematical methods in social science—(Handbook of applicable mathematics).
    1. Social sciences—Mathematics
    I. Title   II. Series
    510′.2′43   H61   80-41593

    ISBN 0 471 27932 3 (cloth)
    ISBN 0 471 27933 1 (paper)

Typeset by Preface Ltd, Salisbury, Wilts.
Printed in the United States of America
by Vail-Ballou Press Inc., Binghampton, N.Y.

Contents

Editorial Note

The *Handbook of Applicable Mathematics* is chiefly addressed to persons who have had little or no academic training in mathematics but who, perhaps at a late stage of their careers, find it necessary to master mathematical concepts and skills that are relevant to their professional work.

We have therefore presented in this Handbook all those topics of mathematics which, we believe, are at least potentially useful in other disciplines. The mathematical material is arranged in six *core volumes* bearing the titles

   I   Algebra
   II Probability
   III Numerical Methods
   IV Analysis
   V   Geometry and Combinatorics
   VI Statistics

However, we feel that a mere collection of mathematical articles is not sufficient for our purpose. Very often the same branch of mathematics (matrix algebra, statistics, differential equations) is required in quite different contexts arising in disparate professions. In order to assist the members of those professions to identify the appropriate mathematical tools we are publishing a number of *guidebooks* of which the present volume is one. Each guidebook discusses why and how mathematics is needed in a particular profession or group of professions. It does not, as a rule, contain detailed expositions of mathematical techniques or results. These will be found in the core volumes, to which the guidebooks will make frequent reference. The two components of the Handbook, that is core volumes and guidebooks, are designed together as complementary aspects of a work which reflects the universal validity and importance of mathematics in our society.

To achieve our goal it is essential to have an efficient reference system at our disposal. This system is explained fully in the 'Introduction' to each core volume; we repeat here the following points. The core volumes are denoted by the Roman numerals mentioned above. Each mathematical item belongs to one of six categories, namely

   (i)   Definitions
   (ii) Theorems, propositions, lemmas and corollaries
   (iii) Equations and other displayed formulae
   (iv) Examples
   (v) Figures
   (vi) Tables

A typical item is designated by a Roman numeral followed by three arabic numerals $a.b.c$, where a refers to the chapter, b to the section and c to the individual item enumerated consecutively in each category. For example, 'Theorem IV 6.2.3' is the third theorem (or proposition or lemma or corollary) of section 2 in Chapter 6 of the core volume IV. We might also have 'Equation IV 6.2.3', the same numbers being possible for items in different categories.

The style and scope of the guidebooks will inevitably differ in accordance with the level of mathematical expertise required in the profession it is intended to serve. But we trust that each guidebook will enhance the usefulness of the set of core volumes which provide the reader with the mathematical information he seeks.

Preface and Acknowledgements

Mathematics is a relative newcomer to social science, which means that there is no established canon setting out what a practitioner should know. The author of a book such as this is therefore faced with the difficult task of deciding where to draw the boundaries of the subject. The decision is, inevitably, a personal one influenced by one's own predilections but there is, nevertheless, a coherent view behind the choice presented in the following pages.

In brief it is that to be scientific, sociology and its near neighbours must be empirical and hence that the collection, analysis and interpretation of observational data are central to the quantitative approach. For this reason the mathematics involved is, very largely, that required for understanding the relevant statistical methods. The variability of individual behaviour and the need to rely on sample data make probability theory the cornerstone of the edifice.

In its positive aspect this line of argument may not be contentious but it does less than justice to the pioneers of the formal mathematical approach to sociological theory as given, for example, by Peter Abell (*Model Building in Sociology*, Weidenfeld and Nicolson, London, 1971). Neither does it include the interesting, if controversial, attempts to use catastrophe theory [see V, Chapter 8] to model qualitative social change. These developments may prove to be of lasting significance but, as yet, they have not unequivocally proved their value in the sense of having contributed to substantive research findings.

This volume was originally planned as a joint venture with Dr Warren K. Bartlett, a psychologist, of the University of Melbourne. Under that arrangement it would have covered psychology as well and so would have resolved several potential demarcation problems. For example, both social psychologists and sociologists are interested in the structure of inter-personal relationships. The recent literature of mathematical sociology contains a good deal about the use of graph theory [see V, Chapter 6] and other modern algebraic methods in this field. In this case we decided to adhere to the allocation of topics between the original joint authors and regard these as being on the psychology side of the border.

Although long distance collaboration eventually defeated us, Warren Bartlett was an equal partner at the planning stage and to him especially my thanks are due—also to Colm O'Muircheartaigh of the London School of Economics for giving me the benefit of his expert knowledge on survey methodology.

London   D. J. Bartholomew

1

Introduction

This guidebook is intended for the social scientist who wishes to follow the mathematical arguments in the literature of his own subject. It is designed to be used in conjunction with the core volumes, to which frequent references are made. The emphasis is on the formulation of problems in mathematical terms and on identifying the techniques necessary to solve them. Inevitably, therefore, it gives a very selective view of social science in general and its quantitative aspects in particular. Many substantively important questions are treated briefly because their mathematical content is slight; conversely some by-ways get more attention than their intrinsic importance justifies because of their mathematical interest.

The term social science is used here to avoid the arbitrary limitations of subject boundaries within the social sciences. However, the focal point of the discussion is in sociology, interpreted broadly, and extending into the territory of political science and social administration. Economics, psychology and geography have become highly quantitative and involve the use of many specialized techniques which require separate treatment. Nevertheless, many of the methods discussed in this book are applied well beyond the field of immediate interest and it could therefore be read with profit by psychologists and others—especially the chapter on multivariate methods.

The widespread use of mathematics and statistics in the social sciences is a relatively recent phenomenon. Although many earlier examples can be found, the modern era may, perhaps, be dated from the publication of Lazarsfeld's *Mathematical Thinking in the Social Sciences* (1954). This was both a symptom of a growing interest in what mathematics might have to offer in the social sciences and a powerful agent in developing that interest. The progress of the mathematical approach has matched the growth of the social sciences themselves and entered fields, like history, which were formerly regarded as beyond its scope.

The position of the social sciences thus stands in marked contrast to the natural sciences with which mathematics has had a long and fundamental relationship. In social science, mathematics is a relative newcomer and many of its applications are elementary and often undeveloped. Whereas the training of a chemist or physicist includes a considerable amount of mathematics in recognition of the needs of the subject it is still uncommon for a social scientist to be so equipped. However, the differences are not

1

simply those of age and sophistication: there are important differences in the nature of the subject matter. Human behaviour is an exceedingly complex phenomenon. Many of the basic concepts, like influence and power, are ill-defined and not easily measured. This had led to the search for suitable kinds of mathematics, sometimes with very little to show in the form of clear-cut results. We shall return to this point, but enough has been said to indicate that both the kind of mathematics and the manner of its use is not simply a pale copy of the more highly developed natural sciences. This fact has considerably influenced the style and content of this particular guide book.

A book of this size cannot hope to cover every use of mathematics in social science. We have tried to select the main mathematical themes the mastery of which will provide the reader with the knowledge and the confidence to go further. Each chapter contains references to the basic text books in each of the areas covered as well as supporting references for the techniques discussed. In addition to these specific references the reader should be aware of the main literature of mathematical social science. In sociology one of the main landmarks is Coleman's *Introduction to Mathematical Sociology* (1964) and, more recently, Farraro's *Mathematical Sociology* (1973) provides a comprehensive picture including much of the basic mathematics. A series of books, under the general title *Progress in Mathematical Social Science*, published by Elsevier, has provided a vehicle for the publication of recent research. An early bibliography was given by Holland and Steuer (1969) and a recent review is provided by Blalock (1975). The annual publication *Sociological Methodology*, of which Heise (1977) is a good example contains many contributions using mathematics. The journals *Quality and Quantity* and the *Journal of Mathematical Sociology* regularly publish quantitative articles but it is characteristic of the field that new material is widely scattered through the literature of sociology and its related disciplines. Beyond the range of our immediate concern, but indicative of the kind of developments taking place, is *Time on the Cross* by Fogel and Engerman (1974). This clearly demonstrates how the quantitative thinking implicit in much historical argument could be made explicit in mathematical terms and subjected to rigorous analysis. Much earlier, Lewis Richardson's pioneering work on the study of war and conflict, published posthumously (1960a, b), had achieved similar results in political science.

In the remainder of this chapter we shall develop in more detail some ideas about the particular character of mathematical applications in social science. These are necessary both in order to understand the organization of the chapters and to appreciate the point of view from which they are written.

One of the fundamental problems in social science research is that of classification and measurement. This is true also, of course, in the natural sciences but there the basic units of measurement are well defined. Time, length, mass and electric charge are capable of being measured to a high degree of accuracy. This places the emphasis on establishing relationships between variables and hence on the mathematics of solving equations—measurement is taken almost for granted. There are, of course, many relevant variables in the social sciences whose magnitudes can be easily measured on a numerical scale, for example cost, response time, income or frequency counts. Very often, however, measurement has to be at a more rudimentary level. It may only be possible to classify individuals into a few categories—the so-called nominal scale. Sometimes one can go farther and arrive at an ordinal scale by ranking individuals, or their judgements of some quantity, according to the value of some underlying variable. Examples of the latter include many human attitudes and abilities. The fact that the basic data often take one or other of these forms has implications for the kinds of mathematics which are relevant. Combinatorial and discrete methods are in widespread use, whereas the ubiquitous differential equation of the natural sciences is less prominent.

All of this, however, does not touch on one of the most distinctive attributes of the measurement problem in social science. The quantities which occur in the discourse of the social scientist are often poorly defined and it may even be debatable as to whether they are a proper subject for measurement at all. Things like social class and aggressiveness are frequently spoken of as though they can be measured on a uni-dimensional scale but, in practice, it is by no means clear whether or not this is so or how it can be done. What we usually have are indicators—that is quantities capable of measurement which we believe reflect the values of the underlying variable, however imperfectly. Thus, for example, it is common to speak about the *quality of life* as though it is a measurable quantity which can exist in varying degrees. However, it is a complex notion which does not lend itself to direct measurement and so the problem has to be approached indirectly. There are a great many measurable quantities which relate to aspects of the central idea, like levels of pollutants in the atmosphere, income, housing conditions and so forth. None of these quantities is a direct measure of the quality of life though each of them contributes something to the total picture. The problem is thus to distil an index from a multitude of possible measurements. On the whole it is not difficult to find things to measure in the social sciences; the real problem is how to select and combine the measures available and this is where the mathematical issues often arise. In particular, many of the techniques of multivariate analysis [see VI, Chapters 16 and 17] described in Chapter 4 have this purpose in view.

The body of the book is divided into four chapters, each dealing with one main aspect of quantitative social science. They are arranged, roughly speaking, in order of increasing mathematical difficulty but each chapter is self-contained and can be read without reference to the others. For this reason references are listed at the end of each chapter at the expense of a small amount of duplication. Social scientists using the book will vary a great deal in their level of mathematical knowledge and it would be impossible to provide a uniform level of treatment equally suited to all readers. The more advanced readers will find their main interest in Chapters 4 and 5 while the beginner may not be able to go beyond Chapters 2 and 3. However, we hope that the total picture conveyed by the book will be useful to all readers regardless of where their main interest lies.

Since this is a guide book it cannot be used in isolation from the material, mathematical or substantive, to which it relates. In particular, the reader will need to consult the basic texts on which we have drawn as well as the research literature. To make this easier the style and notation of each chapter has been designed to make the transition to the wider literature as straightforward as possible. This inevitably means the sacrifice of some degree of uniformity of notation and presentation throughout the book. An example is provided by the treatment of vectors [see I, §5.1]. In Chapter 4 a vector is written as a column since this is the custom in most of the main texts on which that chapter draws. In Chapter 5, on the other hand, vectors are written as rows to conform to the convention most likely to be met in the principal references [see I, §6.2 (iv)]. Such minor variations would not trouble the mathematician but the sociologist, unfamiliar with mathematical language, must tread more carefully.

The longest tradition of quantitative methods in social science is in the application of elementary statistical methods to observational data. Much of this is concerned with the description and inference concerning frequency distributions. The mathematical requirements of this are quite modest. More recently, there has been a growing emphasis on attempts to explain patterns of variation in terms of probability models, and this requires a basic knowledge of the elements of probability [see II, Chapter 2]. This ground is covered in Chapter 2.

Chapter 3 deals with various aspects of the collection of data by means of sample surveys. Mathematical considerations arise at the design stage and in the analysis. The chapter is primarily concerned with the design aspect, though the two cannot be separated and all the chapters have something to say about analysis of data whether it arises from sample surveys or not.

One of the main growth areas is the treatment of multivariate data [see VI, Chapter 16] which is the subject of Chapter 4. Social data have always been multivariate but it was not until powerful computers with suitable software became readily available that the full exploitation of the data available to researchers became feasible. The ease with which such analyses can be performed has meant that they have often been carried out by those without the basic understanding of the methodology necessary to avoid the many pitfalls which beset the unwary. Some of the theory is not easy but we hope that Chapter 4 will ease the path of those seeking a better understanding of widely used methods.

The subject matter of Chapters 2, 3 and 4 is largely concerned with a static view of the world in that it typically involves data collected at a particular point in time. There is a large and growing interest in the dynamic aspects of social processes. Here the focus of interest is on the process of change which, in a social science context, is usually unpredictable in some degree. The appropriate tool for handling dynamical systems of which uncertainty is an integral part is the theory of stochastic processes [see II, Chapter 18]. Chapter 5 provides an account of stochastic models used in social science, including their use for prediction and control.

It is no part of our purpose to enter into debate about the relevance of using mathematical methods in social science. This is obviously an important question, but our treatment begins at the point where the issue has been decided in favour of mathematics. Those who take the opposite view will not wish to read further but, we would argue, until the methods and their purposes have been properly understood their relevance cannot be judged.

References

Blalock, H. M. (Ed.) (1975). *Quantitative Sociology, International Perspectives in Mathematical and Statistical Modeling*, Academic Press, New York.

Coleman, J. S. (1964). *Introduction to Mathematical Sociology*, The Free Press of Glencoe, New York, and Collier–Macmillan, London.

Farraro, T. J. (1973). *Mathematical Sociology: an Introduction to Fundamentals*, Wiley–Interscience, New York.

Fogel, R. W., and Engerman, S. L. (1974). *Time on the Cross: the Economics of Negro Slavery* (2 vols), Wildwood House, London.

Heise, D. R. (ed.) (1977). *Sociological Methodology*, Jossey-Bass Inc., San Francisco.

Holland, J., and Steuer, M. D. (1969). *Mathematical Sociology, a selected annotated bibliography*, Weidenfeld and Nicolson, London.

Lazarsfeld, P. F. (Ed.) (1954). *Mathematical Thinking in the Social Sciences*, The Free Press of Glencoe, New York.

Richardson, L. F. (1960a). *Arms and Insecurity*, Stevens, London.

Richardson, L. F. (1960b). *Statistics of Deadly Quarrels*, Stevens, London.

2

Pattern, Variation and Inference

2.1 A Framework for Discussion

The raw material for most quantitative research in the social sciences is data obtained by observation, questionnaire or experiment. In sociology the sample survey [see VI, §1.1, §2.7] is a prime tool for eliciting information on individual attributes and attitudes. The methods by which such data are obtained are crucial for their proper interpretation and we have therefore discussed the mathematical aspects of the design of surveys and experiments in Chapter 3. In the present chapter we shall suppose that suitable data have been obtained in the form (usually) of simple random samples [see VI, §1.2]. At this stage the analyst will be faced with a substantial quantity of information which is too voluminous and disorganized for its message to be at all clear. The first task will therefore be to introduce some order into the apparent chaos so as to reveal any patterns and relationships which are present. To some extent the path of the analysis will be determined by the purpose for which the data were collected; however, our interest here is not in any particular research strategy but in the mathematical methods which are called into play along the way.

This chapter is concerned with the basic statistical methods which are used to summarize and interpret data and with the mathematics on which these depend. Their use is not, of course, confined to the social sciences but our choice of topics and emphasis has been determined by the demands of social science applications. In particular, we shall devote more attention than is usual outside the social sciences to the patterns of variation which occur. In the physical sciences variation in measurements is usually the result of such things as errors of measurement and is therefore of no interest in itself. The prime object of statistical analysis is then to eliminate the effects of this error or 'noise' in order to lay bare the underlying pattern. Much of the raw material of the social sciences, on the other hand, consists of measurements on people and although there may well be errors of measurement a much more important and interesting source of variation lies in the patterns which arise as a result of individual differences.

The typical sample survey yields information on many variables and, usually, we are interested not only in the behaviour of each one individually but in the relationships between them. In this chapter we shall concentrate (though not exclusively) on univariate analyses, that is those that look at one variable at a time. The inter-relationships between variables are discussed more fully in Chapter 4.

In the social science literature it is common to distinguish four levels of measurement. A nominal scale is one where individuals are assigned to categories as, for example, when we classify people according to the region of the country in which they live or the industry in which they work. Statisticians call this categorical data [see VI, Chapter 10]. An ordinal scale arises where observations can be ranked according to some underlying variable. Human abilities and attitudes often fall into this category. With an interval scale a numerical measure can be assigned to each observation in such a way that equal intervals on the scale correspond to equal increments in the magnitude of the quantity measured. The Fahrenheit and Centigrade scales for measuring temperature are familiar examples. A ratio scale is one which has a natural zero point and hence enables us to give a meaning to ratios which are independent of the unit of measurement. Thus, for example, monetary values are expressed on a ratio scale; it is possible to say that one car is twice as expensive as another and this remains true in whatever currency we choose to express the value. The same is not true of an interval scale such as temperature; a temperature which is twice that of another on the Fahrenheit scale will not yield the same ratio on any other scale. We shall use the term *metrical data* to refer to variables measured on an interval or ratio scale. Each type of measurement poses somewhat different problems of analysis. Those concerned with nominal and ranked data are relatively modest in their mathematical requirements and we shall therefore concentrate on metrical data. For this purpose it will be useful to classify such variables into three groups as follows.

(a) *Counts* A large number of variables that the social scientist meets are obtained by counting how often some item of interest occurs. Industrial sociologists, for example, may count the number of absences, accidents or strikes per unit time in order to see whether they vary systematically over time or from one firm to another. Psychologists may use the same data to throw light on the possible existence of accident or absence proneness. The number of outbreaks of war per century, the number of thefts from a store per week or the number of individual church attendances per year are further examples of variables obtained by counting. A counting scale is a ratio scale and is also *discrete* because the values of the variable are restricted to the non-negative integers.

(b) *Durations* The term *duration* is used here to refer to the length of time (or distance) that some socially interesting phenomenon lasts. There is a duration aspect to most of the phenomena discussed above under (a). Thus, for example, the length of a strike or a period of absence is another way of quantifying that particular phenomenon. As we shall see later, the form of the distribution of such durations can be made to yield useful indications of the social or psychological processes which underlie these happenings. The time interval between stimulus and response, the waiting time for a bus, the time between release from prison and re-conviction or the time between a medical condition and relapse are all further examples of durations. It is convenient to extend the term duration to include length and size as well as time. This enables us to speak of such things as distances between villages as durations. A duration is also measured on a ratio scale but this time it is *continuous* rather than discrete even though, in practice, measurements of time or distance have to be recorded to the nearst day or second, etc.

(c) *Scores* We use this as a convenient term to cover any other numerical scale used in social measurement. A score is a number assigned to an observation in such a way that it reflects the magnitude of some quantity which that individual possesses. A duration or a count can, of course, be thought of as a score as, indeed, can any other straightforward measurement. What we really have in mind, however, are things like the marks awarded in examinations and intelligence tests which are often arrived at by aggregating the number of correct responses or by averaging the scores of different judges. A score can be on an interval or ratio scale, but often it will be the latter.

As already remarked, we start from the position where the data have been collected, perhaps in large quantities, and we wish to discover what can be learnt from them. The stages of analysis to be gone through can be classified as follows:

(i) Description/summarization
(ii) Modelling
(iii) Estimation and/or hypothesis testing [see VI, Chapters 3 and 5]
(iv) Testing goodness of fit [see VI, Chapter 7].

It is important to emphasize that our present concern with mathematics means that some topics of great practical importance will be treated relatively briefly simply because their mathematical content is small. This applies especially to the descriptive part of statistics to which we turn in the next section.

2.2 Summarization of Data

The main methods of summarizing univariate and bivariate data [see VI, §1.2] are straightforward and well known. They are dealt with in virtually all elementary statistical texts and in the core volumes. Here, therefore, we shall merely list them in order to facilitate reference to the primary sources.

When dealing with nominal data there is little to be added to a count of the individuals falling into each category, though it is often useful to express them each as percentages of the total. With several nominal variables the data can be set out in contingency tables [see VI, Chapter 10] with the cell frequencies [see VI, §7.1] expressed as percentages of the marginal totals.

The basic concept for dealing with patterns of variation in interval or ratio variables is the frequency distribution or the cumulative frequency distribution [see II, §4.3.2 or §10.1.1]. These tell us in tabular or pictorial form how frequently each value of the variable has occurred. Such an exercise is informative in itself and it greatly facilitates comparisons between one group and another. The cumulative distribution, in particular, is useful for comparing distributions from different sources because the curves can be superimposed on a single diagram so that the comparison can be made by eye. Bivariate and multivariate distributions [see II, Chapter 6 and §10.5] can also be constructed, though the possibility of presenting a full picture in diagrammatic form becomes more difficult as the dimensionality increases.

A further useful summarization of frequency distributions is in terms of indices designed to measure such things as location, dispersion, skewness and kurtosis [see VI, §1.2 and §2.5.3(b)]. The first two classes of measure are by far the most important although the fact that many social variables have very skew distributions brings the third into greater prominence than is usual in some other fields of application. The two most important measures of location are the arithmetic mean [see VI, §1.2 and §2.5.3(b)] (mean for short) and the median [see II, §10.3.3]. Medians are used very often in social science work both because they are often more 'typical' (e.g. when speaking of such things as incomes) and because the data are liable to be censored [see II, §6.7, and VI, §6.4.3] in which case the median may be easier to calculate. Against this must be set the simpler sampling theory of the mean [see VI, §2.5.3(b)], but distributional assumptions are rarely securely based in social science. This means that distribution-free methods [see VI, Chapter 14] are frequently used in inference and these are often based on the median rather than the mean.

Similar considerations apply to the common measures of dispersion [see II, §9.1]. Although the standard deviation [see II, §9.2] is widely used, the mean deviation [see II, §9.1] and the quartile deviation (or semi-interquartile range [see VI, §1.2, and II, §9.4]), which are easier to interpret intuitively, are also in common use. Ease of interpretation often carries considerable weight with social researchers who may have to deal with consumers of their research who are lacking in numeracy.

Measures of skewness and kurtosis are sometimes useful, though it is often more important to note the existence of these characteristics than to provide measures of them. The usual measures are based on moments [see II, §9.11, and VI, §2.3].

With multivariate data there are many methods of describing the relationships between variables, some of which are covered in Chapter 4. However, the basic measure of the strength of a linear relationship between two variables is the product moment correlation coefficient [see II, §9.8, and VI, §1.5.7]. The calculation of such coefficients is usually a first step in the more sophisticated analyses of multivariate analysis. [see VI, Chapters 16 and 17]. For ranked data [see VI, §14.3, 14.4] there are two principal coefficients of correlation—Spearman's and Kendall's [see VI, §14.9]. The former is simply the product moment coefficient between the ranks rather than the variate values themselves. These correlation coefficients can be adapted to deal with data in contingency tables when the categories of classification are ordered. When they are not ordered numerous other measures of association exist.

All of the foregoing methods are based on the pre-supposition that the order in which the observations occur is of no significance. They would not be appropriate for data obtained serially in time, for example, where there was likely to be dependence between members of the series. A sequence of values in time is called a time series [see VI, Chapter 18]. Monthly unemployment figures, the index of retail prices, annual deaths from influenza and the monthly number of crimes of violence in a city are all examples of series of economic or social interest. Such series will often show a good deal of variation but the main interest will usually centre on the pattern of variation in time, in particular whether there is a trend or a periodic pattern in the sequence. Any such pattern will usually be partly obscured by random variation, and one of the main purposes of time series analysis is to separate out the components of variation.

Time series analysis [see VI, Chapter 18] has been largely developed as a tool for dealing with economic series and hence lies outside the scope of this volume. However, as some of the examples mentioned above show, time series do occur in the other social sciences and it is therefore appropriate to review briefly some of the principal methods. Much of time series analysis is derived from models, some of which will be briefly reviewed in Chapter 5. At the purely descriptive level there are several methods in common use.

All time series analyses should start with a plot of the data against time, since this will reveal to the eye any obvious trends with time. If there is a lot of variation in the short term the series can be smoothed in an attempt to remove the random variation and make the underlying pattern more obvious. One such method is to use a moving average [see VI, §18.7]. This involves replacing each member of the series by an average of a segment of the series centred at the observation in question. Thus if we have the series x_1, x_2, x_3, x_4, x_5, ..., a three-point (unweighted) moving average would give the smoothed series

$$\tfrac{1}{3}(x_1 + x_2 + x_3), \tfrac{1}{3}(x_2 + x_3 + x_4), \tfrac{1}{3}(x_3 + x_4 + x_5), \ldots$$

The idea behind the method is that, over a short period, the random variation will mask the systematic change and that the average will be a better estimate of the trend than is the single value at that point.

A second method of smoothing is to fit a curve of some kind to the data. Thus if there appeared to be a linear trend with time, a straight line might be fitted by least squares [see III, §6.1.1, and/or VI, §§11.1, 11.2, 11.3]. More generally, a polynomial can be fitted either to the whole series or to segments of the series [see III, §6.1.3]. Other functional forms often used are exponential [see IV, §2.11] or harmonic functions [see IV, §9.13]. The latter are especially important when there is a seasonal pattern in the data. The main mathematical requirement is a knowledge of how to fit a curve by the method of least squares, although for the standard problems the formulae required can be obtained directly from textbooks. In this connection the reader is referred especially to Kendall (1976) and Kendall and Stuart (1976).

The degree of dependence between the members of a time series can be investigated by means of the serial correlation coefficient [see VI, §18.5]. This is simply a correlation coefficient between each member of the series and one of its successors. Thus the serial correlation coefficient of *lag 1* is obtained by correlating x_i with x_{i-1} and that of *lag 12* with x_{i-12}. If the serial correlation coefficients are plotted as a function of the lag we obtain the correlogram [see VI, §18.5]. Generally speaking the serial correlation will decrease as the lag increases, but if there is a strong periodic component in the series this will not be so. For example, if we have a series of monthly figures an annual cycle will be revealed by a high serial correlation of *lag 12* meaning that one month's figures are highly correlated with those of the month one year previously.

The interpretation of the correlogram is not altogether easy because of the large sampling variation which may be associated with the coefficients of different lags and of the dependence between them. For this and other reasons it is more convenient to work with the Fourier transform [see IV, §§13.1–13.3] of the correlogram known as the periodogram or the spectrum [see VI, §§18.3, 18.5]. The idea here is to represent the series as a mixture of harmonic terms of different periods and the periodogram gives the weight to be attached to each period. A peak in the periodogram thus indicates a strong periodic component at that point whereas a smooth periodogram shows a lack of periodicity in the data.

2.3 Probability Models for Variation

We now return to the analysis of data in which there is no relevant ordering. The methods of summarization which we listed in Section 2.2 are rarely an end in themselves. Usually, the social scientist will wish to go further and make inferences which go beyond the particular set of data to hand. This may involve estimating or testing hypotheses about parameters of the population from which sample has been drawn. It may involve trying to explain (in some sense) and, maybe, change the underlying process which has generated the data. It may involve trying to predict future patterns of behaviour on the basis of evidence collected in the past. All of these inter-related objectives will involve the use of a probability model for the situation in hand. Probability theory is the branch of mathematics which deals with uncertainty—and hence with variability. The way in which the theory enters will depend a great deal on the circumstances and objectives of the investigation in hand, but it is bound to depend on the basic rules of probability and to involve some fundamental probability distributions. As a foundation for this work we shall describe some of these distributions and ways of manipulating them that arise in social science. This activity can be viewed as the theoretical counterpart of the empirical approach to data dealt with in the preceding section.

A basic model for the distribution of counts

The social scientist is likely to encounter most of the elementary discrete probability distributions [see II, Chapter 5]—the hypergeometric [see II, §5.3], the binomial [see II, §5.2.2], the multinomial [see II, §6.4.2] and the Poisson [see II, §5.4]. Of these all but the Poisson distribution tend to arise in special contexts, particularly in connection with sampling theory. The Poisson distribution on the other hand occurs more widely in social phenomena and even when it does not describe the pattern of variation adequately the Poisson model is a useful building brick for constructing better models.

There are two approaches to the derivation of the Poisson distribution which help to illuminate the meaning of Poisson variation when it occurs in practice. The first is as a distribution of 'rare events'. The derivation may be illustrated using an example of Feller's (1968) concerning outbreaks of fire in the area served by a city fire service. Typically there will be a very large number, n, of locations (buildings, etc.) at which a fire could occur. The probability of a fire at any one location is very small and, to a first approximation at least, outbreaks will be independent. The total number of outbreaks in a day, say, can then be represented as

$$T = \sum_{i=1}^{n} X_i$$

where $X_i = 1$ if a fire occurs at the ith location and is zero otherwise. If $\Pr\{X_i = 1\} = p_i$ [see II, §4.1], if all the p_i's are small and if n is large it may be shown (Feller, 1968) that T is approximately distributed in the Poisson form given [see II, §5.5] by

$$\Pr\{T = j\} = \frac{m^j}{j!} e^{-m} \quad (j = 0, 1, \ldots) \quad \text{where} \quad m = \sum_{i=1}^{n} p_i. \tag{2.1}$$

This is a very general approach to the distribution of a 'count' and is equally applicable in many other spheres. For example, the number of insurance claims made to a motor insurer, the number of aircraft crashes in a year, the number of accidents in a factory and the number of errors made by a punched card operator have the same characteristics. In each case there is a very large number of occasions on which the event of interest could occur, the probability of occurrence is small in any particular case and occurrences are virtually independent. The 'count' consists of the number of occurrences, and probability theory enables us to deduce the form of the distribution. Note that the p_i's do not have to be equal. This is not to say, of course, that counts which can be regarded in this way must have a Poisson distribution, since none of the assumptions is necessarily true. Later in this chapter we shall investigate the consequences of relaxing some of the assumptions.

A second kind of derivation arises where we are interested in the distribution of events in time—like accidents, absences and outbreaks of conflict. In such cases the count arises as the number of events occuring in intervals of time and the empirical frequency distribution will usually be made up from the numbers occurring in a consecutive group of intervals. (Note that these successive numbers form a time series and a full analysis would have to take account of their order. However, the particular assumptions which we are about to make imply that the order is irrelevant.) Kendall (1961), for example, has given examples of distributions of outbreaks of war and strikes which conform very closely to the Poisson form. The distribution arises in this context out of the attempt to give expression to what we mean by a completely random or haphazard distribution of events in time. First of all this requires that the rate (number/unit time) should be constant because if it were not occurrences would be more likely at some times than others and this conflicts with the notion of randomness. Similarly there should be nothing discernible in the pattern of events in the past which would help in predicting the future. All of this is usually formalized by requiring that

$$\Pr\{\text{event in } (t, t + \delta t)\} = \lambda \, \delta t + o(\delta t) \qquad (2.2)$$

where δt is small and λ is the rate of occurrence. A standard technique [see II, (20.1.3)] enables us to deduce that

$$\Pr\{n \text{ events in any interval of length } t\} = P_n(t) = \frac{(\lambda t)^n e^{-\lambda t}}{n!}$$

$$(n = 0, 1, 2, \ldots) \quad (2.3)$$

which is the Poisson distribution in another guise.

The question of how to fit the distribution, that is how to choose the most appropriate value of λ (or m), and of how to judge the adequacy of that fit will be treated later in the chapter.

The Poisson distribution has a number of attractive properties. It involves only one unknown parameter and its mean and variance are both equal to λt (or m). Hence a Poisson distribution will not be a good fit to an empirical distribution unless the mean and variance of the latter are nearly equal. Also, if two or more independent Poisson variables are added the distribution of their sum is also Poisson. This means, for example, that if the number of accidents of different kinds incurred by an individual is Poisson then the total number of accidents of all kinds will be Poisson provided that the independence requirement is met. This result, and its generalization to the sum of any number of variables, may be proved most easily using generating functions [see II, Chapter 12].

Durations: Some relevant functions and a basic model

When constructing models for durations it is helpful to consider not only the density but two other, equivalent, functions. The first of these is the survivor function defined as the function giving the probability that the duration exceeds t [see II, §21.6]. If $f(t)$ is the probability density [see II, §10.1.1] then obviously

$$G(t) = \int_t^\infty f(x)\, dx. \tag{2.4}$$

This is often directly relevant to the questions being asked in a practical study which might, for example, be concerned with the survival of a patient after an operation. The second function goes under a variety of names according to the field of application. We shall call it the hazard function. In mortality studies it is known as the force of mortality, in labour turnover as the force of separation or the length of service specific wastage rate, and so on. It is defined as follows [c.f. II, §21.6]:

$\phi(t)\, \delta t = \mathrm{Pr}$ {duration which has lasted to t, ends in $(t, t + \delta t)$}.

$\phi(t)$ is the hazard function; it measures the propensity to terminate at time t and is a very useful description of the probability process. As the force of mortality it is the propensity to die at age t. This declines in the early months of life, remains low through youth into adulthood and then rises steadily into old age. It may be shown from the definitions that the three functions are related as follows:

$$\left.\begin{aligned} G(t) &= \exp\left(-\int_0^t \phi(x)\, dx\right), \\ \phi(t) &= \frac{f(t)}{G(t)} \\ f(t) &= -\frac{dG(t)}{dt} \end{aligned}\right\} . \tag{2.5}$$

Models for duration have been explored in some detail in Bartholomew (1973). In this chapter we shall concentrate on a few basic distributions, beginning with the most basic of all. This is the exponential distribution [see, II, §11.2] for which $\phi(t) = \lambda$, meaning that the propensity to terminate is independent of age. In this case

$$G(t) = e^{-\lambda t}, \qquad f(t) = \lambda e^{-\lambda t} \qquad (t \geq 0). \tag{2.6}$$

This distribution has

$$\text{Mean} = \lambda^{-1}, \qquad \text{Variance} = \lambda^{-2}. \tag{2.7}$$

The exponential distribution is closely related to the Poisson distribution of counts. In fact if events occur in time according to (2.2) then the distribution of intervals between events will be exponential.

Other useful distributions arise if $\phi(t)$ has other simple forms. In particular if we expected $\phi(t)$ to be monotonic [see IV, Definition 2.7.1] we might take

$$\phi(t) = Kt^a \qquad (K > 0), \tag{2.8}$$

which is monotonic increasing if $a > 0$ and decreasing if $a < 0$. In the latter case we must also have $a > -1$ otherwise $G(t)$ will not tend to zero as t tends to infinity. (In other words there would be a finite probability of an infinite duration.) The distribution having (2.8) as its hazard function is called the Weibull distribution [see II, §11.9].

Another simple functional form for $\phi(t)$ which has found applications in the study of labour turnover and which we shall meet again later in the chapter is

$$\phi(t) = \frac{q}{c + t}. \tag{2.9}$$

This represents a steadily declining propensity to terminate.

Although the foregoing discussion has been conducted in terms of continuous variables there is a parallel treatment in discrete time. For example, if t is discrete taking integer values with

$$\Pr\{t = i\} = f_i \qquad (i = 0, 1, 2, \ldots)$$

then

$$G_i = \Pr\{\text{surviving for } i \text{ or more}\} = \sum_{j=i}^{\infty} f_j \tag{2.10}$$

and [see II, §§3.9.1 and 6.5]

$$\phi_i = \Pr\{\text{terminating at } t = i \mid \text{survival to } t = i\} = f_i/G_i.$$

If $\phi_i = p$ then since $f_i = G_i - G_{i+1}$ it is easy to show that

$$G_i = (1 - p)^i$$

and hence that

$$f_i = p(1 - p)^i \qquad (i = 0, 1, 2, \ldots) \tag{2.11}$$

which is the geometric distribution [see II, §5.2.3].

Network models for duration

A very versatile and useful method for modelling durations is based on the representation of the process as a network. The idea is a natural generalization of the exponential model and may be illustrated on a simple example, due to Clowes (1972), for the length of service of a person in a job. The situation can be represented diagrammatically as follows:

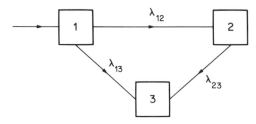

According to this model an individual enters the system (job) in state 1 in which he is undecided about whether he likes the job or not. After a period of time he moves either to state 2—in which case he is committed to the job—or to state 3 which consists of those who have left. If he takes the former route to state 2 he will subsequently leave by making the transition from state 2 to state 3. It is not necessary that the states should be directly observable. In this particular application the time interval between entry to state 1 and exit from the system to state 3 is the only quantity which is directly observable and it is the distribution of this quantity which the theoretical analysis is designed to determine. This is thus an example of what is often called a latent model in that it describes relationships between non-observable states (or variables). It thus represents a theory (in this case a psychological theory) about human behaviour. Using the theory we make predictions about observable quantities. If observation and theory are in agreement we cannot infer that the theory is true, though it is certainly a candidate for serious consideration. On the other hand if observation and theory do not agree the theory must be rejected.

The times spent in states 1 and 2 are determined by the transition rates [see II, §20.4], λ_{ij}, defined by

$$\Pr\{\text{transition from } i \text{ to } j \text{ in } (t, t + \delta t)\} = \lambda_{ij}\delta t + o(\delta t) \tag{2.12}$$

$(i = 1, 2; j = 2, 3; i \neq j)$. The simple exponential model can now be seen to be a special case in which there is only one state.

There are clearly many social processes which can be represented as networks, and all pose common mathematical problems. The model we have just described is, in fact, a continuous time Markov process [see II, Chapter 20] and, as such, will be discussed in Chapter 5. Here we are concerned with only one aspect—the duration—and for this purpose we shall describe a non-rigorous but equivalent analysis of the model based on a deterministic interpretation. The method has been used by Coleman (1964) and others and is of wide applicability.

Suppose that, at time t, the number of individuals in state i is $n_i(t)$, ($i = $, 2, 3). Since $\lambda_{ij} \, \delta t$ is the probability that an individual moves from i to j and since δt is so small that the probability of two or more moves is negligible it follows that the expected number of transitions from i to j in $(t, t + \delta t)$ is $n_i(t)\lambda_{ij} \, \delta t$ [see II, Definition 8.1.1]. If $n_i(t)$ is large enough to be treated as a continuous variable and if we suppose that the actual number of movers can be approximated by its expectation then we can set up equations of the following kind for movements in the interval $(t, t + \delta t)$:

$$n_2(t + \delta t) = n_2(t) - n_2(t)\lambda_{23} \, \delta t + n_1(t) \, \lambda_{12} \, \delta t \tag{2.13}$$

with similar equations for $n_1(t)$ and $n_3(t)$. Taking the limit as $\delta t \to 0$, (2.13) yields

$$\frac{dn_2(t)}{dt} = -\lambda_{23}n_2(t) + \lambda_{12}n_1(t). \tag{2.14}$$

There will be one linear differential equation [cf. IV, (7.23)] like (2.14) for each $n_i(t)$. A complete determination of the state of the system at time t thus requires the solution of a set of simultaneous linear differential equations. Clowes was primarily interested in finding the survivor function for his system which was the only directly observable property. In the present notation this is

$$G(t) = \frac{n_1(0) - n_3(t)}{n_1(0)}$$

with initial conditions $n_2(0) = n_3(0) = 0$. Reference to the general theory of linear differential equations [see IV, §7.2] shows that the solution typically has the form

$$n_i(t) = \sum_j \alpha_{ij} e^{-\beta_{ij}t} \qquad (\beta_{ij} > 0). \tag{2.15}$$

For Clowes' problem this implies that $G(t)$ has the form

$$G(t) = pe^{-\beta_1 t} + (1 - p)e^{-\beta_2 t}. \tag{2.16}$$

In general, the numbers in the states of the network will always have the form of a linear combination of exponentials, though the coefficients $\{\alpha_{ij}\}$ will not necessarily all be non-negative.

Random walk models for duration [see II, §18.3]

There are many other probability models which have been developed for durations, of which we mention only one at this point. This was proposed by Lancaster (1972) for the duration of a strike; other applications have been discussed by Whitmore (1976, 1979) and a general account of the distribution and its properties is given in Folks and Chhikara (1978).

According to this model the two parties to a strike are initially thought of as being separated by a distance *d* on some relevant scale (money, hours, etc.). As time passes and negotiations proceed the gap changes by small amounts such that the change between t and $t + \delta t$ is Normally distributed with mean $\mu \delta t$ and variance $\sigma^2 \delta t$ [see II, §11.4] independently of what happened prior to t. Such a stochastic process is a Wiener process [see II, §18.5]. The problem of finding the distribution of the duration of a strike is thus that of finding the distribution of the time before a Wiener process first reaches d. If $\mu \geq 0$ this will happen with probability one and the distribution in question turns out to have density function given by

$$f(t) = \frac{d}{\sqrt{2\pi}\,\sigma t^{3/2}} \exp\left[-\frac{1}{2}\left(\frac{d - t\mu}{\sigma\sqrt{t}}\right)^2 \right] \qquad (d, \sigma, \mu \geq 0). \qquad (2.17)$$

This is a positively skewed distribution [see II, §9.10] sometimes known as the inverse gaussian distribution. If $\mu < 0$ there is a finite probability that the duration is infinite and the distribution is then described as defective [see II, §18.3.2 (iv)]. Similar models can be set up in discrete time as indicated in Bartholomew (1973, Chapter 6).

Models for scores

Scores may have almost any distribution [see II, Chapter 4] depending on how they are derived. However, a great many are obtained by constructing an index from a largish number of measurements by some such process as averaging or selecting extremes. Sometimes, the mode of construction is sufficient to make deductions about the form of the distribution of the score. From one point of view a model can be regarded as providing an explanation of how a given score distribution has arisen. From another it suggests how an index might be constructed in order to give it desirable distributional properties. Because so much of statistical theory is built around the Normal distribution [see II, §11.4] there are obvious advantages in trying to arrange things so that the distributions with which we have to deal are Normal.

In practice many scores are arrived at by a process which tends to induce Normality–namely that of adding up or averaging. To take a very simple example, suppose that a test of arithmetical ability is constructed by setting 50 sums designed to be of equal difficulty. If each sum is scored 1 or 0 according to whether the answer given is right or wrong then the total score is the sum of 50 individual scores. If the same person took a number of such tests or a group of people with the same ability took the same test one would expect to find an approximately Normal distribution of scores [see II, §11.4.2]. At a slightly more sophisticated level, if a student is asked to answer five questions on an examination paper, with 20 marks awarded for each question, the total score is the sum of 5 marks. Many tests of ability involve some such process of adding up constituent scores to give a total score.

The variation of many other variables—physical as well as mental—associated with people also often show a Normal pattern of variability from one person to another. This may be explained in a similar way by postulating that height, for example, is determined by the independent effects of a number of different genes. If it is further assumed that the effects are additive, total height can be regarded as a sum.

In order to understand the reasons for the approximate Normality of sums and averages it is necessary to refer to Central Limit Theorems [see II, §11.4.2 and §17.3]. These specify the conditions under which sums (or, more generally, linear functions) of random variables have distributions which tend to Normality as the number of terms in the sum tends to infinity. The simplest version requires the constituents to be independently and identically distributed, but weaker versions exist allowing different distributions and a limited degree of dependence.

It is sometimes found that the logarithm [see I, §3.6] of a score is Normally distributed rather than the score itself. Since a Normal distribution may arise as a sum it follows that the log-normal distribution [see II, §11.5] can arise from a product. Thus if

$$y = \prod_{i=1}^{n} x_i$$

then, by the Central Limit Theorem,

$$\log y = \sum_{i=1}^{n} \log x_i \tag{2.18}$$

will tend to be Normal, which is the same as saying that y is log-normal. Therefore, if there is reason to suppose that a score is arrived at by multiplying component scores then the resulting distribution will be approximately log-normal. Further details will be found in Aitchison and Brown (1957). It is a well-attested empirical fact that the length of time that people spend in their jobs or in residence at a given address is log-normally distributed, but it is not easy to see how this duration can be meaningfully expressed as a product (see, however, Bartholomew, 1973, Chapter 6 for two attempts).

Although the Normal distribution has many advantages it also has drawbacks. One of these stems from the fact that its distribution function [see II, §4.3.2 and 10.3.1] cannot be expressed in a simple formula. In applications where one needs to use a distribution function rather than a density there are advantages in using a more tractable distribution. One possibility which is close to the normal in shape is the logistic distribution [see II, §11.10] with distribution function

$$F(x) = \left\{ 1 + \exp\left[-\left(\frac{x - \mu}{\sigma}\right)\right]\right\}^{-1}, \qquad -\infty < x < +\infty. \tag{2.19}$$

This has proved useful in dosage-response analyses and in similar problems in psychology where it is required to estimate $F(x)$ from observations of the proportion of subjects who respond to different levels of a stimulus, x. One can define a log-logistic distribution as one for which the logarithm of the variable has the logistic distribution.

Just as scores may arise from an adding up procedure they may also be extreme values [see II, §§15.5 and 15.6, and II, §14.3]. Thus, for example, it is sometimes the case in systems of continuous assessment that the best (or best k) out of n attempts is counted for examination purposes. Similarly an athlete may be selected for a contest on the basis of his best rather than his average performance. We saw that an average tended to have a Normal distribution subject to very weak conditions on the nature of the random variables being averaged. In the case of extreme values we might wonder whether any similar result holds. The answer is provided by the theory of extreme values (Gumbel, 1958). In this case when all values are identically distributed there are several limiting forms depending on the character of the tails of the constituent distributions [see II, §12.1.4]. The Weibull distribution [see II, §11.9], already encountered in another context, is one of the limiting forms.

In qualitative terms, extreme value distributions tend to be very skew [see II, §9.10]. Scores based on extremes are thus generally more difficult to handle statistically than those based on sums or products.

Mixtures of distributions (Heterogeneity)

Heterogeneity is one of the most pervasive characteristics of social science data. People vary among themselves in almost every way and the behaviour of the same person will vary from one occasion to another. Any serious attempt to model social phenomena must therefore reckon with these facts. For example, while it might be reasonable to suppose that an examination score would be Normal for a given individual on a given occasion it would not be plausible that the same distribution applied to everyone on all occasions. If it did the examination would be a lottery. Instead, we expect individual abilities to vary and hence any observed distribution of marks for a class will be a *mixture* [see II, §14.2] of the distributions for individual candidates. Similar considerations apply to the other examples mentioned in the previous section and many others like them. The social researcher must therefore turn to probability theory for methods of incorporating heterogenity into his models and to statistical theory for the means of identifying a mixture and decomposing it into its constituent parts.

Suppose, by way of illustration, that we are interested in the distribution of the number of accidents per unit time in a factory and that the form of the distribution for a homogeneous group of workers is known. Let us denote this distribution by $P_n(t, \lambda)$ $(n = 0, 1, 2, \ldots)$ where t is the length of the interval and λ is a parameter governing the rate of occurrence. Suppose that the population of workers consists of two groups: a proportion p which we will call the 'accident-prone' for which $\lambda = \lambda_1$ and a proportion $1 - p$ for which $\lambda = \lambda_2$. Then if $P_n(t)$ is the probability of n accidents in time t for the whole population, an elementary probability argument gives that

$$P_n(t) = pP_n(t, \lambda_1) + (1 - p)P_n(t, \lambda_2). \tag{2.20}$$

If there are k groups, an obvious generalization gives

$$P_n(t) = \sum_{i=1}^{k} p_i P_n(t, \lambda_i), \qquad \left(\sum_{i=1}^{k} p_i = 1\right). \tag{2.21}$$

Sometimes it is more appropriate to think of λ as a parameter that varies continuously from zero to infinity in a large population in a manner which can be described by a probability density function $h(\lambda)$, say. In this case

$$P_n(t) = \int_0^{\infty} P_n(t, \lambda)h(\lambda)\, d\lambda \tag{2.22}$$

and the determination of $P_n(t)$ requires the evaluation of an integral. Yet again λ may be partly continuous and partly discrete, in which case (2.21) and (2.22) can be subsumed under the single formula

$$P_n(t) = \int_0^{\infty} P_n(t, \lambda)\, dH(\lambda) \tag{2.23}$$

where $H(\lambda)$ is the distribution function of λ and the integral is an example of a Stieltjes integral [see IV, §4.8]. It is very convenient, both here and in other applications involving this kind of probability calculation, to have such a method of handling discrete and continuous variables in a unified way. For the purpose of illustration we have considered mixtures of a discrete probability distribution, but the argument applies without modification to densities of continuous variables as illustrated below.

Examples of mixtures

Suppose that a duration has an exponential distribution with parameter λ [see II, §11.2] and that λ has the gamma distribution [see II, §11.3] with density

$$h(\lambda) = \frac{c^q}{\Gamma(q)} \lambda^{q-1} e^{-c\lambda} \qquad (\lambda \geq 0). \tag{2.24}$$

The unconditional density of the duration is therefore

$$f(t) = \int_0^\infty h(\lambda) \lambda e^{-\lambda t}\, d\lambda = \frac{q}{c}\left(1 + \frac{t}{c}\right)^{-(q+1)}, \qquad t \geq 0. \tag{2.25}$$

This is a J-shaped density [see II, §9.10.1] like the exponential but with a greater degree of skewness. It was derived by Silcock (1954) as a model of completed length of service in a job. Its force of separation function, $\phi(t)$, was given in (2.9) which shows that it is monotonic decreasing. It may be shown that the standard deviation [see II, §9.2] is greater than that of the exponential with the same mean and, furthermore, that this is true whatever form we choose for $h(\lambda)$. (The proof depends on a result about moments derived below.) Hence, whenever we find an empirical distribution [see VI, §14.2] which departs from the exponential in this way in circumstances where we might have expected an exponential, we may suspect heterogeneity. This is a good illustration of the way in which the analysis of a model can suggest an empirical test for heterogenity. A fruther analysis for this particular model is given in Bartholomew (1973, p. 186).

It is important to realize that a good fit by a mixture model does not imply that the distribution has really arisen in this way. For example, if λ had taken just two values such that $\Pr\{\lambda = \lambda_1\} = p$, $\Pr\{\lambda = \lambda_2] = 1 - p$ the density function of t would be

$$f(t) = p\lambda_1 e^{-\lambda_1 t} + (1 - p)\lambda_2 e^{-\lambda_2 t} \tag{2.26}$$

and this is identical in form with the distribution obtained from Clowes' network model given in (2.16). On the basis of the empirical distribution it is therefore quite impossible to distinguish between the models.

Another important probability distribution used in the social sciences which can be derived by a mixture argument is the negative binomial [see II, §5.2.4]. This arises by taking a continuous mixture of Poisson distributions using the gamma distribution of (2.24). In this case

$$P_n(t) = \int_0^\infty \frac{c^q}{\Gamma(q)} \lambda^{q-1} e^{-c\lambda} \frac{(\lambda t)^n}{n!} e^{-\lambda t}\, d\lambda$$

$$= \frac{\Gamma(n + q)}{\Gamma(q)\Gamma(n + 1)} \left(\frac{t}{c + t}\right)^n \left(\frac{c}{c + t}\right)^q \qquad (n \geq 0). \tag{2.27}$$

This distribution has a greater dispersion than the Poisson and so heterogeneity would be suspected if the variance of a 'count' distribution exceeded its mean.

Sometimes it is useful to approach the problem the other way round. Given that a certain density, $f(t)$, fits the data we may ask whether there exists a mixing distribution such that $f(t)$ is a mixture of some elementary distribution such as the exponential. In this case the answer can be obtained, in principle, with the help of the theory of Laplace transforms [see II, §12.3, and IV, §13.4]. To see this we note that $f(t)$ given by (2.25) is the Laplace transform of $\lambda h(\lambda)$. Therefore, using the inversion formula [see IV, §13.4.2],

$$h(\lambda) = \frac{1}{2\pi i \lambda} \int_{c-i\infty}^{c+i\infty} f(t) e^{t\lambda} \, dt. \tag{2.28}$$

Bartlett and Kendall (1946) used this method to show that if $f(t)$ was a gamma density it was sometimes possible to represent it as a mixture of exponentials. The same approach can be used with mixtures of Poisson distributions since if

$$P_n(t) = \int_0^\infty \frac{(\lambda t)^n}{n!} e^{-\lambda t} h(\lambda) \, d\lambda$$

then $P_n(t)$ is the Laplace transform of $(\lambda t)^n h(\lambda)/n!$

In all of the foregoing examples the mixture had a different form from the components. This means that, in principle, the mixture can be decomposed. Thus, for example, if we were to fit the negative binomial distribution of (2.27) to an observed distribution of counts the estimates of its parameters would determine $h(\lambda)$. In such cases the mixture is said to be identifiable. Unfortunately this is not always the case. For example, if a variable x has a Normal distribution with mean μ and variance σ^2 and if μ has a Normal density $h(\mu)$ with mean ω and variance τ^2 then

$$f(x) = \int_{-\infty}^{+\infty} \frac{1}{\sqrt{2\pi}\sigma} \exp\left[-\frac{1}{2}\left(\frac{x-\mu}{\sigma}\right)^2 \right] h(\mu) \, d\mu. \tag{2.29}$$

Evaluation of this integral shows that $f(x)$ is a Normal density with mean ω and variance $\sigma^2 + \tau^2$. The effect of heterogeneity is thus to increase the variability, but because the form of the distribution remains Normal under mixing (is 'closed' under mixing) one can never discover that mixing has taken place. This is not true of all types of mixing of Normal distributions. For example, if μ were to take just two values the mixture would be identifiable.

The mathematical tools required for constructing and analysing models of mixtures are thus, primarily, those of real or complex integration [see IV, Chapters 4, 6 and 9]. For purposes of estimation [see VI, Chapter 3], among others, it is often useful to be able to find the moments [see II, §9.11, and VI, §2.3] of the mixture without obtaining the full distribution.

This can be done by introducing a double integral and then reversing the order of integration [see IV, Theorem 6.23]. For example, in the exponential case [see II, §11.2]:

$$E(t^r) = \int_0^\infty t^r f(t) \, dt = \int_0^\infty t^r \left\{ \int_0^\infty \lambda e^{-t\lambda} dH(\lambda) \right\} dt$$

$$= \int_0^\infty \int_0^\infty t^r \lambda e^{-\lambda t} \, dH(\lambda) \, dt$$

$$= \int_0^\infty \lambda \left\{ \int_0^\infty t^r e^{-\lambda t} \, dt \right\} dH(\lambda)$$

$$= r! \int_0^\infty \lambda^{-r} \, dH(\lambda) = r! \, E(\lambda^{-r}), \qquad r = 0, 1, 2, \ldots \tag{2.30}$$

The conditions necessary for justifying the reversal of the order of integration in the manner illustrated above are satisfied in this case [see IV, §10.21].

The mathematics of mixing is essentially the same as that which arises in Bayesian statistical analysis [see VI, Chapter 16]. In that context $dH(\lambda)$ would be the prior distribution [see VI, §15.1] and the rest of the integrand the likelihood [see VI §1.2]. The resulting mixture is the marginal distribution [see II, §§6.3 and 13.1.2].

Zipf's Law

One of the most remarkable regularities which has been observed among social phenomena is the relationship which sometimes exists between the sizes and rank orders of objects. Two of the best known examples concern the sizes of towns and of incomes. The latter is discussed in detail by Champernowne (1973).

The form of the relationship in question is revealed if one plots the logarithm of size against the logarithm of rank when the result is a straight line. More precisely, if r denotes the rank of the size of a town, income, etc. and if S is the size then

$$S \propto r^{-a} \tag{2.31}$$

at least for large r and with $1 \le a \le 2$. This is known as Zipf's law; see Zipf (1949) who produced many examples from other fields also. The subject has been pursued by Mandelbrot (1956, 1965) and by Simon (1955). Their empirical results may be viewed merely as an interesting curiosity, but the fact that the law is so widespread suggests that there might be some basic allocation process underlying all these phenomena whose nature might be elucidated by mathematical analysis. The most substantial and convincing investigation of the situation will be found in Hill (1970, 1974) and Hill and Woodroofe (1975). They show that something close to Zipf's law is to be expected under a variety of circumstances either in what they term the 'strong' or the 'weak' form. These results depend on various mathematical and probabilisitic arguments. The reader who wishes to be equipped to follow the derivations and judge the plausibility of the conclusions may find the following outline useful.

The models start with the classical occupancy problem [see II, §5.2.2] in which N balls are allocated among k boxes. (In the towns example the boxes correspond to towns and the balls to people.) As a result of the allocation suppose that the numbers in the boxes are n_1, n_2, ..., n_k ($\Sigma n_i = N$). These are the 'sizes' and after ranking we wish to know under what conditions (2.31) holds.

The successful models start with the so-called Bose–Einstein allocation which assigns equal probability to each possible allocation. Note that $n_i \geq 1$ for all i because if n_i were zero for any i that box would not be known to exist. The number of allocations subject to this restriction is $\binom{N-1}{k-1}$ and, if each has the same probability, that probability is $\binom{N-1}{k-1}^{-1}$. This system of allocation with N and k fixed does not, of itself, produce the law. The essential feature of Hill's models is that k is treated as a random variable with a distribution, conditional on N, which is such that

$$\Pr\left\{\frac{k}{N} \leq x \mid N\right\} = F_N(x)$$

where $F_N(x)$ converges to a limiting form, $F(x)$, as $N \to \infty$. One may thus visualize the allocation process in two stages as follows. N is given and a random number of boxes is selected; the N individuals are then distributed among the boxes according the Bose–Einstein allocation. Hill shows that if this process is generalized by supposing that there are K such sets of boxes and if the boxes are selected in a variety of ways from these sets then the resulting rank-frequency distribution will be approximately of the desired from. The methods employed involve some use of the theory of order statistics [see II, Chapter 15, and VI, §14.3] but, principally, depend on basic probability calculations depending on occupancy probabilities. These arguments lead to exact expressions whose limits, under appropriate conditions, yield the required relationship. Hill (1974) gives a detailed discussion of the nature and plausibility of the assumptions noting, in particular, that the Bose–Einstein allocation implies that expected increases in city sizes (for example) are proportional to existing size.

2.4 Inference about the Parameters of Distributions [see VI, §§1.2 and 3.1]

The models which we have reviewed determine the form of the probability distribution of the variable in question, but the values of the parameters have to be estimated before theory and observation can be compared.

Sometimes the parameters may be of direct interest in themselves as, for example, the proportions in a two-component mixture. In such cases it may also be necessary to test hypotheses about their values. These problems are not peculiar to the social sciences; indeed, they are the central subjects of most standard text books on statistical theory. However, the particular circumstances in which the social scientist finds himself impart a different relative importance to the various facets of the subject.

For example, the social scientist's data are often much more untidy than the natural scientist's. The standard text-book phrase, 'let $x_1, x_2, x_3, \ldots, x_n$ be observations on a continuous random variable with density function $f(x, \theta)$' [see VI, §1.2], which introduces so many discussions of inference represents an unattainable ideal in much social science. It is often the case that any initial randomness [see II, §§3.3 and 3.6.2] on drawing the sample will have been compromised by non-response, or other practical or ethical complications. Censoring, truncation and grouping [see II, §6.7, and VI, §§1.2 and 3.2.2] are other features with which the social scientist habitually has to contend.

Much of the theory of statistical estimation [see VI, Chapter 3] is concerned with questions of efficiency [see VI, §3.3.3]. It is typically assumed, for example, that a random sample [see VI, §1.2] has been drawn from a population distribution of known form and the problem is to obtain the best estimators of its parameters. All work of this kind leans heavily on the assumed distributional form. In the social sciences such assumptions are rarely well-founded, so that the whole analysis takes on a much more suspect character. In these circumstances the achievement of marginally higher efficiency is reminiscent of 'straining out gnats and swallowing camels' (Mtt 23 v24, Jerusalem Bible). In fact few questions in empirical social science research turn on knowing very precisely the value of any parameter of an ill-defined distribution.

Against this background it is easy to see why it is often more important to get an estimate of some kind rather than to be over-much concerned with questions of such things as efficiency, whose meaning is defined within a framework of assumptions of doubtful validity.

These features of social science data mean that the text-book solutions for standard problems are often not directly applicable in practice. We shall therefore place the emphasis here on general methods of inference and, in particular, on point estimation [see VI, §3.1].

Methods of estimation

The most widely used method of point estimation is the method of maximum likelihood [see VI, Chapter 6]. As usually applied this requires an assumption about the mathematical form of the probability distribution involved, and this may present problems. However, the method does provide a widely applicable tool and where we are fitting a probability model of the kind discussed in the last section the distribution and parameters are well-defined. The method can be used if the data are censored [see II, §6.7] or otherwise incomplete although the mathematical and numerical analysis problems may then be more difficult.

In essence the method consists of writing down the joint probability [see II, Definition 6.1.1] (in the case of a discrete variable) or the joint probability density (for a continuous variable) [see II, §13.1] and then maximizing it with respect to the unknown parameters. Thus if we have n independent observations $x_1, x_2, \ldots, x_n$ on a random variable x with density function $f(x, \theta)$ the likelihood function is

$$l = \prod_{i=1}^{n} f(x_i, \theta). \tag{2.32}$$

For this purpose l is regarded as a function of θ with respect to which the maximization is carried out. In practice it is often more convenient to maximize the logarithm of l. If the variables are not independent or identically distributed the likelihood function may not be a simple product as in (2.32), but the nature of the mathematical problem is unchanged.

With k unknown parameters $\boldsymbol{\theta} = (\theta_1, \theta_2, \ldots, \theta_k)$ the basic mathematical problem is to maximize a function

$$\psi(\theta_1, \theta_2, \ldots, \theta_k).$$

In straightforward cases this problem can be solved by standard calculus methods which involve solving the k simultaneous equations

$$\frac{\partial \psi}{\partial \theta_i} = 0 \qquad (i = 1, 2, \ldots, k)$$

and checking whether the solution obtained is a maximum, a minimum [see IV, Definition 5.6.3] or a saddle point [see IV, Figure 5.6.4]. The method by which the equations will be solved in practice will depend on their number and their form [see III, §5.6]. A common method is to use an interative technique by which a guessed solution is systematically improved. The general problem of the numerical solution of simultaneous equations is one of the main topics treated in numerical analysis [see III, Chapters 3 and 5]. We shall meet examples of maximum likelihood estimation in Chapter 4.

It is not necessarily the case that the greatest value of the likelihood function occurs at a point where the derivatives vanish [see IV, Definition 5.6.1]. If the values of the parameters are constrained the maximum may lie on a boundary of the parameter space. Such situations often occur in social science and one important class of such problems arises when the parameters are subject to order restrictions. To illustrate the point consider one of the earliest problems posed by Jonckheere (1954). It concerned an experimental situation where a score was obtained in different groups of subjects at different levels of 'stress'. There was reason to suppose that the scores within each group were distributed about a mean level which increased with stress. If we were to estimate the group means by, say, the sample means we would be making no use of our knowledge about the monotonic relationship between stress level and the mean. To express the matter formally let θ_i denote the mean response level for the distribution of the ith group. Suppose that the groups are numbered so that the higher the subscript of θ the higher the stress; then our prior knowledge amounts to the statement that $\theta_1 \le \theta_2 \le \ldots \le \theta_k$ where k is the number of groups. The problem of maximizing the likelihood is now that of finding the largest value of $\psi(\theta)$ within the region defined by these inequalities or on the boundary. Maximization of a function subject to (linear) inequalities (or equalities) is a problem of mathematical programming [see IV, Chapter 15]. If the θ's are means of Normal distributions the log-likelihood is a quadratic function and then the problem is one of quadratic programming [see IV, Chapter 15].

Because the social sciences often deal with quantities which can be ranked fairly easily but not measured on an interval or ratio scale it is quite common to have prior knowledge in the form of order restrictions on parameters. An account of the theory of estimation under order restrictions will be found in Barlow and co-workers (1972).

The following two examples illustrate the method of maximum likelihood on two elementary but non-standard cases. The first is an example of truncation which is afforded by the Poisson distribution with the zero-class missing [see II, §6.7]. Suppose that we suspect that a distribution of counts can be fitted by a Poisson distribution but that cases with zero occurrences have not been recorded. This might arise when accident statistics are collected at a first-aid post. An accident will only be recorded for individuals who had at least one; those who avoided accidents altogether will not be counted and hence their number will be unknown. To estimate the mean of the Poisson distribution by maximum likelihood we must work with the probability distribution conditional on at least one event occurring [see II, §6.5]. A simple probability argument shows this to be

$$P_n = \frac{m^n}{n!} e^{-m}(1 - e^{-m})^{-1} \qquad (n = 1, 2, \ldots). \tag{2.33}$$

If the data consist of k observations of $n : n_1, n_2, \ldots, n_k$ then the likelihood function is

$$l = \frac{m^{\Sigma n_i}}{\prod n_i!} e^{-km}(1 - e^{-m})^{-k}, \tag{2.34}$$

which has to be maximized with respect to m. There is no simple explicit expression for the maximum likelihood estimator but the maximization can easily be effected by numerical methods.

The second example illustrates the use of maximum likelihood estimation in a case of incomplete data when the form of the probability distribution in question is unknown. It is typical of a kind of problem which is quite common in social applications of statistics. Suppose that we are interested in estimating the distribution of a duration. Data are available on n individuals, but all that is known about each is whether or not the duration had terminated at a given time. For example, suppose that one is interested in estimating the duration of residence, x, on a housing estate. For each house the date of construction is available together with a note of whether the original occupant is still in residence. Suppose that the ith house is aged t_i and that the duration of residence of the first occupant of that house was x_i. The information available only tells us that $x_i < t_i$ (if the present occupant is new) or that $x_i \geq t_i$ (if the original occupant is still in residence). If the distribution function of duration is $F(x)$ then the contribution to the likelihood is $F(t_i)$ in those cases where $x_i < t_i$ and $1 - F(t_i)$ otherwise. The likelihood may thus be written

$$l = \prod_{i=1}^{n} \{F(t_i)\}^{a_i} \{1 - F(t_i)\}^{1-a_i} \tag{2.35}$$

where $a_i = 1$ if $x_i < t_i$ and $a_i = 0$ if $x_i \geq t_i$. The 'unknowns' in this case are the values of the distribution function at the points $t_i (i = 1, 2, \ldots, n)$. However, since $F(t)$ is a distribution function it must be monotonically increasing in x [see II, Figure 10.3.1]. Hence if $t_1 \leq t_2 \leq \ldots \leq t_k$ we must have $F(t_1) \leq F(t_2) \leq \ldots \leq F(t_k)$ and hence (2.35) must be maximized with respect to $F(t_1)$, $F(t_2)$, $\ldots$, $F(t_k)$ subject to these order restrictions. The solution to this particular problem can be obtained fairly easily as shown in Barlow and co-workers (1972). Similar problems arise in other areas of application. For example, we might be interested in the length of time before symptoms recur after medical treatment or before a response is observed to some psychological stimulus. If all that is recorded is whether or not the response has occurred after some fixed period of time—perhaps when the individual is lost to observation—the problem will be amenable to treatment by this method. How complete a picture we get of the function $F(x)$ depends on whether the values t_i span the range of x. One might interpolate between the points at which estimates are obtained by fitting some appropriate distribution to the estimates.

Two other methods of estimation involve very similar mathematical operations to those of maximum likelihood. The method of minimum χ^2 [see VI, §3.7] differs only with respect to the form of the function to be optimized. Bayesian approaches to point estimation involve the minimization of an expected loss or the determination of the mode [see II, §10.1.3] of a posterior distribution [see VI, §15.1].

We have already remarked that high precision may not be necessary in social science applications and hence, when a method such as maximum likelihood would prove too costly, simpler *ad hoc* methods may serve equally well. One useful approach is to take some numerical characteristics of the observed distribution and equate them to their theoretical counterparts. This is frequently done with percentage points [see II, §10.3.3]. The 100α percentile of $F(\mathbf{x}, \theta)$ is the solution of

$$F(x, \theta) = \alpha \tag{2.36}$$

which we may write as $x(\alpha, \theta)$. If this is equated to the same percentile of the empirical distribution we have an equation for the unknown vector-valued parameter θ. By choosing as many percentiles as there are unknown parameters, k say, we have the set of simultaneous equations

$$F(x_i, \theta) = \alpha_i \qquad (i = 1, 2, \ldots, k) \tag{2.37}$$

which, in general, will have a unique solution for θ. The essence of the method is thus to choose θ such that the observed and theoretical distribution functions coincide at k points. An interesting statistical problem concerns how best to choose the x_i's (or the α_i's) so that the resulting estimates are as good as possible. A discussion of this problem in relation to the log-normal distribution will be found in Aitchison and Brown (1957) but, in practice, the choice is likely to be highly constrained by what data are available. Indeed, one of the advantages of the method of percentage points is that it can be applied to data which are censored or grouped. Its advantages over maximum likelihood are well illustrated by reference to fitting the two-term mixed exponential distribution. Given a random sample $x_1, x_2, \ldots, x_n$ the likelihood function will be

$$l = \prod_{i=1}^{n} \{p\lambda_1 e^{-\lambda_1 x_i} + (1 - p)\lambda_2 e^{-\lambda_2 x_i}\}. \tag{2.38}$$

Viewed as a function of p, λ_1 and λ_2 this is very awkward to maximize and the problem is made more difficult by the fact that the likelihood 'surface' may have a 'ridge' so that many different sets of parameter values give nearly the same value of l as the maximum. Using the method of percentage points one would choose three values of α and find the associated x's from the empirical distribution. The system of simultaneous equations would then have the form

$$pe^{-\lambda_1 x(i)} + (1 - p)e^{-\lambda_2 x(i)} = \alpha_i \qquad (i = 1, 2, 3) \tag{2.39}$$

where $x(i)$ denotes the ith percentage point. These equations are still not easy to solve but they pose simpler problems of numerical analysis than does the maximization of (2.38). The problem can be greatly simplified if it is possible to choose the $x(i)$'s to be multiples of one another. The equations of (2.39) can then be expressed as polynomials in $e^{-\lambda_1}$ and $e^{-\lambda_2}$ as shown in Bartholomew (1959). Elimination methods can then be used to reduce the problem to one of finding the roots of a polynomial.

Another commonly-used method is to equate the theoretical and sample moments [see VI, §3.5]. Sometimes this turns out to be the same as the method of maximum likelihood and if often gives fairly simple estimating equations. It cannot be used, however, with data that have been censored or are otherwise incomplete.

We have had many occasions to remark on the occurrence of data which are incomplete through failure to obtain full information on the sample members. This situation arises because the social researcher often has limited control over the circumstances in which he makes his observations. Two sorts of incompleteness occur commonly in social investigation which pose special estimation problems, especially in the study of duration. In longitudinal studies, for example, it is usual to follow cohorts of individuals over a period of time. Thus a group of patients undergoing surgery may be observed to see how long it is before they have a recurrence of the trouble or exhibit other symptoms of interest. The length of time before re-conviction for released prisoners and the length of time that recruits to a firm stay in their jobs are further subjects on which data can be collected by observation of the process over a period of time. At the end of the period an estimate of the survivor function may be required from data which include some incomplete durations. If the patients, employees, etc. have entered the system at different times each individual will have been observed for a different length of time. The problem of estimating parameters can be approached via the likelihood function, though the traditional methods use actuarial techniques. These two approaches have been brought together by Chiang (1968) and Bartholomew and Forbes (1979).

A second, and very common, form of data on durations arises from cross-sectional studies in which a process is observed over a short interval of time. This is often referred to as *census* or *current* data. Because such data frequently arise in acturial work, the methods for handling it have been largely confined to mortality studies in the actuarial literature. In order to illustrate the kind of problem which arises, consider an application made by Marshall (1971) to the study of mobility. The aim was to estimate the distribution of the length of time that a house occupier lives at a particular address in different parts of a town in South East England. The data available consisted of the distribution of length of occupancy at the beginning and end of a certain calendar year together with the number in each length of occupancy group who moved during that year. In tabular form the data are as follows.

Length of occupancy	Average number at risk of moving	Number of movers
$0 \rightarrow x_1$	R_0	M_0
$x_1 \rightarrow x_2$	R_1	M_1
$x_2 \rightarrow x_3$	R_2	M_2
$\vdots$	$\vdots$	$\vdots$

The numbers in the middle column would be averages of the beginning and end of year numbers in the group. The last column gives the distribution by length of occupancy for leavers, but it is not an estimate of the frequency distribution of length of occupancy since it depends on the rate at which people have moved into the area. For example, a large influx 3 years ago would lead to a large number of movers with 3 years of occupancy during the current year. It is, however, possible to estimate the propensity-to-move function and from this to find $G(x)$ and $f(x)$ via the relationships given in (2.5). The basis of the method, described in Bartholomew and Forbes (1979), is first to approximate $\phi(x)$ by a step function which is constant in each of the intervals (x_i, x_{i+1}). If ϕ_i is the constant value in (x_i, x_{i+1}) it is easily shown that an estimate of this value is provided by M_i/R_i.

So far we have been concerned with what is called point estimation. Usually, it will be desirable to accompany such an estimate by some indication of the error associated with it. This may be done by quoting the standard error [see VI, §1.2]—the standard deviation of the sampling distribution of the estimator [see VI, Chapter 2]. One can then have about 95% confidence that the true value lies within two standard errors of the estimate, for example. This is exact for a Normal sampling distribution and quite a good approximation unless the distribution is very non-Normal. If an estimator is a linear function of the sample values then it is possible to appeal to the Central Limit Theorem to justify the Normal approximation. For maximum likelihood estimators the asymptotic distribution [see VI, §6.2] is known to be Normal under rather general conditions and the asymptotic standard errors can be easily obtained from the second derivative of the logarithm of the likelihood function [see VI, §3.3.3]. If the sampling distribution is markedly non-Normal, as it may be if the sample size is small, a more exact specification of the error associated with an estimator will be required. For this the theory of confidence intervals is required [see VI, Chapter 4]. One useful and general method of finding a confidence interval for a single parameter is as follows. Let $\hat{\theta}$ be the maximum likelihood estimator of the parameter and let the distribution function of its sampling distribution be $F(\hat{\theta} \mid \theta)$. Then it is easy to show that $y = F(\hat{\theta} \mid \theta)$ has uniform distribution on the interval $(0, 1)$ [see II, Theorem 10.7.2] and, in particular that

$$\Pr\{\alpha_1 \leq F(\hat{\theta} \mid \theta) \leq 1 - \alpha_2\} = 1 - (\alpha_1 + \alpha_2). \tag{2.40}$$

If $F(\hat{\theta} \mid \theta)$ is monotonic in θ these inequalities may be inverted to give an equivalent statement of the form

$$\Pr\{\theta_1 \leq \theta \leq \theta_2\} = 1 - (\alpha_1 + \alpha_2)$$

where θ_1 and θ_2 are the roots of

$$F(\hat{\theta} \mid \theta) = \alpha_1 \quad \text{and} \quad F(\hat{\theta} \mid \theta) = 1 - \alpha_2.$$

Significance tests (Hypothesis testing) [see VI, Chapter 5]

A second mode of inference about the parameters of probability distributions is provided by significance testing. Indeed, this often assumes a more prominent role in social science statistics than do methods of estimation. In part this is a reflection of the fact that quantitative work in social science is at an early stage and it is in these circumstances that significance testing is more relevant. It also springs from a somewhat over-enthusiastic and uncritical view of what such tests can achieve.

A statistical hypothesis is a statement about probability distributions. A test of a statistical hypothesis is designed to show whether the data available are compatible with that statement. It is in this sense that the hypothesis is under test and if it fails it will be rejected. If it passes we cannot conclude that it is true—merely that on the evidence to hand there is insufficient reason to reject it. It is therefore somewhat misleading to speak of accepting a hypothesis, as many texts for social scientists do, since this tempts one to equate acceptance with truth. Hypotheses that arise naturally in practice often concern means and proportions. A hypothesis may specify the value of the mean of some distribution or that the means of several distributions are the same. Thus, for example, if one were comparing retail price levels of some item in different regions of the country on the basis of samples of prices it might be reasonable to test the hypothesis that the mean prices were the same in each region. The reason for setting up such a hypothesis would be a desire to adopt the simplest explanation until compelled by the data to do otherwise. This is merely an application of the principle, common to all scientific investigation, of seeking the simplest explanation for the data in hand. As a canon of science this principle may be sound but its relevance to each application should not be taken for granted. A second, and common, example arises when considering the relationship between variables. In the simple linear regression model [see VI, §9.11] the mean value of a variable y is assumed to depend linearly on another variable x so that [see II, §8.9] $E(y \mid x) = \alpha + \beta x$. One might test the hypothesis $\beta = 0$ on the grounds that the variable x should not be invoked to explain the value of y unless the simpler hypothesis $E(y) = \alpha$ can be shown to be inadequate. The result of a test of significance is never final and irreversible. It is an aid to judgement whose main purpose is to set up standards of evidence necessary to justify replacing a simple model by a more complicated one.

A full discussion of significance testing would be out of place here. It is part of the foundation of any statistics course and it is treated, at the appropriate level, in virtually all texts. Kendall and Stuart (1979) provide a full account of the theory and Knott and O'Muircheartaigh (1977) give an outline covering estimation as well as hypothesis testing for the benefit of those concerned with the analysis of survey data. The common tests for means, proportions and variances (t-, χ^2- and F-tests [see VI, §5.2]) are frequently used by social scientists. They are well documented and make minimal mathematical demands on the user. However, social scientists are liable to meet new situations for which standard tests are not available. These require general methods which do make mathematical demands and it is these with which we shall be concerned here. First we give just sufficient background and terminology to render the discussion intelligible to those unfamiliar with the area.

The main elements of a test procedure can be set out as follows.

(a) A *null* hypothesis [see VI, §5.4] which is to be tested; this will often be that a set of parameters are equal or zero or that they are subject to certain constraints.
(b) A test statistic [see VI, §1.2] which is some function of the sample data chosen to discriminate as effectively as possible between the null hypothesis and the likely alternatives.
(c) The sampling distribution [see VI, Chapter 2] of the test statistic.
(d) A rule for deciding what values of the test statistic would justify the rejection of the null hypothesis.

The mathematical demands of the subject arise mainly under (b) and (c); (a) is a substantive question and (d) is concerned with the logic rather than the mathematics of testing. Nevertheless, the mathematical problems under (b) and (c) cannot be formulated until (d) has been settled.

The choice of a rule is influenced by the desire to reconcile two conflicting requirements. First, one wishes to avoid rejecting a null hypothesis when it is really true (the so-called Type I error) and, secondly, one wants to avoid failing to reject the null hypothesis when it is false (the Type II error). In the classical theory the dilemma is resolved by arguing that the Type I error is the more serious and hence that this should be held at an acceptably small level. Having ensured this we may then seek to minimize the risk of a Type II error.

To pose the mathematical problem we use geometrical terminology by referring to the set of all possible samples as the sample space. The object is then to partition the sample space into two regions—the rejection (or critical) region and its complement. The critical region has to be constructed so that the probability that a sample falls in the region when the null hypothesis is true is small (often 0.05 or 0.01) but that it is as large as possible for relevant alternative hypotheses. The solution to the simplest such problem, on which the general solution is based, is provided by the Neyman–Pearson lemma [see VI, §5.4]. This relates to the case where it is desired to test a hypothesis about the value of a single parameter, θ, of a probability distribution. Let the null hypothesis be that $\theta = \theta_0$ and suppose that the only possible alternative is that $\theta = \theta_1$. (This is highly unrealistic but it paves the way for a treatment of the more general problem.) Suppose that the joint density function of the sample $\mathbf{x} = (x_1, x_2, \ldots, x_n)$ is $f(\mathbf{x} \mid \theta)$ (assumed continuous), then we have to find a region R in the x-space such that

$$\int_R f(\mathbf{x} \mid \theta_1)\, d\mathbf{x}$$

is maximized, subject to the requirement that

$$\int_R f(\mathbf{x} \mid \theta_0)\, d\mathbf{x} = \alpha$$

where α is the chosen probability of wrongly rejecting the null hypothesis (the significance level or size of the test). The lemma states that on the boundary of R the likelihood ratio

$$\lambda = f(\mathbf{x} \mid \theta_0)/f(\mathbf{x} \mid \theta_1) \tag{2.41}$$

is constant. A point is in the rejection region if $\lambda \le \lambda_0$ where λ_0 is the critical value. The ratio λ may therefore be used as the test statistic and the critical value λ_0 may be determined from the sampling distribution of λ that is so that

$$\Pr\{\lambda \le \lambda_0 \mid \theta = \theta_0\} = \alpha.$$

If the critical region turns out to have the same form whatever the value of θ_1 in some interval the test is said to be uniformly most powerful [see VI, §5.4] against that set of θ's. (Power is the complement of the probability of the Type II error.)

In general the probability distribution of the x's may involve several parameters and the null hypothesis may not involve them all. Those which do not enter into the specification of the null hypothesis are called 'nuisance' parameters [see VI, §5.2]. A general method of finding a test statistic in this case derives its motivation from the likelihood ratio statistic of (2.41). Suppose now that θ is vector-valued, taking values in a space Ω. The null hypothesis specifies that θ lies in some subspace ω of Ω. Let $f(\mathbf{x} \mid \hat{\theta}_0)$ denote the maximum value of the likelihood when $\theta \in \omega$ and $f(\mathbf{x} \mid \hat{\theta}_1)$ the maximum when $\theta \in \Omega - \omega$. Then a suitable test statistic is

$$\lambda = f(\mathbf{x} \mid \hat{\theta}_0)/f(\mathbf{x} \mid \hat{\theta}_1). \tag{2.42}$$

The mathematical steps in deriving λ are therefore exactly the same as in finding maximum likelihood estimators. The likelihood ratio statistic λ is a function of the sample values and its sampling distribution under the null hypothesis can, in principle, be found using the calculus of random variables. In practice this may be difficult and the resulting distribution may turn out to depend on the nuisance parameters. However, there is a general asymptotic result, which often provides a good approximation, to the effect that

$$-2 \ln \lambda \sim \chi_r^2, \tag{2.43}$$

i.e. $-2 \ln \lambda$ is distributed as chi-squared, the number of degrees of freedom depending on the exact form of the null hypothesis. This result requires certain conditions to be satisfied. In particular, if ω results from imposing r linear restraints on the θ's then (2.43) holds asymptotically with r as the degrees of freedom. Many of the tests used in multivariate analysis are based on this result.

The probability that a real departure from the null hypothesis is detected by the test is known as the power. It is, of course, a function of the unknown parameters. Also, it is a function of the sample size and is therefore useful in helping to decide what the sample size should be. There is no point in carrying out a survey if the sample size is too small to detect the sort of effects which are practically important. The determination of the sample size required to achieve a given power is simply a matter of solving an equation in one variable.

Distribution-free methods (Non-parametric methods) [see VI, Chapter 14]

The approach to inference followed throughout this section requires an assumption about the form of the distribution of the observations. Without this the likelihood cannot be written down and hence neither maximum likelihood estimators nor likelihood ratio statistics can be obtained. The various probability models described in Section 2.3 may provide a basis for a suitable assumption, but sometimes it will be difficult to justify any distributional form. In these circumstances one would prefer to use methods which dispense with distributional assumptions altogether. This need has been felt by social scientists, particularly psychologists, among whom such methods are widely used. In the absence of an assumed distributional form there are no parameters in the ordinary sense and so the problems have to be re-formulated. Thus instead of asking whether two samples come from Normal populations with the same mean we now have to ask whether they come from the same distribution (of unspecified form). The test criterion will then be chosen with a view to detecting differences in location.

Many distribution-free tests statistics are based on ranks [see VI, §14.3] rather than variate values (hence they can be used where only ordinal measures are available). Quite often, they use essentially the same test statistics as the corresponding 'Normal theory' tests but are calculated instead from the ranks. Thus, for example, the rank sum statistic for testing for a difference in location can be viewed as being based on the difference in mean rank for the two samples—the ranks are those for the pooled samples. The novelty arises in finding the sampling distribution of the statistic. This is done by assuming that all permutations of the sample members are equally likely on the null hypothesis. The mathematical problem is then the combinatorial one of enumerating cases. With small samples this can be done by listing all possible cases, but for larger sample sizes asymptotic results are usually available which often have their justification in some version of the Central Limit theorem.

Distribution-free methods are covered in most statistics texts, especially those written for social scientists. Especially recommended is Hollander and Wolfe (1973) or, for a rather earlier treatment, Noether (1967). Siegel (1956) is widely used and provides a convenient listing of methods and their properties. A much more theoretical account is contained in the symposium proceedings edited by Puri (1970). A comprehensive bibliography is available in Singer (1979).

Goodness of fit [see VI, Chapter 7]

Having fitted a theoretical frequency distribution to data it is natural to ask whether the agreement between data and theory is adequate. Traditionally this problem has been treated in statistical theory under the heading of 'goodness of fit'. The most common method is to tabulate the observed distribution in the form of a frequency table [see VI, §3.2.2] and draw up a table comparing the observed and theoretical (or 'expected') frequencies. A measure of the closeness of the fit is then constructed using the chi-squared statistic [see VI, §7.12] defined by

$$\chi^2 = \Sigma \frac{(O - E)^2}{E} \tag{2.44}$$

where O and E denote observed and expected frequencies, respectively. The significance of the deviations between the two sets of frequencies is then judged by reference to the sampling distribution of χ^2 calculated on the assumption that the data have been randomly sampled from the distribution being fitted. Other measures of goodness of fit can be constructed from the observed and expected frequencies of which

$$\Lambda = -2 \Sigma O \ln O/E$$

is based on the likelihood ratio method (see below). Yet another group of tests is based on the difference between the observed sample distribution function and the theoretical distribution. The best known of these is the Kolmogorov–Smirnov statistic [see VI, §7.2.1] which uses the largest deviation between the two distributions.

Although a goodness of fit test answers a well-defined question it must be recognized that this is not always the question that is being asked. To clarify ideas we may list three possible purposes for fitting a model to data as follows.

(i) To help decide whether the model is 'true'.

(ii) To provide a parsimonious description of the data [see VI, §1.2].

(iii) Because we wish to carry out some further analysis which assumes that the model is true.

A classical goodness of fit test is designed for the first situation and is not directly relevant to the other two. For example, if we fit a log-normal distribution to data on completed length of service in a firm we may well

38

find that the fit is poor as judged by a χ^2-test. Nevertheless, as a concise description of the data or as a tool for forecasting it may be sufficiently accurate for practical purposes. The real question is whether the tool is sufficiently good for its purpose and not whether it is perfect, and this is not a purely statistical question.

References

Aitchison, J., and Brown, J. A. C. (1957). *The Lognormal Distribution*, Cambridge University Press, London.

Barlow, R. E., Bartholomew, D. J., Bremner, J. M., and Brunk, H. D. (1972). *Statistical Inference under Order Restrictions*, Wiley, London.

Bartlett, M. S., and Kendall, D. G. (1946). The statistical analysis of variance-heterogeneity and the logarithmic transformation. *Suppl. J. Roy. Statist. Soc.*, **8**, 128–138.

Bartholomew, D. J. (1959). Note on the measurement and prediction of labour turnover. *J. Roy. Statist. Soc.*, A, **122**, 232–239.

Bartholomew, D. J. (1973). *Stochastic Models for Social Processes*, 2nd ed. Wiley, London.

Bartholomew, D. J., and Forbes, A. F. (1979). *Statistical Techniques for Manpower Planning*, Wiley, London.

Champernowne, D. G. (1973). *The Distribution of Incomes Between Persons*, Cambridge University Press, London.

Chiang, C. L. (1968). *Introduction to Stochastic Processes in Biostatistics*, Wiley, New York.

Clowes, G. A. (1972). A dynamic model for the analysis of labour turnover. *J. Roy. Statist. Soc.*, A, **135**, 242–256.

Coleman, J. S. (1964). *Introduction to Mathematical Sociology*, The Free Press of Glencoe, New York, and Collier-Macmillan, London.

Feller, W. (1968). *An Introduction to Probability Theory and Its Applications*, Vol. I, 3rd ed. Wiley, New York.

Folks, J. L., and Chhikara, R. S. (1978). The inverse gaussian distribution and its applications. *J. Roy. Statist. Soc.*, B, **40**, 263–289.

Gumbel, E. J. (1958). *The Statistics of Extremes*, Columbia University Press, New York.

Hill, B. M. (1970). Zipf's law and prior distributions for the composition of a population. *J. Amer. Statist. Ass.*, **65**, 1220–1232.

Hill, B. M. (1974). The rank-frequency form of Zipf's law. *J. Amer. Statist. Ass.*, **69**, 1017–1026.

Hill, B. M., and Woodroofe, M. (1975). Stronger forms of Zipf's law. *J. Amer. Statist. Ass.*, **70**, 212–219.

Hollander, M., and Wolfe, D. A. (1973). *Non-parametric Statistical Methods*, Wiley, New York.

Jonckheere, A. R. (1954). A distribution free k-sample test against ordered alternatives. *Biometrika*, **41**, 133–145.

Kendall, M. G. (1961). Natural law in the social sciences. *J. Roy. Statist. Soc.*, A, **124**, 1–19.

Kendall, M. G. (1976). *Time Series*, 2nd ed. Griffin, London and High Wycombe.

Kendall, M. G., and Stuart, A. (1979). *The Advanced Theory of Statistics*, Vol. 2, (4th ed.) Griffin, London and High Wycombe.

Knott, M., and O'Muircheartaigh, C. A. (1977). Estimation and hypothesis testing. In C. A. O'Muircheartaigh and C. Payne (Eds.), *The Analysis of Survey Data, Vol. 2, Model Fitting*, Wiley, London, pp. 1–34.

Lancaster, A. (1972). A stochastic model for the duration of a strike. *J. Roy. Statist. Soc.*, A, **135**, 257–271.

Mandelbrot, B. (1956). On the language of taxonomy: an outline of a 'thermostatical' theory of systems of categories with Willis (natural) structure. In C. Cherry (Ed.), *Information Theory: Third London Symposium*, Butterworths, London. pp. 135–148.

Mandelbrot, B. (1965). A class of long-tailed probability distributions and the empirical distribution of city sizes. In F. Massarik and P. Ratoosh (Eds), *Mathematical Explorations in Behavioural Science*, Richard D. Irwin Inc. and the Dorsey Press, Homewood Ill. pp. 322–332.

Marshall, M. L. (1971). The use of probability distributions for comparing the turnover of families in a residential area. In A. G. Wilson (Ed.), *London Papers in Regional Science*, **2**, Urban Regional Planning, Pion, London. pp. 171–193.

Noether, G. E. (1967). *Elements of Non-parametric Statistics*, Wiley, New York.

Puri, M. L. (Ed.) (1970). *Non-parametric Techniques of Statistical Inference*, Cambridge University Press, London.

Siegel, S. (1956). *Non-parametric Statistics for Behavioral Sciences*, McGraw-Hill, New York.

Silcock, H. (1954). The phenomenon of labour turnover. *J. Roy. Statist. Soc.*, A, **117**, 429–440.

Simon, H. A. (1955). On a class of skew distribution functions. *Biometrika*, **42**, 425–440.

Singer, B. (1979). Distribution-free methods for non-parametric problems: a classified and selected bibliography. *Brit. J. Math. Statist. Psych.*, **32**, 1–60.

Whitmore, G. A. (1976). Management applications of the inverse gaussian distribution. *Omega*, **4**, 215–223.

Whitmore, G. A. (1979). An inverse Gausian model for labour turnover. *J. Roy. Statist. Soc.* A **142**, 468–478.

Zipf, G. K. (1949). *Human Behaviour and the Principle of Least Effort*, Addison-Wesley, Reading, Mass.

3

Collection of Data:
Design and Analysis of Surveys

3.1 The Background

A great deal of the data used by social scientists is obtained by means of social surveys. The information is often acquired by using interviewers who visit the sampled respondents and ask questions about attitudes, attributes and relationships. Sometimes a postal survey is used and the respondents are then invited to complete the questionnaire themselves. Familiar examples are provided by opinion polls and market research enquiries, but many research studies in social psychology, sociology and political studies also rely heavily on survey methods. Some surveys involve little more than estimating a few proportions or totals while others require elaborate exercises in scaling and multivariate analysis [see VI, Chapter 17]. In all cases the reasons for using a sample rather than the whole population are likely to lie in limitations on resources in the shape of time, money and skilled personnel.

Once the population has been defined and a sampling frame drawn up the conduct of a survey involves two stages, viz.

(a) The design of the sampling procedure, including the choice of sample size, the selection of people to be interviewed, the procedures to be adopted in following up respondents who are not at home and so on.

(b) The analysis of the data arising from the survey with a view to making inferences about the population from which the sample has been drawn.

Although it is convenient to treat these aspects separately for purposes of exposition they are, of course, intimately related. The question of what data to collect can only be adequately answered if the purposes for which they are to be used have been defined.

By no means all facets of survey work involve mathematical arguments and those that do tend to be less demanding in this respect than many others discussed elsewhere in this book. For example, the problems of questionnaire design, coding of responses and the training of interviewers are often crucial for the success of a piece of research but they place no mathematical demands on the survey practitioner. Much of the sampling theory for the basic designs depends only on techniques for finding means and variances of linear functions of random variables. However, the literature of sampling is so voluminous and varied that it would be useful for social scientists coming new to the field to have a guide to the theory which is available and to the mathematical knowledge which is required to understand it. This chapter is designed to provide such a guide. It cannot claim to be exhaustive but we believe that no major area of the subject requiring mathematical knowledge has been omitted.

3.2 The Literature

In this section we shall confine ourselves to books and certain key papers since the newcomer to the field is likely to find this less overwhelming than an attempt at a full bibliography.

At the most basic level Stuart (1976) provides an introduction to the ideas of sampling theory in a treatment which is almost devoid of mathematics. Sampford (1962) is also an introductory account designed for practitioners with the emphasis on agricultural applications while Moser and Kalton (1971) does much the same for the social sciences with relatively little emphasis on sampling theory. In the early nineteen-fifties there were published several books giving systematic accounts of survey theory which are still standard works on the subject. These include Yates (1949), Deming (1950), Cochran (1953), Hansen, Hurwitz and Madow (1953) and Sukhatme (1954). The latest edition of Yates appeared in 1980 and the second and third editions of Cochran in 1963 and 1977 respectively. Murthy (1967) and Raj (1968) give more recent but substantially similar treatments of the theory while Kish (1965) provides what is, perhaps, the best all-round treatment of survey practice and theory. Johnson and Smith (1969) contains the proceedings of a symposium on developments in survey theory. More recently Barnett (1974) has provided an introductory account of sampling theory and Konijn (1973) and Cassel, Wretman and Sarndal (1977) more advanced treatments. Some general texts on statistical theory include sections on the theory of sampling from finite populations as, for example, Kendall and Stuart, Vol. III (1976). Two volumes on the analysis of survey data edited by O'Muircheartaigh and Payne (1977) give a wide coverage of modern techniques with particular emphasis on multivariate methods.

Papers on sampling theory and method can be found in most of the main statistical journals. Neyman (1934) marks the beginning of the modern approach to sampling theory and the subject has been reviewed at intervals, by, for example, Yates (1946), Dalenius (1962) and Smith (1976). This last paper is especially interesting in that it attempts to relate finite population theory to the mainstream of statistical theory which, hitherto, have tended to be developed in separate compartments. Ericson (1969) and Godambe (1955, 1966) have also approached the subject with somewhat similar objectives. In many respects the analysis of survey data has lagged behind design and it has been commonplace for data from complex designs to be treated as though they had been obtained by simple random sampling. Steps to rectify this oversimplification have been taken by Kish and Frankel (1974) and Bebbington and Smith (1977) (see also Section 3.9).

It is possible to understand and use the standard sampling designs with very little mathematical and statistical knowledge. However, practical conditions rarely correspond closely with the ideals of the textbook and in such circumstances a deeper understanding of the technicalities is invaluable. Since the estimation of means and totals figures prominently in most survey work the sampling behaviour of linear functions of random variables is central. In particular we have to find means and variances of such functions and appeal to relevant forms of the Central Limit Theorem to establish their approximate normality. Attempts to construct designs in ways which maximize precision or minimize cost lead to the maximization of functions of several variables subject to constraints which take the form either of equalities or inequalities. These require the traditional calculus methods using Lagrange multipliers [see IV, §5.15] or the techniques of mathematical programming [see IV, Chapter 15].

Several types of sampling technique are used in practice, but only those based on probability ideas can be treated theoretically. We shall therefore not deal with quota sampling (which is widely used in practice) or other, less formal or 'purposive', ways of selecting samples. A probability sampling method is one such that there is a known non-zero probability of choosing each possible sample. In classical theory it is this feature which establishes the link between the sample and the population from which it comes and which therefore makes a theory possible. The calculus of probability thus lies at the root of sampling theory and, for the most part, the results required will be found in the core volumes on Probability and Statistics.

In remaining sections we shall review those aspects of sampling theory which involve mathematics. It is not our intention to provide a text-book approach with full derivations of results, but we shall have to give a summary sufficient to enable the reader to identify those parts of the sampling literature and the core volumes which are relevant for his purposes. This involves establishing a common notation and terminology which, so far as possible, conforms to common usage.

3.3 Sample Designs

Suppose that we label the members of a population, in any order, with the consecutive integers 1, 2, 3, . . ., N where N, the population size, will usually be very large. A sample of size n—often a few hundreds—is to be drawn from this population and used as a basis for drawing inferences about the population. Let y denote some variable measured on members of the population, y_i being the value of y for the individual numbered i. The population total is thus $\sum_{i=1}^{N} y_i$ and the mean is

$$\mu = \frac{1}{N} \sum_{i=1}^{N} y_i. \tag{3.1}$$

This notation also covers the case where y refers to the presence or absence of some attribute. Let $y_i = 1$ if the ith individual possesses the attribute and $y_1 = 0$ otherwise. Then μ as given above will be the proportion of the population who possess the attribute. In such cases we shall replace μ by P. The population variance will be defined by

$$\sigma^2 = \frac{1}{N - 1} \sum_{i=1}^{N} (y_i - \mu)^2. \tag{3.2}$$

(The use of $N - 1$ rather than N in the divisor leads to some simplification in the subsequent formulae but is of no practical significance.) In the case where y represents an attribute [see VI, §1.2] it may easily be shown that

$$\sigma^2 = \frac{N}{N - 1} P(1 - P) \simeq P(1 - P). \tag{3.3}$$

In practice, we are rarely interested in a single variable but in many. Although we shall usually wish to look at each variable separately it is often the relationships between the variables which are of greater importance. The theory required for this is much less well-developed and our treatment will therefore have to be over-weighted towards single variables and, especially, means and proportions.

Simple random sampling without replacement [see II, Definition 3.8.1]

The simplest sampling method is the one in which all possible samples are equally likely to be chosen. This embodies an obvious principle of 'fairness' which might be expected to produce a sample which was, in some sense, representative. For its application we require a list of all members of the population (the sampling frame) and a method for drawing the sample members. In the case of small populations this can be done by representing the members by cards or discs and drawing the sample from a well-shuffled pack or bag. With the large populations common in social science work this is impacticable and the same result is achieved by using random numbers [see II, §§5.1 and 5.6]. In practice pseudo-random numbers [see VI, §20.3] are usually used since these can be readily generated within a computer.

Although there are $\binom{N}{n}$ possible samples and if they are all equally likely to be drawn it is a straightforward matter, in principle, to calculate the sampling properties of any sample statistics. The easiest of all is the case of a proportion where the exact sampling distribution is *hypergeometric* [see II, §5.3]: more exactly if d is the number who possess the attribute in a sample of size n then

$$P(d) = \frac{\binom{NP}{d}\binom{N(1-P)}{n-d}}{\binom{N}{n}}, \qquad \{0 \le d \le \min(NP, N(1-P))\}. \qquad (3.4)$$

When N is large compared with n this is close to a binomial distribution [see II, §5.2.2] which, in turn, is well approximated by a Normal distribution [see II, §11.4]. In practice, therefore, we almost always use the Normal approximation [see II, §11.4.3]

$$\frac{d}{n} \sim N\left[P, \frac{P(1-P)}{n}\left(1 - \frac{n}{N}\right)\right]. \qquad (3.5)$$

(Here, as elsewhere in this volume, the symbol '$\sim$' means 'is distributed as'.)

In the case of the sample mean a Normal approximation based on the following representation is always used. Introduce random variables $\{a_i\}$ such that

$a_i = 1$ if the ith population member is included in the sample
$\quad = 0$ otherwise.

Then the sample mean can be written

$$\bar{y} = \frac{1}{n}\sum_{i=1}^{N} a_i y_i. \qquad (3.6)$$

We have now expressed $\bar{y}$ as a linear function of the random variables $\{a_i\}$ and hence can appeal to standard distributional theory to find the distribution. The a_i's are not, in general, independent and their distribution will be determined by the sampling procedure. For the present case of simple random sampling

$$\Pr\{a_i = 1\} = \frac{n}{N}, \qquad \Pr\{a_i = 1, a_j = 1\} = \frac{n(n-1)}{N(N-1)} \qquad (i \ne j) \qquad (3.7)$$

and so on. Using these results it may be shown that

$$E(\bar{y}) = \mu, \qquad \operatorname{var}(\bar{y}) = \left(1 - \frac{n}{N}\right)\frac{\sigma^2}{n}. \qquad (3.8)$$

(This includes the foregoing results for a proportion as a special case.) This result shows that the sample mean is an unbiased estimator [see VI, §3.3.1(d)] of the population mean. There are versions of the Central Limit Theorem applicable to linear functions of dependent variables which establish the approximate Normality of $\bar{y}$. To summarize, then,

$$\bar{y} \sim N\left[\mu, \frac{\sigma^2}{n}\left(1 - \frac{n}{N}\right)\right] \qquad (3.9)$$

and this can be made the basis of inference procedures for μ. In practice σ^2 will be unknown but can be replaced by the sample variance,

$$s^2 = \frac{1}{n-1} \sum_{i=1}^{N} a_i(y_i - \bar{y})^2.$$

These basic results underlie the sampling theory for the more complicated designs to which we now turn.

Stratified random sampling

In this case the population is first divided into k strata and a simple random sample is drawn from each stratum. Such a design may be selected for one of several reasons. Firstly, the strata may be of interest in their own right; secondly the introduction of stratification often leads to greater precision in estimating overall population characteristics; and, thirdly, stratification allows flexibility in design which is useful in multi-stage designs. In practice the strata may be based on such things as sex, place of residence or social status. The design of a stratified sample involves the choice of relevant strata and of the sample size to be drawn from each stratum. To do this in an optimal way requires a knowledge of the sampling properties of the relevant test statistics or estimators. These can be simply obtained from the foregoing results for simple random sampling.

Let the stratum sizes be N_1, N_2, ..., N_k with means μ_1, μ_2, ..., μ_k respectively. We draw samples of sizes n_1, n_2, ..., n_k from the strata and denote the means by $\bar{y}_1$, $\bar{y}_2$, ..., $\bar{y}_k$. Any two strata means can be compared using the fact that

$$\bar{y}_i - \bar{y}_j \sim N\left[\mu_i - \mu_j, \frac{\sigma_i^2}{n_i}\left(1 - \frac{n_i}{N_i}\right) + \frac{\sigma_j^2}{n_j}\left(1 - \frac{n_j}{N_j}\right)\right] \qquad (3.10)$$

where σ_i^2 and σ_j^2 are the stratum variances which may be estimated by their sample counterparts. The set of stratum means can be compared by the techniques of the one-way analysis of variance and multiple comparison methods [see VI, §§8.3 and 11.4]. For these purposes the finite population correction factors $[1 - (n_i/N_i)]$ are usually ignored as they are usually close to one in practice.

To estimate the overall population mean, μ, we proceed as follows. Clearly,

$$\mu = \sum_{i=1}^{N} N_i \mu_i / N$$

which may be estimated by

$$\hat{\mu} = \sum_{i=1}^{N} N_i \bar{y}_i / N. \tag{3.11}$$

Since $\hat{\mu}$ is a linear function of k independent $\bar{y}_i$'s we may use the standard theory to show that

$$\hat{\mu} \sim N\left[\mu, \sum_{i=1}^{k} \frac{\sigma_i^2}{n_i}\left(1 - \frac{n_i}{N_i}\right)\left(\frac{N_i}{N}\right)^2\right]. \tag{3.12}$$

The expression for the variance plays a key role in answering the design questions posed above (see Section 3.5).

Cluster sampling

In many populations the members are grouped into what may be termed clusters, which have the property of being close together in some sense. For example, a cluster might be an area like a street or block of flats. It will then be cheaper to interview a given number of people in such a cluster than if the same number were selected at random from the whole population. By this means the sample size for a given cost can often be substantially increased. In cluster sampling a random sample of clusters is chosen and all members of the clusters selected are included in the sample. In a purely formal sense the division of a population into clusters and into strata is the same. In practice, however, strata are usually relatively few in number and large in size whereas clusters are usually numerous and fairly small. Furthermore, whereas one usually aims to make strata as homogeneous as possible, it is desirable to have clusters as heterogeneous as possible. The difference between the two schemes is that in stratified random sampling we take random samples from all strata, while in cluster sampling we take only a sample of clusters but include all members of the chosen clusters.

Unless the clusters happen to be of equal size it is not possible to fix the sample size in advance since it obviously depends on which clusters happen to be selected. Suppose, therefore, that we take c clusters (if we have some idea of cluster sizes we can clearly choose c to give, approximately, the desired sample size). Let T_i denote the sum of the y's in the ith cluster then

$$\mu = \sum_{i=1}^{k} \frac{T_i}{N} = \frac{k}{N}\left(\frac{1}{k}\sum_{i=1}^{k} T_i\right) \tag{3.13}$$

where k is now the total number of clusters in the population. An estimator of μ and its sampling distribution can now be obtained by treating the clusters as individual sampling units with the T_i's as their values. Thus $\sum T_i/k$ can be estimated by the mean of the sampled cluster totals ($\bar{T}$ say) and hence μ may be estimated by

$$\hat{\mu} = \frac{k}{N} \bar{T} \tag{3.14}$$

with variance

$$\text{var}(\hat{\mu}) = \frac{k^2}{N^2} \left(1 - \frac{c}{k}\right) \frac{\sigma_T^2}{c} \tag{3.15}$$

where σ_T^2 is the population variance of the cluster totals. In practice σ_T^2 must be estimated from the sampled clusters and the approximate normality of $\hat{\mu}$, required for inference procedures, deduced from the Central Limit Theorem.

In Section 3.4 we shall wish to compare (3.15) with the variance of μ from a simple random sample of the same size. This is most easily done when the cluster sizes are equal. In that case the sample size $n = c(N/k)$, in which case (3.15) becomes

$$\text{var}(\hat{\mu}) = \frac{k}{N} \frac{\sigma_T^2}{n} \left(1 - \frac{n}{N}\right). \tag{3.16}$$

Systematic sampling

This is the name given to the method of sampling in which members are drawn at equal intervals from a list of the population. Thus if the individuals are numbered consecutively from 1 to N and we require a sample of size n chosen so that $N/n = k$ is an integer we would take every kth name on the list starting with an individual chosen at random from among the first k. Such a procedure is clearly a special case of cluster sampling since each of the k possible samples may be thought of as a cluster and we sample just one cluster ($c = 1$). The estimator given by (3.14) becomes the sample mean and will be unbiased. The variance of the estimator cannot now be estimated from (3.16) because only one observation of T_i is available, but this formula can still be used to make theoretical comparisons between systematic and random sampling (Section 3.4).

Cluster sampling with sub-sampling

If the clusters are relatively large—as they might be if one were selecting a sample of school children using schools as clusters—it may be desirable to introduce a second stage of sampling by taking random samples from each cluster. The first stage would thus involve selecting clusters and the second stage selecting individuals within clusters. Estimates of the population mean and variance can be constructed in two stages as follows. We know from (3.14) how to estimate μ if the sampled cluster totals are known. We also know how to estimate a cluster total from a random sample drawn from within that cluster. Therefore, replacing $\bar{T}$ in (3.14) by its sample estimate we now have

$$\hat{\mu} = \frac{k}{N} \left(\frac{1}{c} \sum_{i=1}^{k} a_i N_i \bar{y}_i \right) \tag{3.17}$$

where $\bar{y}_i$ is now the sample mean for the ith cluster and $a_i = 1$ if the ith cluster is included in the sample and zero otherwise. To establish that $\hat{\mu}$ is unbiased its expectation can be taken in two stages using a standard result from probability theory [see II, §16.3] that if X and Y are two random variables then $E(XY) = E(XE(Y \mid X))$. The same technique also leads to the following formula for the variance:

$$\text{var}(\hat{\mu}) = \frac{k}{c} \sum_{i=1}^{k} \left(\frac{N_i}{N} \right) \frac{\sigma_i^2}{n_i} \left(1 - \frac{n_i}{N_i} \right) + \left(\frac{k}{n} \right)^2 \frac{\sigma_T^2}{c} \left(1 - \frac{c}{k} \right) \tag{3.18}$$

$$= \frac{(k/c) \text{ (variance for stratified sampling)}}{+ \text{ (variance for cluster sampling)}}.$$

This formula also demonstrates the relationship between cluster sampling and stratified sampling. Thus, if $k = c$ the method reduces to stratified sampling whereas if $n_i = N_i$ for all i, we are back to one-stage cluster sampling.

These ideas can be extended to designs involving three or more stages or different kinds of two-stage design. For example, if the clusters are defined as all those living within given areas on a map the clusters might be selected by drawing map references at random. Clusters would then be chosen with probability proportional to size; sub-samples of equal size might then be taken from each cluster. Similar techniques to those mentioned above are required for deriving the sampling properties of estimators in such cases.

Estimation of variance from replicated sub-samples

It is sometimes possible to estimate sampling variances of estimators using internal evidence provided by the sample itself and without explicit reference to the sample design. Suppose that the sample size can be expressed as $n = mb$ where both m and b are integers and further that the full sample can be divided into b independent sub-samples in each of which the same sample design is used. Let $t^{(i)}$ denote some sample statistic of interest calculated from a sample of size i. Then from each of the b sub-samples we can calculate values of this statistic $t_1^{(m)}, t_2^{(m)}, \ldots, t_b^{(m)}$, say. An estimator of the variance of $t^{(m)}$ is thus

$$s_m^2 = \frac{1}{b-1} \sum_{i=1}^{b} (t_i^{(m)} - \bar{t}^{(m)})^2.$$

If t is a statistic such that

$$t^{(n)} = \frac{1}{b} \sum_{i=1}^{b} t_i^{(m)}$$

then, if we regard our b sub-samples as a simple random sample of N/m possible sub-samples, the finite population correction will be

$$\left(1 - \frac{b}{N/m}\right) = \left(1 - \frac{n}{N}\right)$$

and so

$$S_n^2 = \frac{S_m^2}{b}\left(1 - \frac{n}{N}\right). \tag{3.19}$$

This and related methods of estimating sampling variances are reviewed in Kish and Frankel (1974).

Except for the passing reference to pps (probability proportional to size) sampling, all of the designs discussed here have involved equal probabilities of selection at each stage. It is perfectly possible to have unequal probabilities of selection and then the algebra becomes more complicated but the principles remain the same.

3.4 The Design Effect and Methods for Increasing Precision

It is convenient to measure the efficiency of any given design by comparing it with simple random sampling. This is usually done by forming the quotient of the sampling variances of the estimator for the two designs. Thus if var($\hat{\mu}$) is the variance of an estimator of the population mean for the design in question, the 'design effect' is defined as

$$D = \mathrm{var}(\hat{\mu}) \Big/ \frac{\sigma^2}{n}\left(1 - \frac{n}{N}\right). \tag{3.20}$$

In the case of differences between means or other sample statistics the denominator would be the appropriate random sampling variance.

In stratified random sampling, when the finite population correction is negligible, it can be shown (see, for example, Cochran, 1963, p. 98) that $D \leq 1$. This means that we never get a less precise estimate with stratified sampling and so the design can be said to increase the efficiency of the survey. Whether the gain is sufficient to justify the extra cost which may be involved is more questionable, especially in view of the fact that D tends to be close to one for comparisons between means and for some other statistics (see Kish and Frankel, 1974, for example).

Similar calculations can be made for cluster sampling. If the cluster sizes are all equal to m the variance of the estimator of μ may be written

$$\text{var}(\hat{\mu}) = \frac{\sigma^2}{n}\left(1 - \frac{n}{N}\right)\{1 + \rho(m - 1)\} \tag{3.21}$$

where ρ is the intra-cluster correlation coefficient measuring the degree of similarity between members of the same cluster. In practice, members of the same cluster often tend to be alike and this means that ρ is positive (often of the order 0.04). Hence, especially if the cluster size is large, D can be substantially greater than one. This disadvantage may be more than offset by the reduced cost of collecting a cluster sample.

The increase in efficiency which results from stratification may be viewed as a way of using prior knowledge about the population to improve the estimates. The same effect can sometimes be achieved by other means, in particular by ratio and regression estimators.

Ratio and regression estimators

Suppose that we are interested in the population mean of a variable y which is known to be correlated with another variable x[see II, §9.8.3]. If it also happens that the population mean of x is known *a priori* the precision of our estimate can often be increased by taking account of the known relationship existing between y and x. For example, x might denote some variable recorded for each member of the population at a recent census and y might be its current value. The population mean of x is therefore known and we would usually expect a strong positive relationship between y and x.

A simple way of taking our prior knowledge into account in a simple random sample is to use the ratio estimator

$$\hat{\mu}_y = \bar{y}\left[\frac{\mu_x}{\bar{x}}\right] \tag{3.22}$$

where μ_x and μ_y are the population means and $\bar{x}$ and $\bar{y}$ the sample means. The rationale of this estimator is as follows. If $\bar{x}$ happens to exceed μ_x we know that we have a sample in which the x-values are, on average, too large. Since the x's and y's are correlated we may surmise that the y's are also too large, on average. To correct for this anticipated upward bias we therefore assume that the ratios $\mu_y/\bar{y}$ and $\mu_x/\bar{x}$ will be about the same and this argument leads to (3.22).

Finding the sampling distribution of $\hat{\mu}_y$ involves dealing with the ratio $\bar{y}/\bar{x}$. The exact distribution is difficult but there are well-known methods (see core volumes) for finding the distribution of ratios. These depend on a Taylor series expansion obtained by writing

$$\bar{x}^{-1} = \mu_x^{-1}\left[1 + \frac{\bar{x} - \mu_x}{\mu_x}\right]^{-1}$$

and using the fact that $(\bar{x} - \mu_x)$ is of order $n^{-1/2}$. The determination of the moments of $\hat{\mu}_y$ therefore depends on finding the moments and product moments of $\bar{y}$ and $\bar{x}$. By such means it can be shown that

$$\hat{\mu}_y \sim N\left[\mu_y\left\{\sigma_y^2 - \frac{2\mu_y}{\mu_x}\sigma_{xy} + \left(\frac{\mu_y}{\mu_x}\right)^2\sigma_x^2\right\}\frac{1}{n}\left(1 - \frac{n}{N}\right)\right] \tag{3.23}$$

where σ_{xy} is the covariance of x and y and σ_x^2 and σ_y^2 are the respective variances of x and y.

The variance of μ_y is not necessarily less than in the case of simple random sampling. A necessary (but not sufficient) condition for this to be so is that $\sigma_{xy} > 0$ that is, that x and y are positively correlated. To estimate the variance in practice it is necessary to estimate the σ's which are unknown and μ_y from the sample.

The rationale behind (3.22) is most convincing if the regression of y on x is a straight line through the origin. One might therefore expect to improve the estimate, in general, by relaxing the requirement of passing through the origin. This leads to the idea of the regression estimator of a mean given by

$$\hat{\mu} = \bar{y} + b(\mu_x - \bar{x}) \tag{3.24}$$

where b is some constant. This is an unbiased estimator of μ whatever value is chosen for b. Being a linear function of $\bar{y}$ and $\bar{x}$ its variance is easily found to be

$$\text{var}(\hat{\mu}) = \{\sigma_y^2 - 2b\sigma_{xy} + b^2\sigma_x^2\}\frac{1}{n}\left(1 - \frac{n}{N}\right) \tag{3.25}$$

and approximate Normality is established in the usual way. It is easy to show by the usual calculus method that the variance is minimized by choosing

$$b = \frac{\sigma_{xy}}{\sigma x^2}$$

in which case

$$\text{var}(\hat{\mu}) = \frac{\sigma_y^2}{n}\left(1 - \frac{n}{N}\right)(1 - \rho_{xy}^2) \tag{3.26}$$

where ρ_{xy} is the product moment correlation coefficient of x and y [see II, §9.8.1]. This variance is never greater than that for simple random sampling. Thus the higher the correlation the greater the gain in precision. The minimizing value of b will be recognized as the linear regression coefficient of y on x in the population. Since this is unlikely to be known in practice the minimum will not be achieved in general but we can get close to it by replacing b by the sample regression coefficient [see VI, §9.2]. In this case $\hat{\mu}_y$ is no longer a linear function and hence the determination of its sampling properties is more difficult. The series expansion method can be used to show that the resulting estimator is nearly unbiased and that its approximate variance can be found by substituting sample estimates in (3.26). The ratio estimator emerges as a special case of (3.24) when b is estimated by $\bar{y}/\bar{x}$, which would be appropriate if the line was known to pass through the origin.

Ratio and regression estimators can be used in more complicated designs. For example, in a stratified random sample, the strata means can be estimated by this method and then substituted into (3.11) in place of the $\bar{y}_i$'s. In this case a choice has to be made as to whether the regression coefficient is to be assumed the same in each stratum or not. In the latter event a different value of b will be estimated for each stratum. In the former case a common estimator will be needed. The method can also be extended to make use of information on several different x-variables using the multiple regression of y on the x's [see II, §13.6, and VI, §9.11].

Double or two-phase sampling

There may be occasions when information on a relevant supplementary variable x is lacking for the population as a whole but where it is worth collecting it as a separate exercise. This need not involve observing x for every member of the population but for a sufficiently large sample. The procedure is thus to select a first sample to obtain the information on x and then to draw a random sub-sample on which y is observed. If x is cheap to obtain and y is expensive and if the two variables are correlated this may be a good way of getting some of the benefits of the larger sample without having to incur the full cost. In the case of the regression estimator, μ_x would be replaced by the mean of x in the larger sample. Again, this complicates the distribution theory somewhat but if the first stage sample is large compared with the second the original theory for the regression estimator will be a good approximation.

Double sampling can also be used in the stratified design to estimate the strata sizes if these are unknown *a priori*. In the first phase of sampling we would merely observe into which stratum each member fell; the value of y would then be observed on the members selected for the second phase.

3.5 Choice and Allocation of Sample Size

One of the most basic questions in sample survey design concerns the choice of sample size. This involves not only the total size but its allocation between strata or within clusters as the case may be. Not all the relevant factors are quantifiable, but two important factors which can be measured are *cost* and *precision*.

Of the two, precision is a relatively straightforward matter which can be expressed in terms of variance or mean square error. Cost is more difficult as it includes not only the cost of collecting the sample values but also the penalties of making errors in the estimates.

The easist case is that of simple random sampling where the object is to estimate a single parameter. The question of how large a sample to take can be related to the precision required in the estimate. This may often be expressed as a requirement to be 'correct to within 1%'. The statistician interprets this to mean 'to within 1% with high probability, say 99%'. In the case of the mean this is tantamount to requiring the standard error of the sample mean to be less than some constant. That is, an n has to be found such that

$$\frac{\sigma^2}{n}\left(1 - \frac{n}{N}\right) \le C. \tag{3.27}$$

It is the smallest n which is required and this is obtained by rearranging the inequality. Unfortunately σ^2 will rarely be known. In the absence of such knowledge it may be possible to make a plausible guess or, better still, to use an estimate derived from a pilot survey. In the case of estimating a proportion the problem is simplified because $\sigma^2 = P(1 - P) \le \frac{1}{4}$ so by taking the largest possible value of σ^2 we shall err on the safe side. Alternatively P can be estimated from pilot survey data if this is available.

If a specific decision is to be based on the outcome of the sample analysis it may be possible to choose the sample size by balancing the cost of sampling against the precision of the estimator. To do this we need to assign costs and losses as follows. Let $C(n)$ be the cost of sampling when the sample size is n. Denote the error of the estimate obtained from the sample by e (this will be $|\bar{y} - \mu|$ in the case of a mean) and let the loss associated with this error be $l(e)$. If $l(e)$ and $C(n)$ are expressed in the same units the total cost will be $C(n) + l(e)$. Since e is a random variable it seems reasonable to minimize the expected cost and so the mathematical problem is to minimize

$$\phi(n) = C(n) + El(e) \tag{3.28}$$

with respect to n (on which $El(e)$ depends). It is common to take $l(e) \propto e^2$, in which case

$$El(e) \propto \text{var}(e) = \frac{\sigma^2}{n}\left(1 - \frac{n}{N}\right)$$

in the case of the mean. Although n must be an integer it is usually treated as continuous so that calculus methods can be employed and the answer is then rounded to the nearest integer. Instead of expressing the problem in terms of loss we can talk about the gains of increased precision and we then have an equivalent maximization problem.

In more complicated designs we shall be concerned not only with choosing the total sample size but with the allocation of that total to different parts of the design. This problem may be formulated in various ways which we now illustrate in the case of stratified random sampling. First, suppose that the total sample size has been decided upon and it remains to fix the allocation between strata. We might then aim to choose the allocation so as to minimize the variance of the estimator. In the case of the mean the problem becomes:

$$\text{minimize } V = \sum_{i=1}^{k} \frac{\sigma_i^2}{n_i} \left(\frac{N_i}{N}\right) \quad \text{(from 3.12)}$$

with respect to $n_1, n_2, \ldots, n_k$ subject to the restriction

$$\sum_{i=1}^{k} n_i = n.$$

(3.29)

(Notice that the finite population correction has been omitted from V above because its inclusion only introduces a term not depending on the n_i's.) This is a simple example of restricted minimization which can be solved by the method of Lagrange multipliers [see IV, §15.1.4]. Other restrictions might be imposed in practice such as, for example, that the number in any stratum should not fall below some minimum value. This would introduce inequality constraints of the form $n_i \geq m_i$ and the minimization would then require quadratic programming techniques [see IV, Chapter 75]. The solution to the simpler problem of (3.29) requires

$$n_i \propto N_i \sigma_i$$

which, again, depends on the unknown strata variances. A simpler allocation rule is to take $n_i \propto N_i$ which will be optimal in the above sense if the σ_i's are equal.

Another approach is to choose the n_i's so as to minimize the variance of the estimator for a given cost. Suppose the cost of having sample numbers $n_1, n_2, \ldots, n_k$ is $C(n_1, n_2, \ldots, n_k)$; then the problem is:

minimize V

subject to

$$C(n_1, n_2, \ldots, n_k) = C$$

(3.30)

which is the same kind of problem as (3.29).

The roles of variance and cost can be reversed so as to minimize the cost for a given precision, thus:

minimize $C(n_1, n_2, \ldots, n_k)$

subject to

$$V = V_0, \text{ say,}$$

(3.31)

where V_0 is the required precision. The two problems are equivalent from a mathematical point of view since the Lagrangean method requires finding the unrestricted minimum of a linear combination of C and V.

If C is a linear function of the n's (as it is likely to be) the foregoing problems can be solved more elegantly using the Schwarz inequality [see IV, §21.3] as shown by Stuart (1954) and Kokan (1963). Writing

$$V = \sum_{i=1}^{k} \frac{a_i}{n_i} \quad \text{and} \quad C = c_0 + \sum_{i=1}^{k} c_i n_i$$

then

$$V(C - C_0) = \left(\sum_{i=1}^{k} \frac{A_i}{n_i} \right) \left(\sum_{i=1}^{k} C_i n_i \right) \geq \left(\sum_{i=1}^{k} \sqrt{A_i C_i} \right)^2$$

with equality holding when $\sqrt{(A_i/n_i)} \propto (C_i n_i)$, that is, when $n_i \propto \sqrt{(A_i/C_i)}$ which implies $n_i \propto N_i \sigma_i / \sqrt{C_i}$. The constant of proportionality is determined using the fact that C or V is fixed. For example, if V is fixed the minimum value of C is

$$C_0 + \left(\sum_{i=1}^{k} \frac{N_i}{N} \sigma_i \sqrt{C_i} \right)^2 \bigg/ V.$$

Similar approaches may be used with other designs, for example with two-stage cluster sampling. For a given sample size we may choose a few clusters with large sub-samples from each of a large number of clusters with small sub-samples. A suitable cost function in this case might be

$$C = C_0 + C_1 c + C_2 mc$$

where c is the number of clusters and m the sample size in each cluster (assumed the same for all clusters for simplicity).

It will be obvious that although the precise form of the problem will depend very much on the practical circumstances as well as on the sample design, the mathematical problem is essentially the same in all cases. First a function to minimize (or maximize) is chosen by reference to cost or precision and then restrictions are added under which the minimization is to be carried out.

3.6 Response Errors

The 'errors' considered so far arise from the fact that the sample will not have the same mean or other characteristics as the population. They are thus attributable to sampling variation and are not errors in the sense of mistakes on the part of the surveyor. In practice other errors arise, including what are referred to as 'response errors'. An individual response error occurs whenever the recorded value for that individual differs from the true value. With simple factual matters like family size, sex and occupation, response errors may be negligible but with more sensitive matters like age, income or attitudes they may be much more serious. Errors of this kind may arise from deliberate or unintentional misrepresentation by the interviewee, by misunderstanding or misleading phraseology on the part of the interviewer or from failure of communication involving them both. There is a large literature on response errors and much of it is concerned with the practical matters which make no mathematical demands on the user. However, there is a substantial body of theory designed to quantify the effects of non-response on sample estimates which does depend on statistical and mathematical methods. In this section we shall indicate the ideas and methods which underlie some of the theory. Further discussions will be found in O'Muircheartaigh (1977) and Kish (1965) in which further references will be found.

Much of the theory starts from a simple additive model of the kind,

$$y_i = \mu_i + \beta_i + e_i \tag{3.32}$$

where
  y_i is the actual value recorded for the ith member
  μ_i is the true value
  β_i is the bias of the ith member
  e_i is the error of measurement (or recording).

The bias [see VI, §3.3.1(d)], β_i, is assumed fixed and represents the inherent tendency to over- or under-estimate on the part of the respondent or the interviewer. The error term expresses the fact that one would expect the response to vary from one occasion to another due to the variability of the respondent/interviewer environment. Without loss of generality we may suppose $E(e_i) = 0$ for all i and we assume that e_i has constant variance σ_e^2. It would not be reasonable to assume that the e_i's are independent because, for example, members of the same family might tend to react in the same way or the same interviewer may tend to err in the same direction on different occasions. To allow for this we shall begin by supposing that $\text{corr}(e_i, e_j) = \rho$ [see II, §9.8]. Later we shall generalize this to allow correlations between errors for the same interviewer while having independence between interviewers.

Starting from (3.32) we can study the sampling behaviour of the sample mean using elementary arguments involving expectations. We may write

$$\bar{y} = \frac{1}{n} \sum_{i=1}^{N} a_i \mu_i + \frac{1}{n} \sum_{i=1}^{N} a_i \beta_i + \frac{1}{n} \sum_{i=1}^{N} a_i e_i \tag{3.33}$$

where the a_i's are the random variables appropriate to a simple random sample first introduced in (3.6). The only novelty here is in the last sum where products of random variables occur. These can be handled using the conditional expectation technique by conditioning first on the a_i's. As a result we find

$$E(\bar{y}) = \mu + \bar{\beta}$$

$$\text{var}(\bar{y}) = \left(1 - \frac{n}{N}\right) \frac{\sigma^2_{\mu+\beta}}{n} + \frac{\sigma^2_e}{n}\{1 + (n - 1)\rho\} \Bigg\} \qquad (3.34)$$

where $\bar{\beta}$ is the average β_i and

$$\sigma^2_{\mu+\beta} = \left(\frac{1}{N - 1}\right) \sum_{i=1}^{N} (\mu_i + \beta_i - \bar{\mu} - \bar{\beta})^2.$$

The mean square error of $\bar{y}$, which is a more relevant measure of error for a biased estimator, is then $\text{var}(\bar{y}) + \bar{\beta}^2$. In general, $\sigma^2_{\mu+\beta}$ will be greater than σ^2_μ (though it need not be). These formulae show that the existence of differential biases between people is likely to increase the variance and the the existence of response error (e) will certainly do so. This increase can be greatly magnified by the presence of l, the correlation between the response errors. The factor $\{1 + (n - 1)\rho\}$ increases linearly with the sample size and even if ρ is only of the order of 0.01 or 0.05 its effect can be quite substantial. Note, in particular, that the term $\sigma^2_e \rho (n - 1)/n$ is virtually independent of the sample size so it is not the case with response errors that the error of estimation decreases with sample size.

The foregoing model may be reasonable if applied to the work of a single interviewer. In practice, where there would be more than one interviewer, it might be more realistic to assume a stronger correlation 'within interviewers' than 'between interviewers'. Indeed, the method of *inter-penetrating samples* is designed to ensure that there are no correlations of response errors between interviewers.

Suppose there are k interviewers who each visit m respondents, then $n = mk$. Each group of m respondents is a random sub-sample of the population. The estimator of the population mean obtained from any one interviewer will therefore have variance given by (3.34) with n replaced by m. The overall estimate of the population mean is the average of the interviewer means, and to obtain its variance we must divide the single interviewer variance by k. Hence,

$$\text{var}(\hat{\mu}) = \frac{1}{mk}\left\{\sigma^2_{\mu+\beta}\left(1 - \frac{n}{N}\right) + \sigma^2_e\{1 + (m - 1)\rho\}\right\}. \qquad (3.35)$$

For given $n = mk$ we might ask how best to choose m and k. Inspection of (3.35) shows that the variance is minimized by taking $m = 1$, that is, by having one interviewer for each sample member. In practice, this would be prohibitively expensive but, in any case, the model is likely to be unrealistic under such extreme conditions. For example, σ^2_e might well be a function of the number of interviewers, increasing with k as a result of poorer training and supervision. Likewise ρ might depend on m being larger when m is small than when it is large. Nevertheless the formula suggests that there are advantages in having a relatively large number of interviewers.

If $m > 1$ we can do an analysis of variance [see VI, §11.4] between and within interviewers as shown in the table.

	Degrees of freedom	E (Mean Square) (ignoring finite population correction)
Between interviewers	$k - 1$	$\sigma_{\mu+\beta}^2 + \sigma_e^2\{1 + (m - 1)\rho\}$
Within interviewers	$k(m - 1)$	$\sigma_{\mu+\beta}^2 + \sigma_e^2(1 - \rho)$
Total	$km - 1$	

A comparison of the two mean squares provides some information about ρ. If $\rho = 0$ the two expectations will be equal and an approximate F-test enables us to test this hypothesis. Also $\rho\sigma_e^2$ can be estimated from the difference of the two mean squares. In order to estimate ρ we first need an estimate of ρ_e^2 from some other source. It may be possible to obtain this by re-interviewing some members of the sample and estimating σ_e^2 from the variation in response from one occasion to another.

We have based the foregoing discussion on the case of estimating the mean of a single variable in a simple random sample. The ideas can be extended to more complicated designs and can take in questions arising in the analysis of multivariate data (see O'Muircheartaigh, 1977). The essence of the method in these cases is to set up a linear model as in (3.32) in which assumptions are made about the distributional properties appropriate to the sample design. The variances of estimators can then be found using the standard techniques illustrated here and the various components of variance [see VI, §12.3] can be found by analysis of variance methods.

3.7 Non-Response

Another way in which bias may enter into survey work is through non-response. This may arise because respondents are not at home, too ill, have removed or refuse to co-operate. If non-responders were a random sub-sample of those originally selected there would be no bias and the only price to pay would be in the loss of precision resulting from the smaller sample size. In practice, however, it is usually the case that presence or absence in the final sample is correlated with the subject of the enquiry. In other words, those who do not respond will be different, on average, from those who do.

The effect of non-response on estimation can be investigated by setting up a model for the contact process. The usual way to do this, stemming from Deming (1950), is to regard the population as divided into classes according to the probability of being found at home. Let π_j be the proportion of the population in class j and let μ_j and σ_j^2 be the mean and variance of y for the jth group. Then the population mean is

$$\mu = \sum_j \pi_j \mu_j. \tag{3.36}$$

Suppose that interviewers make repeated calls and let p_{ij} be the probability that a respondent in class j will be found at home on or before the ith call. If $\bar{y}_i$ is the sample mean calculated after i calls we wish to find the mean and variance of $\bar{y}_i$ and to compare it with those for the complete sample. Writing $\bar{y}_{ij}$ for the mean y for those in category j contacted after i calls and n_{ij} for the number of such persons it is clear that

$$\bar{y}_i = \frac{\sum_j n_{ij} \bar{y}_{ij}}{\sum_j n_{ij}}. \tag{3.37}$$

In this formula the n_{ij} and $\bar{y}_{ij}$'s are random variables. The determination of the mean and variance of $\bar{y}_i$ depends on showing that, for fixed $n_i = \sum_j n_{ij}$, the set $\{n_{ij}\}$ has a multinomial distribution [see II, §6.4] and that n_i has a binomial distribution [see II, §§5.2.2]. Approximate methods for dealing with ratios using conditional expectation techniques [see II, §8.9] then yield the required results. For example,

$$E(\bar{y}_i) \doteq \sum_j p_{ij} \pi_j \mu_j \bigg/ \sum_j p_{ij} \pi_j. \tag{3.38}$$

By means of such formulae the bias and precision of estimators after a given number of call-backs can be weighed against the cost of further call-backs.

There are several methods for eliminating or, at any rate, reducing not-at-home bias which are less expensive than repeated calling back.

The Politz-Simmons method

This method requires only one call but uses the interview to obtain supplementary data from which the respondents' probability of being at home can be estimated. This is done by asking the respondent on how many of the preceding 5 week-nights he was at home at the time of calling. If the answer is t then the probability of that individual being found at home on a randomly selected occasion is estimated to be $(t + 1)/6$. In forming the estimate of the population mean those with low probabilities of contact are given more weight since, proportionately, more of these will have been missed. The estimator is

$$\hat{\mu} = \frac{\sum_{t=0}^{5} 6n_t \bar{y}_t / (t+1)}{\sum_{t=0}^{5} 6n_t / (t+1)} \tag{3.39}$$

where n_t is the number interviewed who were at home on the t previous evenings and $\bar{y}_t$ is their mean response. The calculation of the mean and variance of this estimator again involves dealing with a ratio. If n_{jt} denotes the number from category j who were at home on t previous evenings $(n_t = \Sigma_j n_{jt})$ then the argument depends on the assumption that the probability that a person in category j is at home on t previous evenings is the binomial probability [see II, §5.2.2]

$$\binom{5}{t} p_j^t (1 - p_j)^{5-t} \qquad (t = 0, 1, \ldots, 5)$$

where p_j is the fraction of time that those in category j are at home. The expected value of the estimator of the population mean is

$$E(\hat{\mu}) \doteq \frac{\sum_j \pi_j \mu_j \{1 - (1 - p_j)^6\}}{\sum_j \pi_j \{1 - (1 - p_j)^6\}} \tag{3.40}$$

where π_j is the proportion of the population in category j, as before. This is not, in general, equal to μ but will usually have much less bias than the unweighted mean of the incomplete sample. The expression for the variance is more complicated but a formula is given in Cochran (1963) where it is stated that it tends to be 25 to 35% higher than the variance of the unweighted mean.

Hansen–Hurwitz method

Another way of dealing with non-response is to follow up only a fraction of the non-responders. This may be particularly appropriate if the 'first call' is a postal survey and the second call is by an interviewer. To be successful it is necessary that the interviewers should obtain a near 100% response at the second call. The method is as follows. An initial sample of size n is selected of which, we suppose, n_1, respond. A random sample of n_2 of the $(n - n_1)$ non-responders is then selected and interviewed. If all the calls are successful an unbiased estimator of μ is given by

$$\hat{\mu} = \frac{1}{n} \{n_1 \bar{y}_1 + (n - n_1) \bar{y}_2\} \tag{3.41}$$

where $\bar{y}_1$ and $\bar{y}_2$ are the sample means of the first and second call samples.

The proof of this result requires us first to find the expectation of $\hat{\mu}$ conditional on $(n_1, \bar{y}_1)$ and on having drawn the original sample and then to average over all possible samples.

Since n_2 is at choice the question arises of how large this should be. If we write $n_2 = (n - n_1)/F$ then the average sampling fraction at the first call is F times that at the second. The cost of the second call by an interviewer will usually be higher than the first call and so we are again faced with the need to balance cost and precision. Hansen and Hurwitz (1946) (see also Cochran, 1963) showed how to find the optimum value of F which minimizes the cost for a given precision. This calculation requires finding the variance of (3.41) by appropriate conditioning techniques and then carrying out a restrained minimization after the manner of Section 3.5.

Bartholomew method

Superficially this is very similar to Hansen and Hurwitz's method in that the estimator of the population mean has exactly the same form as in (3.41). However, the rationale and sampling method are different. The idea behind the method is that the bias among those contacted at the first call (by an interviewer) is likely to be greater than among those contacted subsequently. The reason for this is that the interviewer can obtain information (and/or make appointments) about non-responders at the first call and so make the probabilities of contact at the second call more nearly equal. The form of the estimator is exactly the same as (3.41) where, in this case, $\bar{y}_1$ is the mean of the 'first call' sample and $\bar{y}_2$ is the mean of the second. The estimator was investigated by Thomsen (1975) who found, among other things, an upper bound for the bias. Some further theory and numerical examples are given in Bartholomew (1961).

3.8 Randomized Response Methods

Even if the respondent is contacted he may refuse to give the information requested, especially if it is of a sensitive nature. This is liable to be a further source of bias and efforts have been made to devise ways of reducing the refusal rate. A group of such methods, depending on elementary probability arguments, are known as randomized response methods. The basic idea was introduced by Warner (1965) and it has been discussed by Horvitz, Shah and Simmons (1967), Abdul-Ela, Greenberg and Horvitz (1967), Krotki and McDaniel (1975), Greenberg, Abdul-Ela, Simmons and Horvitz (1969), Abernathy, Greenberg and Horvitz (1970), Moors (1971), Folsom, Greenberg, Horvitz and Abernathy (1973), Sen (1974, 1975), Anderson (1975), Lanke (1975), Bourke and Dalenius (1975) and Shimizu and Bonham (1978). A textbook account of the methods is given in Cochran (1977).

The original method, as proposed by Warner (1965), is as follows.

Suppose that we wish to estimate the proportion of individuals in a population who possess the property A. In a simple random sampling design (see Section 3.9) the respondent would be asked 'Are you an A?' and the proportion who answered 'yes' would be used as an estimate of the population proportion. In the new method the respondent is given a spinner (or some such randomizing device) whose circumference is marked off into two parts, A and $\bar{A}$, with a known probability of showing A ($= p$, say). The respondent spins the spinner, out of sight of the interviewer, and says 'yes' or 'no' according to whether the result coincides with his state or not. If π is the proportion of A's in the population then clearly

$$\begin{aligned}\Pr\{\text{yes}\} &= \pi \Pr\{\text{yes}\,|\,A\} + (1 - \pi) \Pr\{\text{yes}\,|\,\bar{A}\} \\ &= \pi p + (1 - \pi)(1 - p).\end{aligned} \tag{3.42}$$

Now since p is known and $\Pr\{\text{yes}\}$ can be estimated from the proportion of 'yes' answers, (3.42) can be made to yield an estimate of the unknown π. In fact the maximum likelihood estimator of π is

$$\hat{\pi} = \frac{1 - p - n_1/n}{(1 - p) - p} \tag{3.43}$$

where n is the sample size and n_1 the number of 'yes' answers. This is an unbiased estimator and has variance

$$\text{var}(\hat{\pi}) = \frac{\pi(1 - \pi)}{n} + \left\{\frac{1}{16(p - \tfrac{1}{2})^2} - \frac{1}{4}\right\} \Big/ n. \tag{3.44}$$

The estimator does not exist if $p = \tfrac{1}{2}$ since then the reply is completely uninformative. At the extremes $p = 0$ and $p = 1$ we would have complete information (there being no randomization). An important design question concerns how to choose p so that π can be estimated with reasonable precision but without revealing too much about the respondent's views. Unless there is still a fair degree of uncertainty about the interviewee's state after the interview, his reluctance to take part is unlikely to be overcome. In probability terms this requires that probabilities like [see II, §3.9.1]

$$\Pr\{\text{individual is } A \,|\, \text{yes}\}$$

should not be too close to 0 or 1 because, if they were, we would have nearly certain knowledge of the respondent's state. Such probabilities can be calculated by Bayes' theorem [see II, §16.4, and VI, Chapter 15] giving

$$\Pr\{A\,|\,\text{yes}\} = \Pr\{A\}\Pr\{\text{yes}\,|\,A\}/\Pr\{\text{yes}\}$$

which, in this case, becomes

$$\Pr\{A\,|\,\text{yes}\} = \pi p/\{\pi p + (1 - p)(1 - \pi)\}. \tag{3.45}$$

A variant of the randomized response idea is to couple the sensitive question with one which is insensitive. In this case the respondent uses the random mechanism to decide which question to answer and the interviewer does not know which question is being answered. Suppose the two questions are: (i) are you an A? (ii) are you a B? If the answer is 'yes' then we know that

$$\Pr\{\text{yes}\} = \Pr\{\text{question 1 chosen}\}\Pr\{A\} + \Pr\{\text{question 2 chosen}\}\Pr\{B\}$$
$$= p\Pr\{A\} + (1 - p)\Pr\{B\}. \tag{3.46}$$

If B is a characteristic for which the population proportion is already known then $\Pr\{A\}$ can be expressed as

$$\Pr\{A\} = \frac{\Pr\{\text{yes}\} - (1 - p)\Pr\{B\}}{p}$$

which yields the estimator

$$\hat{\pi} = \frac{n_1/n - (1 - p)\Pr\{B\}}{p} \tag{3.47}$$

which has variance

$$\text{var}(\hat{\pi}) = \frac{1}{p^2}\frac{\pi(1 - \pi)}{n}. \tag{3.48}$$

This is always greater than the variance of the usual binomial estimator. Ideally we would like p to be as near 1 as the respondent will accept, but the value $p = \frac{1}{2}$ leaves us in the greatest uncertainty about the respondent's true state.

If $\Pr\{B\}$ is not known we take a second sample with a different value of p. This leads to two estimating equations for the two unknown probabilities (see Abdul-Ela, Greenberg and Horvitz, 1967). The basic idea has been extended to deal with responses having several categories and with variables.

3.9 Inference in Sample Surveys

The theoretical basis of the methods which we have reviewed is relatively elementary when judged in terms of its mathematical pre-requisites. In particular, the methods of inference depend on little more than the calculations of means and standard errors [see VI, §1.2]. The former have turned out to be simple (usually linear) functions of random variables which can be handled by well-known techniques. For most practising social scientists this level of treatment will be sufficient but they should be aware that there is a debate going on about the foundations of the subject which may, eventually, have far-reaching effects on survey practice.

We have already noted that whereas the theory is mainly concerned with means and proportions of a single variable most serious social investigations give rise to multivariate data which can now be analysed in sophisticated ways using computer software packages. The theory of inference for such situations is poorly developed, though a start has been made by Kish and Frankel (1974) from a frequentist point of view [see VI, §15.1].

The debate about the foundations of statistical inference in general has not left the survey field untouched. The question of the existence of best linear unbiased estimators [see II, §3.3.2] has been discussed and answered by Godambe (1955) and Basu (1971). The likelihood [see VI, §1.2] approach to inference has been investigated by Godambe (1966) and Basu (1969) among others. The last-named author has also discussed the concept of sufficiency [see VI, §3.4] in the context of sampling theory. The Bayesian approach to inference [see VI, Chapter 15] was introduced into this field by Ericson (1969) who makes use of the notion of exchangeability of random variables [see VI, §3.3.1(b)] in setting up a framework for inference. Perhaps the best starting point for someone wishing to explore this territory is the review paper by Smith (1976).

References

Abdul-Ela, A-L. A., Greenberg, B. G., and Horvitz, D. G. (1967). A multi-proportions randomized response model. *J. Amer. Statist. Ass.*, **62**, 990–1008.

Abernathy, J., Greenberg, B. G., and Horvitz, D. G. (1970). Estimates of induced abortion in urban North Carolina. *Demography*, **7**, 19–29.

Anderson, H. (1975). Estimation of a proportion through randomized response. *Bull. Int. Statist. Inst.*, **46**, Book 3, 26–29.

Barnett, V. (1974). *Elements of Sampling Theory*, English Universities Press, London.

Bartholomew, D. J. (1961). A method of allowing for 'not-at-home' bias in sample surveys. *App. Statist.*, **10**, 52–59.

Basu, D. (1969). Role of sufficiency and likelihood principles in sample survey theory. *Sankhya*, **31**, 441–454.

Basu, D. (1971). An essay on the logical foundations of survey sampling, Part I. In V. P. Godambe, and D. A. Sprott (Eds), *Foundations of Statistical Inference*, Holt, Rinehart and Winston, Toronto, pp. 203–242.

Bebbington, A. C. and Smith, T. M. F., (1977). The effect of survey design on multivariate analysis. In C.A. O'Muircheartaigh and C. Payne (Eds), *The Analysis of Survey Data*, Vol. II, Wiley, London. pp. 175–192.

Bourke, P. D., and Dalenius, T. (1975). Some new ideas in the realm of randomized enquiries. *Bull. Int. Statist. Inst.*, **46**, Book 3, 126–129.

Cassel, C. M., Wretman, J. H., and Sarndal, C. E. (1977). *Foundations of Inference in Survey Sampling*, Wiley, New York.

Cochran, W. G. (1953). *Sampling Techniques*, 1st ed.; 2nd ed. (1963); 3rd ed. (1977). Wiley, New York.

Dalenius, T. (1962). Recent advances in sample survey theory and methods. *Ann. Math. Statist.*, **33**, 325–349.

Deming, W. E. (1950). *Some Theory of Sampling*, Wiley, New York.

Ericson, W. A. (1969). Subjective Bayesian models in sampling finite populations I. *J. Roy. Statist. Soc.*, B, **31**, 195–234.

Folsom, R. E., Greenberg, B. G., Horvitz, D. G. and Abernathy, J. (1973). The two alternative questions randomized response model for human surveys. *J. Amer. Statist. Ass.*, **68**, 525–530.

Godambe, V. P. (1955). A unified theory of sampling from finite populations. *J. Roy. Statist. Soc.*, B, **17**, 269–278.

Godambe, V. P. (1966). A new approach to sampling from finite populations. I and II *J. Roy. Statist. Soc.*, B, **28**, 310–328.

Greenberg, B. G., Abdul-Ela, A-L. A., Simmons, W. R., and Horvitz, D. G. (1969). The unrelated question randomized response model: theoretical framework. *J. Amer. Statist. Ass.*, **64**, 520–539.

Hansen, M. H. and Hurwitz, W. N. (1946). The problem of non-response in sample surveys. *J. Amer. Statist. Ass.*, **41**, 517–529.

Hansen, M. H., Hurwitz, W. N. and Madow, W. G. (1953). *Sample Survey Methods and Theory*, Vols. I and II, Wiley, New York.

Horvitz, D. G., Shah, B. V., and Simmons, W. R. (1967). The unrelated question randomized response model. *1967 Social Statistics Proceedings of the American Statistical Association*, 65–72.

Johnson, N. L., and Smith, H. (Eds.) (1969). *New Developments in Survey Sampling*, Wiley-Interscience, New York.

Kendall, M. G., and Stuart, A. (1976). *The Advanced Theory of Statistics*, Vol. III, 3rd ed. Griffin, London.

Kish, L. (1965). *Survey Sampling*, Wiley New York.

Kish, L. and Frankel, M. R. (1974). Inference from complex samples. *J. Roy. Statist. Soc.*, B, **36**, 1–37.

Kokan, A. R. (1963). Optimum allocation in multivariate surveys. *J. Roy. Statist. Soc.*, A, **126**, 557–565.

Konijn, H. S. (1973). *Statistical Theory of Sample Survey Design and Analysis*, North Holland, Amsterdam and London; American Elsevier, New York.

Krotki, K. J., and McDaniel, S. A. (1975). Three estimates of illegal abortion in Alberta, Canada: survey, mail-back questionnaire and randomized response technique. *Bull. Int. Statist. Inst.*, **46**, Book 4, 67–70.

Lanke, J. (1975). On the choice of unrelated question in Simmons' version of randomized response. *J. Amer. Statist. Ass.*, **70**, 80–83.

Moors, J. J. A. (1971). Optimization of the unrelated question randomized response model. *J. Amer. Statist. Ass.*, **66**, 627–629.

Moser, C. A. and Kalton, G. G. W. (1971). *Survey Methods in Social Investigation*, Heinemann, London.

Murthy, M. N. (1967). *Sampling Theory and Methods*, Statistical Publishing Society, Calcutta.

Neyman, J. (1934). On the two different aspects of the representative method: the method of stratified sampling and the method of purposive selection. *J. Roy. Statist. Soc.*, **97**, 558–625.

O'Muircheartaigh, C. A. (1977). Response errors. In C. A. O'Muircheartaigh and C. Payne (Eds.), *The Analysis of Survey Data*, Vol. II, Wiley, London, 193–239.

O'Muircheartaigh, C. A. and Payne, C. (1977). *The Analysis of Survey Data*, Vols I and II, Wiley, London.

Raj, D. (1968). *Sampling Theory*, McGraw-Hill, New York.

Sampford, M. R. (1962). *An Introduction to Sampling Theory, with Applications to Agriculture*, Oliver and Boyd, Edinburgh.

Sen, P. K. (1974). On unbiased estimation for randomized response models. *J. Amer. Statist. Ass.*, **69**, 997–1001.

Sen, P. K. (1975). Asymptotically optimal estimators of general parameters in randomized response models. *Bull. Int. Statist. Inst.*, **46**, Book 4, 323–326.

Shimizu, I. M., and Bonham, G. S. (1978). Randomized response technique in a national survey. *J. Amer. Statist. Ass.*, **73**, 35–39.

Smith, T. M. F. (1976). The foundations of survey sampling: a review. *J. Roy. Statist. Soc.*, A, **139**, 183–204.

Stuart, A. (1954). A simple presentation of optimum sampling results. *J. Roy. Statist. Soc.*, B., **16**, 239–241.

Stuart, A. (1976). *Basic Ideas of Scientific Sampling*, 2nd ed. Griffin, London and High Wycombe: Griffin.

Sukhatme, P. V. (1954). *Sampling Theory of Surveys with Applications*, Iowa State College Press, Ames, Iowa.

Thomsen, I. B. (1975). Evaluating the efficiency of two weighting procedures to reduce non-response bias: An application of Cochran's non-response stratum approach. *Bull. Int. Statist. Inst.*, **46**, Book 4, 396–401.

Warner, S. L. (1965). Randomized response: a survey technique for eliminating evasive answer bias. *J. Amer. Statist. Ass.*, **60**, 63–69.

Yates, F. (1946). A review of recent statistical developments in sampling and sample surveys. *J. Roy. Statist. Soc.*, **109**, 12–43.

Yates, F. (1949). *Sampling Methods for Census and Surveys*, 1st ed.; 2nd ed. (1953); 3rd ed. (1960); 4th ed. (1980). Griffin, London.

4

Multivariate Methods in Social Science

4.1 An Overview

The application of multivariate methods in sociology, and social science generally, has enjoyed an enormous popularity in the last decade or so. Sociological data, especially those arising from surveys, have always been multivariate [see VI, Chapters 16 and 17]. A typical enquiry conducted by means of a questionnaire will usually provide information on a large number of variables relating to the individuals questioned. However, until recently the analysis of such data had not proceeded much beyond the computing of summary measures for each variable separately and simple cross-tabulations of pairs of variables. What is new is the systematic attempt to investigate the inter-relationships between all variables simultaneously and so lay bare, so far as possible, the structure of the data. The greatest single force in bringing about this change has been the availability of cheap computing facilities and, especially, of software packages designed for use by social scientists.

Multivariate methods not only involve heavy computation, they also make heavier mathematical demands than the simple univariate methods like those described in Chapter 2. It is, of course, possible to use the methods on a computer without any understanding of their theoretical bases. This is frequently done and sometimes leads to inappropriate and misleading analyses. Multivariate methods are very useful, but also very delicate, tools which cannot be used effectively without a basic understanding of their mode of operation and their limitations. The primary aim of this chapter is to help the sociologist provide himself with the mathematical foundation required for this purpose. Fortunately, this is an easier task than might appear at first sight from the bewildering variety of techniques occurring in the literature. Although 11 different techniques will be covered in this chapter they almost all draw on a relatively small body of mathematics. The ordering of the material has been chosen with a view to emphasizing the common mathematical structure rather than the diverse purposes which the techniques serve. Our account is in no sense a manual, and taken by itself it would give a misleading idea of the relative importance of the various methods. It is essentially a bridge between the practical world of social science data analysis and the mathematical roots of the methods used.

In order to set the scene for what follows we require some terminology and notation. Suppose that we obtain p items of information on n individuals as, for example, when n people each answer p questions. The items of information may be values of a continuous variable like age, income or seniority or they may be categorized as with sex, religion or voting intention. Let x_{ij} denote the response of the ith individual on the jth item (appropriately coded in the case of categorical variables). The complete set of data may be set out in an array, or *data matrix* as follows

$$
\mathbf{X} = \begin{bmatrix} x_{11} & x_{12} & \cdots & x_{1p} \\ x_{21} & x_{22} & \cdots & x_{2p} \\ \vdots & \vdots & & \\ x_{n1} & x_{n2} & \cdots & x_{np} \end{bmatrix}
$$

This constitutes the raw material for multivariate analysis. The variables may or may not all have the same status. In analyses concerned with prediction and causality the aim will be to see how far one group of variables (the explanatory or independent variables) determines the remaining variable(s) (the dependent variable(s)). This might be described as 'dependence' analysis. In other circumstances the variables all have the same status and the analysis looks at the structure of the relationships. This can be called 'inter-dependence' analysis. The distinction is the same as that between regression and correlation analysis [see VI, §8.3] in elementary bivariate statistics.

It is common and useful to think in geometrical terms when considering multivariate methods. If the x's are continuous variables the set of observations on the ith individual can be regarded as the cartesian coordinates of a point in p-dimensional space. The total data set is therefore a cluster of points whose structure can be described in terms of the configuration of the points in space. Thus, for example, in cluster analysis [see §4.4] we shall be looking for a tendency for the points to separate into distinct groups and in principal component analysis [see VI, §17.2] at whether the dimensionality of the set is largely confined to a space of fewer than p dimensions. Some properties of the configuration will depend on the origin chosen and on the scale of the variables. Those properties which are independent of scale and origin are particularly important in multivariate analysis. Even if some or all of the x's are categorical [see VI, Chapter 10] it is still convenient to use the geometrical terminology of the continuous case.

An alternative way of representing the data in geometrical terms is to treat the columns as determining points in n-dimensional space [see I, Example 5.2.2]. In this case points correspond to variables rather than to individuals.

In view of the geometrical interpretation of multivariate data it is not surprising to find that the theory of the subject centres on geometrical concepts such as distance, rotation and translation of axes [see V, §1.2.6] and projection. In algebraic terms, the methods depend heavily on linear algebra including the properties of matrices [see I, §6.2] and their associated eigenvalues and vectors [see I, §7.2].

Multivariate analysis has a descriptive and an inferential aspect. In social science the emphasis has been on description, with the aim being to reduce a large mass of data to manageable and comprehensible proportions. Techniques for this purpose are designed to explore and describe the set of data points. They are thus essentially concerned with the geometry of the set. Inference from the sample of points to the population from which they have been drawn is more difficult and, in social science at least, not always possible or relevant. The data may not have been obtained by simple random sampling and, even if they have, biases may have been introduced by such things as non-response. More generally, inference implies a probability model of the data which is often lacking in the exploratory investigations which are characteristic of many social investigations. Nevertheless it is sometimes desirable to make inferences, and for this to be done an assumption must be made about the joint probability distribution of the x's [see II, Chapter 6]. This part of the subject has been dominated by the assumption of multivariate Normality [see II, §13.4, and VI, §16.2] and hence the properties of the multivariate normal distribution are central to an understanding of multivariate methods. Such a distribution is completely determined by the means and covariances of the variables [see II, §9.6]. Hence the covariances, or correlation coefficients [see II, §9.8], are the starting point of most analyses [see VI, §2.5.7, §18.5 and §18.8]. Also of particular importance are the facts that the marginal distributions [see II, §6.3 and §13.1.2] are Normal [see II, §11.4] and the expected value of any variable given the others is a linear function of those other variables [see II, §8.9].

4.2 The Literature of Multivariate Methods

The literature of the subject has grown rapidly in recent years and no attempt will be made to provide a comprehensive review. Instead we shall indicate the directions in which the sociologist should look if he wishes to strengthen his theoretical foundations. This reading, coupled with the resources of the core volumes, should provide ample material.

There are books written by statisticians for statisticians of which Anderson (1958), Rao (1973) and Kendall (1980) are good examples. On regression theory and the general linear model we may add Scheffé (1959) and Graybill (1961) but these by no means exhaust the possibilities. Such books are essential for those who wish to go deeply into the subject.

However, insofar as they deal largely with the inferential side and lean heavily on the distributional assumptions of multivariate normality they are unlikely to have high priority for most social scientists.

There are also books written by statisticians for social scientists and by social scientists for one another. It is this group that the beginner is likely to find most useful. A useful starting point is O'Muircheartaigh and Payne (1977) which contains discussion and examples of almost all multivariate techniques. This is written for practitioners in largely non-technical language and hence the mathematical framework of the methods is not always apparent. Nevertheless the extensive list of references to each chapter will take the reader into deeper water. Of the many other general texts which are likely to be of particular value to social scientists we mention van der Geer (1971) and Maxwell (1977). The latter, although written with psychologists in mind, is simply presented and contains one chapter on matrices and determinants. For discrete data, Bishop, Fienberg and Holland (1975) is excellent.

There is a *Journal of Multivariate Analysis* but it is more concerned with distribution theory than with techniques of analysis as such.

A book which is concerned with multivariate data analysis, and especially with graphical methods, is Gnanadesikan (1977).

There are many books on particular techniques and we shall refer to these as we proceed.

4.3 The General Linear Model

What is termed the general linear model underlies a large area of statistical method. The linear regression model [see VI, Chapter 8] is an important special case which gives rise to what is possibly the most widely used technique in social science data analysis. In fact it is rather more than a special case since, appropriately interpreted, all methods derived from the general linear model may be viewed as regression methods. As we shall see, path analysis and binary segmentation are, mathematically speaking, members of the same family of techniques. For this reason this section is largely devoted to regression analysis with relatively brief sub-sections on other techniques which make use of the same mathematical foundations. Not only is regression analysis widely used but it is often mis-used, especially by those who rely on computer packages without a clear understanding of the theory underlying the methods. By emphasizing the common mathematical structure and the assumptions of the various methods this section aims to provide social scientists with the means of exploring the foundations.

Regression Analysis

Regression falls into that class of multivariate methods which we termed 'dependence' analysis in Section 4.1. That is it is concerned with the way in which the value of some variable y, say, depends on the values of a set of other variables which we denote by x_1, x_2, ..., x_k. In particular, the technique is concerned with how best to predict y when the values of the x's are given. Multiple regression starts with an assumption about the form of the relationship and then proceeds to estimate and test hypotheses about the values of its parameters. in particular the basic assumptions are that

$$E(y) = \sum_{j=1}^{k} \beta_j x_j$$

$$\text{var}(y) = \sigma^2$$

(4.1)

and that different observations on y are mutually independent. Note that the variance of y does not depend on the x's. The assumption of independence can easily be relaxed and we shall meet a case later where this is necessary. If n observations are made on the y's the model may be written

$$\mathbf{y} = \mathbf{X}\boldsymbol{\beta} + \mathbf{e}$$

(4.2)

[see I, §5.7] where $\mathbf{y}' = (y_1, y_2, \ldots, y_n)$, $\boldsymbol{\beta}' = (\beta_1, \beta_2, \ldots, \beta_k)$; $\mathbf{X}$ is the $n \times k$ matrix $\{x_{ij}\}$ where the first suffix indexes the observations; $\mathbf{e}$ is the vector of 'errors', which are the amounts by which y differs from its expectation. The distributional assumptions made above imply that $E(\mathbf{e}) = \mathbf{0}$ and $\mathbf{D}(\mathbf{e}) = \sigma^2 \mathbf{I}$ where $\mathbf{D}$ is the dispersion (variance–covariance) matrix and $\mathbf{I}$ is the unit matrix [see II, §13.3.1]. $\mathbf{X}\boldsymbol{\beta}$ is called the regression function and the model is described as 'linear' because it is linear in the β's. As defined, it is also linear in the x's but it could be that $x_{i2} = (x_{i1})^2$. This would be an example of polynomial regression but it would still be a linear model in the sense of this section. (It is particularly confusing that the adjective 'linear' in the general linear model refers to the β's and in linear regression to the x's, but the practice is deeply ingrained.) Likewise, the theory does not require the x's to be measured on a continuous or discrete scale; they can be 'dummy' variables with 1 indicating the presence and 0 the absence of some attribute. Where all the variables are of this kind we have what is often termed an analysis of variance model, and where there is a mixture of the two kinds it is an analysis of covariance model.

The matrix $\mathbf{X}$ is not quite the full data matrix of Section 4.1 because the values of the y variable have been excluded. The latter is called the dependent variable because it depends on the values of the x's. The x's are often called, by contrast, the independent variables but this is in quite a different sense from the use of this phrase in probability theory. In fact the x's may very well be statistically dependent. We prefer to call them explanatory variables, but some writers use the term factors and others instrumental variables.

The most difficult problems which the social scientist has to face have more to do with the appropriateness of the model and the interpretation of the analysis than with the mathematics underlying the methodology. These aspects do not concern us here and we shall therefore proceed directly to the mathematics.

Two prime concerns in regression analysis are to estimate the parameters of the model and to test hypotheses about their values—in particular whether they differ significantly from zero. Inferential statements require a further assumption to be made about the distribution of y and, where necessary, this is taken to be Normal. Point estimates [see VI, §3.1] can be obtained without this distributional assumption by the method of least squares [see VI, Chapter 11]. Its application here requires the minimization of a quadratic function of many variables followed by the solution of simultaneous linear equations. It may be shown that the estimators obtained by this method have smallest variance among the class of unbiased estimates which are linear in the observations (the Gauss–Markov theorem [see VI, §11.1]). If the Normality assumption is invoked the estimators are also the same as those obtained by maximum likelihood [see VI, Chapter 6]. If we generalize to the case where the y's are not independent, $D(e) = \sigma^2 G$ where G is not the identity matrix. If G is non-singular [see I, Definition 6.4.2] the model can be reduced to (4.1) by a linear transformation. However, if G is singular ($|G| = 0$) the standard theory breaks down and the notion of a generalized inverse has to be introduced (see Rao (1973), Chapter 1).

The theory of regression is covered in virtually all textbooks on statistics and, in particular, in the general texts on multivariate analysis mentioned at the beginning of this chapter. Chapter 4 of Rao (1973) is particularly useful and the earlier chapters of his book cover most of the mathematical pre-requisites. Draper and Smith (1966) and Plackett (1960) are devoted entirely to regression analysis, the first more concerned with applications and the second with theory. Scheffé's (1959) *Analysis of Variance* begins with an account of the theory of the general linear model before dealing with the many special cases which constitute the analysis of variance.

Estimation

Estimation of the β's by least squares involves the minimization of

$$\sum_{i=1}^{n} \left(y_i - \sum_{j=1}^{k} \beta_j x_{ij} \right)^2 = (y - X\beta)'(y - X\beta) \tag{4.3}$$

with respect to β. Differentiating and setting the partial derivatives equal to zero [see IV, §5.6] gives the estimating equations

$$X'X\beta = X'y. \tag{4.4}$$

If $S = X'X$ is non-singular then [see I, Theorem 6.4.2]

$$\hat{\beta} = S^{-1}X'y. \tag{4.5}$$

If, as sometimes happens, there is prior knowledge to the effect that, say, all of the β's are non-negative then (4.3) must be minimized subject to these further constraints. The problem then becomes one of quadratic programming [see IV, Chapter 15] and the estimators no longer have the same properties as before.

An estimator of σ^2 may be obtained using the fact that

$$E(y - X\hat{\beta})'(y - X\hat{\beta}) = (n - k)\sigma^2. \tag{4.6}$$

The proof of this result makes use of several theorems of matrix algebra. Substituting for $\hat{\beta}$ from (4.5) we have

$$E(y - XS^{-1}X'y)'(y - XS^{-1}X'y) = E(y'A'Ay) \tag{4.7}$$

where $A = I - XS^{-1}X'$. It then has to be verified that A is symmetric $(A = A')$ and idempotent $(A = A^2)$ so that the right-hand side of (4.7) is

$$E(y'Ay).$$

Further progress depends upon results about the expectations of quadratic forms [see I, §6.7(v)], in particular that [see I, Definition 7.3.1]

$$E(y'Ay) = \sigma^2 \operatorname{trace} A + E(y')A\, E(y). \tag{4.8}$$

In the present case $E(y) = X\beta$ and simple algebra then shows that

$$E(y'Ay) = \sigma^2 \operatorname{trace} A. \tag{4.9}$$

Because A is idempotent, trace A = rank A [see I, (6.7.22)] and hence (4.6) follows. An unbiased estimator of σ^2 is therefore obtained from

$$\hat{\sigma}^2 = \frac{1}{n - k}(y - X\hat{\beta})'(y - X\hat{\beta}); \tag{4.10}$$

$(y - X\hat{\beta})'(y - X\hat{\beta})$ is the sum of squares of deviations from the fitted regression function and is known as the residual sum of squares.

The dispersion matrix of the $\hat{\beta}$'s may be found using standard methods for linear functions of random variables. Because $\hat{\beta}$ is unbiased the required dispersion matrix is given by

$$D(\hat{\beta}) = E(\hat{\beta} - \beta)(\hat{\beta} - \beta)'.$$

Now

$$\hat{\beta} - \beta = S^{-1}X'(y - E(y))$$

and straightforward manipulation using $E(y - E(y))'(y - E(y)) = \sigma^2 I$ gives

$$D(\hat{\beta}) = S^{-1}\sigma^2. \tag{4.11}$$

Hypothesis testing

If we assume that the y's are Normal then the $\hat{\beta}$'s will also be Normal since they are linear functions of the y's [see II, Theorem 13.4.3]. For example, we shall have

$$\hat{\beta}_1 \sim N(\beta_1, \sigma^2 s^{11})$$

where s^{11} is the element in the first row and first column of $\mathbf{S}^{-1}$. If σ^2 were known the hypothesis $\beta_1 = 0$ could be tested by treating $\hat{\beta}_1/\sigma\sqrt{s^{11}}$ as a standard Normal variable [see II, §11.4.1]. If σ^2 is unknown it may be replaced by $\hat{\sigma}^2$ and then the ratio $\hat{\beta}_1/\hat{\sigma}\sqrt{s^{11}}$ will have a t-distribution with $n - k$ degrees of freedom. This result depends on establishing that $(n - k)\hat{\sigma}^2$ has a χ^2-distribution [see II, §11.4.11, and VI, §7.1.2] independent of $\hat{\beta}_1$ which is a special case of a more general result mentioned below.

Test statistics for more general hypotheses about the β's may be derived by the likelihood ratio method [see VI, §5.5]. Suppose that the null hypothesis which one wishes to test requires that r linear combinations of the β's be zero. (This includes as a special and important case the hypothesis that in some sub-set the β's are equal to one another or are zero). The likelihood ratio method then leads to the statistic

$$F = \frac{\left\{ \min_{\omega} (\mathbf{y} - \mathbf{X}\boldsymbol{\beta})'(\mathbf{y} - \mathbf{X}\boldsymbol{\beta}) - (\mathbf{y} - \mathbf{X}\hat{\boldsymbol{\beta}})'(\mathbf{y} - \mathbf{X}\hat{\boldsymbol{\beta}}) \right\} \Big/ r}{(\mathbf{y} - \mathbf{X}\hat{\boldsymbol{\beta}})'(\mathbf{y} - \mathbf{X}\hat{\boldsymbol{\beta}})/(n - k)} \tag{4.12}$$

where ω refers to the set of all β's satisfying the r linear restraints. The determination of the minimum thus requires the minimization of a quadratic form subject to linear restraints. A large value of $F(> 1)$ indicates a departure from the null hypothesis, but to judge its significance we need to know the sampling distribution [see VI, Chapter 2] of F under the null hypothesis [see VI, §5.4]. This depends on establishing that the quadratic forms in the numerator and denominator of (4.12) have independent χ^2 distributions. In that case the ratio has the F-distribution [see VI, §2.5.6].

The quadratic forms which arise in statistics such as (4.12) may be arrived at by decomposing the total sum of squares $\mathbf{y}'\mathbf{y}$ on the following lines:

$$\mathbf{y}'\mathbf{y} = \mathbf{y}'\mathbf{A}_1\mathbf{y} + \mathbf{y}'\mathbf{A}_2\mathbf{y} + \ldots + \mathbf{y}'\mathbf{A}_r\mathbf{y}. \tag{4.13}$$

In the case given above this takes the form

$$\mathbf{y}'\mathbf{y} = \left[\min_{\omega} (\mathbf{y} - \mathbf{X}\boldsymbol{\beta})'(\mathbf{y} - \mathbf{X}\boldsymbol{\beta}) - (\mathbf{y} - \mathbf{X}\hat{\boldsymbol{\beta}})'(\mathbf{y} - \mathbf{X}\hat{\boldsymbol{\beta}}) \right]$$
$$+ (\mathbf{y} - \mathbf{X}\hat{\boldsymbol{\beta}})'(\mathbf{y} - \mathbf{X}\hat{\boldsymbol{\beta}}) + [\mathbf{y}'\mathbf{y} - \min_{\omega} (\mathbf{y} - \mathbf{X}\boldsymbol{\beta})'(\mathbf{y} - \mathbf{X}\boldsymbol{\beta})]. \tag{4.14}$$

The point of such a representation is that there is a powerful theorem, known as Cochran's theorem (or Fisher–Cochran) [see VI, §2.5.8] which provides necessary and sufficient conditions for the quadratic forms on the right-hand side of (4.13) to have independent χ^2 distributions. The theorem states that this is true if and only if the ranks [see I, §5.6] $n_1, n_2, \ldots, n_r$ of $\mathbf{A}_1, \mathbf{A}_2, \ldots, \mathbf{A}_r$ add up to n (the dimension of $\mathbf{y}$). Various corollaries of this theorem are useful; in particular, if either (a) $\mathbf{A}_1, \mathbf{A}_2, \ldots, \mathbf{A}_r$ are each idempotent [see I, §6.7, (xiii)] or (b) $\mathbf{A}_i\mathbf{A}_j = \mathbf{0}$ for all $i \neq j$ then the quadratic forms are independent, the ith member having a χ^2 distribution with n_i degrees of freedom. It follows from this that the ratio of two mean squares will have an F-distribution.

The applications of the basic regression model are many and diverse and the reader may not find it easy to relate the foregoing algebra to the bewildering array of sums of squares appearing in the textbooks on the subject. Nevertheless, all methods derived from the general linear model depend on the basic mathematical arguments set out above. To illustrate the generality of the formulation we shall now show how it leads to the standard one-way analysis of variance [see VI, §11.4]. This, of course, is usually obtained by more direct methods based on a direct partitioning of the total sum of squares into 'between' and 'within' group components.

Suppose that there are n observations divided into k groups, n_1 in the first, n_2 in the second and so on. The model supposes that, in the jth group, y is distributed normally with mean β_j. This arises as a special case of the general model

$$y_i = \sum_{j=1}^{k} \beta_j x_{ij} + e_i$$

when

$$x_{i1} = 1, \qquad i = 1, 2, \ldots, n_1$$
$$\qquad = 0 \quad \text{otherwise}$$
$$x_{i2} = 1, \qquad i = n_1 + 1, n_1 + 2, \ldots, n_1 + n_2$$
$$\qquad = 0 \quad \text{otherwise}$$
$$\vdots$$
$$x_{ik} = 1, \qquad i = n - n_k + 1, n - n_k + 2, \ldots, n$$
$$\qquad = 0 \quad \text{otherwise.}$$

Hence

$$\mathbf{X} = (\mathbf{x}_1, \mathbf{x}_2, \ldots, \mathbf{x}_k)$$

where

$$\mathbf{x}_j = (x_{1j}, x_{2j}, \ldots, x_{kj})'$$

and

$$S = X'X = \begin{bmatrix} n_1 & 0 & 0 & \cdots & 0 \\ 0 & n_2 & 0 & \cdots & 0 \\ \vdots & & & & \vdots \\ & & & & \\ 0 & & \cdots\cdots\cdots & & n_k \end{bmatrix}.$$

The least squares estimators of the β_i's are therefore given by

$$\hat{\beta} = S^{-1}X'y = (\bar{y}_1, \bar{y}_2, \ldots, \bar{y}_k)'$$

and

$$D(\hat{\beta}) = \begin{bmatrix} \dfrac{1}{n_1} & 0 & \cdots\cdots & 0 \\ 0 & \dfrac{1}{n_2} & \cdots\cdots & 0 \\ \vdots & & & \vdots \\ & & & \\ 0 & & \cdots\cdots\cdots & \dfrac{1}{n_k} \end{bmatrix} \sigma^2,$$

results which are otherwise obvious. Likewise

$$\hat{\sigma}^2 = \frac{1}{n-k}\left[\sum_{i=1}^{n_1}(y_i - \bar{y}_1)^2 + \sum_{i=n_1+1}^{n_1+n_2}(y_i - \bar{y}_2)^2 + \ldots + \sum_{i=n_1+\ldots+n_{k-1}+1}^{n}(y_i - \bar{y}_k)^2 \right]$$

where $\bar{y}_j$ is the mean y in the jth group. In the usual analysis of variance terminology this is the within groups (or, residual) mean square. In the one-way analysis of variance the hypothesis which is usually tested is that $\beta_1 = \beta_2 = \ldots = \beta_k$. This is equivalent to the $k-1$ linear restraints $\beta_1 - \beta_2 = 0$, $\beta_2 - \beta_3 = 0$, $\ldots$, $\beta_{k-1} - \beta_k = 0$ so that $r = k-1$ in (4.12). The usual analysis of variance is based on the decomposition

$$y'y - n\bar{y}^2 = (y - X\hat{\beta})'(y - X\hat{\beta}) + \{\hat{\beta}'X'X\hat{\beta} - n\bar{y}^2\}$$

where

$$\bar{y} = \frac{1}{n}\sum_{i=1}^{n}y_i = \frac{1}{n}\sum_{i=1}^{k}n_i\hat{\beta}_i.$$

The two quadratic forms on the right-hand side are distributed independently as χ^2 with $(n-k)$ and $(k-1)$ degrees of freedom, respectively. These are the 'within' and 'between' groups sums of squares expressed in the notation of the general linear model.

Similar arguments apply if the groups into which the observations are divided are cross-classified according to the levels of different factors. In this case it is usual to re-parameterize the models so that its parameters correspond to what are termed the 'main effects' and 'interactions' [see VI, §12.7]. For a two-factor model that data may be set out in the cells of a two-way table with rows corresponding to levels of one factor and columns to the other. Multiple subscripts are used so that rows and columns can be identified. Thus we might write the model for a table with H rows and I columns as

$$y_{hij} = \beta_{hi} + e_{hij} \qquad (h = 1, 2, \ldots, H; i = 1, 2, \ldots, I; j = 1, 2, \ldots, n_{hi})$$

n_{hi} being the number in the cell in row h and column i. There are various hypotheses that one might wish to test about such a model—for example that $\beta_{hi} = \alpha_h + \gamma_i$ for all h and i. This is the hypothesis of additivity, meaning that the effect of a given level of the row factor is unaffected by the level of the column factor. An F-test for such an hypothesis can be found using the likelihood ratio method. One way of re-parameterizing the model, used when the n_{hi}'s are equal, is based on the identity

$$\beta_{hi} = \bar{\beta} + (\bar{\beta}_{h.} - \bar{\beta}) + (\bar{\beta}_{.i} - \bar{\beta}) + (\beta_{hi} - \bar{\beta}_{h.} - \bar{\beta}_{.i} + \bar{\beta})$$

where

$$\bar{\beta} = \frac{1}{HI} \sum_h \sum_i \beta_{hi}, \qquad \bar{\beta}_{h.} = \frac{1}{I} \sum_i \beta_{hi}, \qquad \bar{\beta}_{.i} = \frac{1}{N} \sum_h \beta_{hi}.$$

The last term measures the interaction, or departure from additivity, as may be seen from the fact that the substitution of $\beta_{hi} = \alpha_h + \gamma_i$ makes it zero. The middle two terms are main effects in that they measure the effect of one factor averaged over the levels of the other. The point of this representation is that the hypotheses which it is natural to test involve setting the main effect or interaction terms equal to zero.

Similar ideas underlie the application of the analysis of variance to other types of classification. There are many ramifications of the linear model with which there is no space to deal here. Tests of hypotheses of the kind discussed above are often followed by multiple comparison procedures designed to identify in which part of the parameter space the true β lies. The mathematical bases of such methods are discussed in Scheffé (1959) and Rao (1973). In certain contexts, rare in the social sciences, it may be more meaningful to regard the β's as random variables. Methods for handling this case usually start with the analysis of variance table for the fixed effects model.

In later sections we shall meet examples where the y's are $(0,1)$ variables, which means that the assumption of constant variance breaks down.

So-called *monotone regression* will arise when we come to consider non-metric multi-dimensional scaling. Instead of making the strong assumption that the regression function is linear we merely require that it shall be monotone in the explanatory variables [see IV, Definition 2.7.1]. The theory of such models is treated fully in Barlow and co-workers (1972).

Path Analysis

In essence, this is the application of multiple regression methods to the study of the inter-relationships of temporally ordered variables. From a mathematical point of view, therefore, nothing needs to be added to what has been said above about regression analysis. Not all of the discussions of path analysis in the literature make this point clear and we shall therefore briefly indicate the connection between the two.

The notion of 'causation' implies a temporal ordering of events. Thus an event can be held to be a 'cause' of another event which occurs later but not vice versa. Path analysis is a technique designed to estimate the strengths of the causal links between variables. It is not concerned with determining from the data which variables are so linked. The pattern of the linkages is part of the assumptions of the model which have to be decided upon by the analyst. These are often expressed diagrammatically in the form of a path diagram; the following is a very simple example.

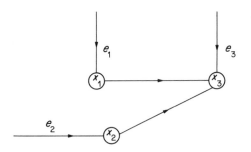

The three variables in which we are interested are x_1, x_2 and x_3; x_3 is assumed to be influenced by both x_1 and x_2 and this is shown in the diagram by the direction of the connecting arrows. In addition, all three variables are affected by 'outside' factors called exogenous variables: their influence is indicated by the three arrows labelled e_1, e_2 and e_3. On these assumptions it is natural to ask how much of x_3's value can be attributed to the influence of x_1 how much to x_2 and how much to the exogenous effects represented by e_3. This is what path analysis seeks to discover by use of regression methods. Here we merely outline the way in which regression analysis arises. Further theory and examples will be found in Duncan (1975), Macdonald and Doreian (1977) and Macdonald (1977).

Suppose that a path analysis diagram has been constructed in which a variable x_9 is causally related to temporally prior variables x_1, x_3, x_5 and x_8, say. Then one would fit the regression equation

$$x_9 = \beta_1 x_1 + \beta_3 x_3 + \beta_5 x_5 + \beta_8 x_8 + e. \tag{4.15}$$

The interpretation of this equation is made in terms of the 'path coefficients'. These are the regression coefficients either as fitted or in a standardized form. In the former case the path coefficient of x_3 on x_9 in the case above would be

$$\alpha_{9,3} = \beta_3 \sigma(x_3)/\sigma(x_9). \tag{4.16}$$

This is what the regression coefficient of x_3 would have been if all the variables had first been standardized so as to have zero mean and unit standard deviation. The path coefficient measures the strength of the influence of x_3 on x_9 in the following sense. The numerator of $\alpha_{9,3}$ would be the standard deviation of x_9 if all the other variables, including the exogenous term e, were fixed. The denominator is its actual standard deviation and so the ratio of the two represents the proportion of the overall standard deviation that can be attributed to x_3. The sign of $\sigma_{9,3}$ indicates the direction of the influence which x_3 has on x_9.

It is possible to express path coefficients in terms of the correlation coefficients between the x's, and it has sometimes been suggested that these relationships should form the basis for the estimation of the path coefficients. However, such methods offer no obvious advantage over the routine application of regression methods.

Binary Segmentation

This is an exploratory technique for investigating the dependence of one set of variables (usually only one) on a set of explanatory variables. It is therefore similar in purpose to regression analysis but does not seek to quantify the relationship by means of a regression function. Instead its aim is to identify which explanatory variables account for most of the variation in the independent variable. The mathematical demands are slight since the solution is reached on a computer by a systematic investigation of cases. In fact there is very little theory for the method, which is closely linked to a series of computer algorithms developed by the Institute for Social Research at the University of Michigan under the name of the automatic interaction detector (AID). A useful account of the method is given by Fielding (1977b).

Briefly, the method proceeds as follows. Suppose there is one independent variable denoted by y and a set of explanatory variables, usually categorical, $x_1, x_2, \ldots$. Start with one of the explanatory variables, x_1 say, and seek to partition individuals into two exhaustive and disjoint groups according to their values of x_1 in such a way that the y-values are as widely separated as possible. The degree of separation of the two groups is measured by comparing the 'between groups' sum of squares with the total sum of squares [see VI, §11.4]. A large value of the ratio indicates a successful split and vice versa. The aim is thus to maximize the proportion of the total sum of squares which can be accounted for by such a binary split on some other variable. Each such variable must therefore be examined in the same way so that the optimum x can be selected as a basis for the partition. Having divided the data into two parts, each part is treated in exactly the same way as before but omitting the explanatory variable used to make the first split. This procedure can be continued as far as desired; various *ad hoc* rules are used for deciding when to stop. The essence of the algorithm is that it has to examine a large number of possible partitions and compute the separation criterion for each one. This would be impossible without a computer which is well-suited to performing the large number of simple repetitive operations.

The main extension of the method is to the case where there are several y's instead of one. The same kind of procedure can be followed if a suitable way of measuring the distance apart of the groups can be agreed. This can be done using a multivariate analysis of variance in which the dispersion matrix of the set of y's is partitioned into 'between' and 'within' matrices. Thus

$$\mathbf{T} = \mathbf{B} + \mathbf{W}$$

where $\mathbf{T}$ is the total dispersion matrix and $\mathbf{B}$ and $\mathbf{W}$ the between and within groups matrices formed from the binary split. The separation can be measured by

$$\frac{\text{trace } \mathbf{B}}{\text{trace } \mathbf{T}}$$

and the algorithm has to search for the split which maximizes this ratio. Since the y's will normally be correlated they can be transformed to a set of uncorrelated variables by the method of principal components (see below) prior to the application of the binary segmentation algorithm.

Log-linear models for contingency tables [see VI, §10.2]

The great majority of multivariate methods have been developed for use with continuous variables. In social science many variables are categorical [see VI, Chapter 10] and this fact has provided a considerable impetus towards developing techniques which will cope with categorical variables. We have seen [see sub-section on regression analysis, above] that there is no difficulty in incorporating categorical variables as explanatory variables into regression analysis. Log-linear models have been developed to provide a model analogous to the general linear model for categorical data in many-way contingency tables [see VI, Chapter 10].

Convenient sources of information about log-linear models are Birch

(1963), Haberman (1973), Plackett (1974), Bishop, Fienberg and Holland (1975), Payne (1977) and Upton (1978).

In order to illustrate the means by which probability models for dependence between categorical variables can be expressed in terms of a linear model we consider the case of a 3-way contingency table. Data in such tables may arise from a variety of sampling schemes. It is important to distinguish these, for example, when deciding what hypotheses it is reasonable to test, but for our more limited purpose of describing the mathematics on which the methods depend it will suffice to consider one such model. Suppose, therefore, that we have taken a random sample of size n whose members have been subject to a threefold classification. The set of cell frequencies will therefore have a multinomial distribution [see II, §6.4.2] according to which the probability of falling into cell (h,i,j) is p_{hij} ($h = 1, 2, \ldots, H; i = 1, 2, \ldots, I; j = 1, 2, \ldots, J$). We may also introduce marginal probabilities such as

$$p_{hi.} = \sum_j p_{hij}, \qquad p_{h..} = \sum_i \sum_j p_{hij} \quad \text{etc.}$$

Suppose that we were interested in the hypothesis that the three variables are mutually independent [see II, §§3.5, 6.1, 6.6, 10.5 and 13.1]. According to the product rule for probabilities [see II, Definition 3.5.1] this would imply that

$$p_{hij} = p_{h..} \, p_{.i.} \, p_{..j}$$

or that

$$\log p_{hij} = \log p_{h..} + \log p_{.i.} + \log p_{..j} \tag{4.17}$$

for all h, i and j. Another possible hypothesis is that a pair of variables are independent given the value of the third. Letting A and B denote such a pair with C being the third variable and using elementary conditional probability [see II, §3.9] arguments this implies that

$$\Pr(AB \mid C) = \Pr(A \mid C)\Pr(B \mid C). \tag{4.18}$$

If this is true A and B may be said to be conditionally independent [see II, §13.1.6]. Given (4.18)

$$\Pr(ABC) = \Pr(C)\Pr(AB \mid C) = \Pr(C)\Pr(A \mid C)\Pr(B \mid C)$$

which, from the definition of a conditional probability may also be written

$$\Pr(ABC) = \Pr(C) \frac{\Pr(AC)}{\Pr(C)} \frac{\Pr(BC)}{\Pr(C)} .$$

Translated into the notation for the cell probabilities this requires that

$$p_{hij} = p_{h.j} p_{.ij}/p_{..j}$$

or

$$\log p_{hij} = \log p_{h.j} + \log p_{.ij} - \log p_{..j} .$$ (4.19)

We note from (4.17) and (4.19) that both hypotheses imply that $\log p_{hij}$ is linear in quantities which involve logarithms of marginal probabilities [see II, §6.3]. The hypothesis of complete independence involves marginal probabilities obtained by summing over two dimensions of the table; that of conditional independence brings in those obtained by summing only over the A and B dimensions.

The results suggest that the analysis of the model might proceed by analogy with the analysis of variance. In the 3-way case, for example, we might adopt the model

$$\log f_{hij} = \log F_{hij} + e_{hij}$$ (4.20)

where f_{hij} is the observed frequency in the cell (h,i,j) and $F_{ijh} = np_{ijh}$ is the expected frequency. The hypothesis of complete independence given by (4.17) then becomes the hypothesis of additivity (i.e. no interaction [see VI, §12.7]). In these terms the conditional independence hypothesis means that the first order interaction between A and B is zero but that the other two first order interactions are not. By re-parameterizing the model as in the analysis of variance one can therefore test a whole range of hypotheses concerning linear contrasts among the $\log F_{hij}$'s.

The error terms in (4.20) are not, of course, Normal and independent since they arise from multinomial sampling. The estimation of the parameters cannot therefore proceed on the Normal assumptions. Generalized least squares can be used to take account of the correlations and unequal variances but this requires the calculation of the dispersion matrix of the e's. A more satisfactory method is to use maximum likelihood [see VI, Chapter 6]. With multinomial sampling [see II, §10.3] the log(likelihood) is, apart from a constant, given by

$$L = \sum_h \sum_i \sum_j f_{hij} \log p_{hij}.$$

This may be maximized subject to the constraints imposed on the parameters by the hypothesis under test. In some cases there will be simple explicit solutions for the estimators but, in general, they will have to be obtained by iterative techniques. Nelder and Wedderburn (1972) describe such a method which may be implemented using the GLIM computer program. An iterative scaling method due to Fienberg (1970) achieves the same end.

The logit model

A similar approach may be used when one of the classifications in a contingency table takes the role of a dependent variable. This gives rise to a regression type of problem. If the dependent variable is a dichotomy with categories A and $\bar{A}$ the aim would be to predict the probability of A given the individual's placing on the other variables. If p is the proportion in question the logit model takes the form

$$E[\log\{p/(1 - p)\}] = \sum_{j=1}^{k} \beta_j x_j. \tag{4.21}$$

If the explanatory variables are categorical the x's will be indicator variables [see VI, §8.2] but the model can perfectly well accommodate variables measured on a continuous scale. The error term will not be Normal because p is binomial, but it may be shown that $\log\{p/(1 - p)\}$ has a variance which is almost constant and hence methods based on ordinary least squares are applicable. If all of the x's are categorical it may also be shown (see Payne, 1977, for example) that the logit model is a special case of the log-linear model.

4.4 Classification Methods

Cluster analysis

This term is used for a very varied body of techniques whose object is to search for clusters in a population of individuals. It is not easy to give a precise definition of what is meant by a cluster but the general idea is clear enough. A cluster is a set of individuals who are sufficiently alike to distinguish them, as a group, from the remainder of the population. Cluster analysis is therefore often used when it is suspected that the population under investigation is composed of several more or less distinct sub-populations. If we find evidence for such a rudimentary structure in the data this may well be a valuable means of describing the population or it may form a basis for more detailed analysis. Several other terms have been used to describe an essentially similar activity in various sciences, including taxonomy, typology and classification. Biologists, for example, have a long history of classifying members of the plant and animal kingdoms and clinicians have similar problems in medical diagnosis. Recently, social scientists have turned to cluster analysis as a means of introducing a degree of order into the confusing picture which is often presented by multiple observations on many individuals.

Cormack (1971) provided a review of classification methods and Jardine and Sibson (1971) have subjected many clustering techniques to a critical examination in the light of various mathematical *desiderata*. Few methods emerge unscathed from their examination but some social scientists have objected that the critieria used are less appropriate in the social sciences than in biology. One of the most useful accounts of clustering methods is that of Everitt (1974) and this author has also contributed accounts of the subject to O'Muircheartaigh and Payne (1977) and Maxwell (1977).

Several of the simpler methods in use are virtually devoid of mathematical content and almost all can be used via computer packages with little understanding of their mathematical foundations. However, this is a recipe for error and this section is therefore concerned with the mathematics involved in the two approaches to cluster analysis which are most demanding in this respect.

The starting point will be the data matrix X of Section 4.1 where the element x_{ij} is the score given to the ith individual on the jth variable. The term *score* is used here to include any kind of measurement, qualitative or quantitative. The justification for placing individuals in the same cluster will be that they are 'alike' in some sense. It is therefore necessary to begin by constructing measures of similarity (or dissimilarity) between pairs of individuals. The choice of such measures is not, primarily, a mathematical question but must be decided upon in the context of the practical problem.

Two kinds of similarity measure are commonly used. If we think of X as defining a set of n points in p-dimensional space it is natural to think of their distance apart (Euclidean or otherwise [see IV, §11.1]) as measuring their similarity—the closer the points the greater the similarity. Both approaches to cluster analysis discussed in this section are based on such measures. The other way of measuring similarity can be simply explained as follows. If the five measurements on two individuals were

$$
\begin{array}{llllll}
\text{I} & 3 & 2 & 9 & 7 & 5 \\
\text{II} & 6 & 4 & 18 & 14 & 10
\end{array}
$$

we might argue that although the two individuals are well-separated in terms of distance they nevertheless exhibit the same 'profile'. In fact, the numbers for individual II are exactly twice those of I. This is an extreme example of the kind of similarity which can be measured by a correlation coefficient (between p variables on 2 individuals rather than between two variables on n individuals as is more usual). If some of the variables are categorical a similar purpose is served by measures of association.

The first of the two approaches to be discussed involves the optimization of a clustering criterion. The idea behind such a method is that if we can devise a measure of the success of any classification procedure then we should adopt that classification which makes the measure as large as possible. Such a measure can easily be constructed using the ideas of one-way multivariate analysis of variance. Suppose that the individuals are arbitrarily divided into k groups. This would be regarded as a satisfactory clustering if those individuals within a group were closer together, in general, than members of different groups. Closeness in this sense can be measured by the dispersion matrix [see II, §13.3.1] of the observations.

Let $\mathbf{T}$ represent the dispersion matrix for the complete data set ($\mathbf{X'X}$ if the x's in the data matrix are measured about their column means) and let $\mathbf{W}_i$ be the dispersion matrix of those in the ith group with $\mathbf{W} = \Sigma_{i=1}^g \mathbf{W}_i$, g being the number of groups. Then the between groups dispersion matrix is $\mathbf{B} = \mathbf{T} - \mathbf{W}$. A good attempt at clustering the data will be indicated if $\mathbf{W}$ is small, in some sense, compared to $\mathbf{B}$. If $p = 1$ the matrices are scalars and we can set out to find the clustering which makes $\mathbf{W}$ a minimum. If $p > 1$ some function of the elements of the matrices must be selected for minimization. There is no obviously best choice though it can be shown that some choices are better than others if the clusters have particular shapes (e.g. spherical). In the absence of such information *a priori* one might explore several different possibilities. Three measures for which computer programs exist are (a) trace $\mathbf{W}$, (b) $|\mathbf{W}|$ (the determinant) and (c) trace $\mathbf{BW}^{-1}$ [see I, §6.4]. The trace of a matrix is the sum of the diagonal elements [cf. I, Definition 7.3.1] which, in the present case, are sums of squares measuring the distance apart of individuals in the same group. The determinant of $\mathbf{W}$ [see I, §6.9] is, apart from a constant, a generalized variance.

For a given value of g the optimum allocation could, in principle, be found by computing the criterion for every possible allocation of n individuals to g categories. In practice this is impossible except for very small g or n because of the very large number of cases. The algorithms used are therefore 'hill-climbing' (or 'descending') methods which take a given allocation and seek to adjust it by seeing whether the criterion can be improved by moving any individual to another group. The procedure then continues until no such move can be made. The problem, as with all such search methods, is that they may reach a local rather than a global minimum. There is no certain check against this but if the same minimum is reached from several widely different starting points there is a strong presumption that the optimum has been achieved. However, the final test of a method is whether the clusters produced are meaningful in the practical context. Those yielded by a local optimum may therefore be quite acceptable.

The second approach postulates a probability model for the data. Cluster analysis then reduces to the problem of estimating the parameters of the model. Suppose that there are distinct groups or clusters in the population and that for all individuals in the ith cluster the p variables are distributed in the multivariate normal form with mean vector $\boldsymbol{\mu}_i$ and dispersion matrix $\boldsymbol{\Sigma}_i$. Let the proportion of the population in the ith cluster be α_i; then the data may be viewed as a random sample from the population with density function

$$f(\mathbf{x}) = \sum_{i=1}^g \alpha_i N(\mathbf{x}; \boldsymbol{\mu}_i, \boldsymbol{\Sigma}_i) \tag{4.22}$$

where $N(.)$ denotes the multivariate Normal density function. The first step is to estimate the parameters of this distribution and the second to allocate the individuals to the sub-populations. The parameters may be estimated by the method of maximum likelihood, for each g, using a modified Newton–Raphson method [see III, §5.4.1]. The number of parameters is typically large, and unless n is very large the estimates are liable to be imprecise. A simpler version of the model involves the assumption that the dispersion matrices are equal.

Once parameter estimates are available they can be used to estimate the probability that any given individual comes from any particular sub-population. Let $P(i \mid \mathbf{x})$ be the conditional probability that the individual with observed vector $\mathbf{x}$ comes from sub-population i. Then standard conditional probability arguments give

$$P(i \mid \mathbf{x}) = \alpha_i N(\mathbf{x}; \boldsymbol{\mu}_i, \boldsymbol{\Sigma}_i)/f(\mathbf{x}) \qquad (i = 1, 2, \ldots, g). \tag{4.23}$$

Each individual would then be allocated to that group for which this probability was the highest.

There are many other methods of cluster analysis, some of which are more widely used than those outlined above. However, once the measures of similarity have been agreed upon, the mathematical demands they place on the user are negligible.

Discriminant analysis [see VI, §16.4]

This is concerned with the problem of allocating an individual to one of a set of populations on the basis of knowledge about those populations derived from samples. It thus differs from cluster analysis in several respects. The number of populations, g, is known and the parameters of each one can be estimated from a sample known to have come from that population. This part of the problem is therefore a standard one of statistical inference and will not concern us further. Our account will be concerned with rules for allocating a new individual to one of the groups.

Applications of discriminant analysis have been mainly in psychology and archaeology and it is difficult to find examples in social science. However, it is easy to think of examples of cases where the technique might be useful. For example, in a voting study one might have data on a number of variables for groups of Conservative and Labour voters. If similar data were available for individuals who were unwilling to disclose their voting intention, discriminant analysis could be used to assign such persons to one or other group for purposes of subsequent analysis. In psychology, applications have been concerned with such things as the selection of individuals for education or training, and for diagnosing mental illness.

In the case where there are only two groups, regression analysis can be adapted to yield a discriminant function. Thus we score $y = 1$ if an individual belongs to one group and $y = 0$ if he belongs to the other. The regression of y on the explanatory variables x_1, x_2, ... then provides a means of predicting y for a new individual from his x-values. An allocation to the first group might then be made if the predicted y is nearer to 1 than 0 and vice versa.

There have been two general approaches to the solution of the discrimination problem. The first, for details of which see Rao (1973), formulates the problem in decision theory [see VI, Chapter 19] terms by seeking an allocation rule which minimizes the expected loss arising from mis-classification. The second approach aims to find a set of indices which distinguish as sharply as possible between the groups. Such methods are described, for example, in Kendall and Stuart (1976) and Maxwell (1977).

The basic set-up for both approaches is as follows. Suppose that an individual belongs to one and only one of g populations. Measurements are available on p variables $\mathbf{x} = (x_1, x_2, \ldots, x_p)'$ and we denote the density function of $\mathbf{x}$ in the ith population by $f_i(\mathbf{x})$. The (unknown) probability that an individual comes from the ith population is denoted by π_i ($\Sigma_{i=1}^g \pi_i = 1$). Finally let r_{ij} be the loss incurred by allocating a member of the ith population to category j (this will be a positive number).

The first approach aims to minimize the expected loss. Mathematically this involves partitioning the x-space into g mutually exclusive and exhaustive regions R_1, R_2, ..., R_g; an individual is then allocated to population i if his $\mathbf{x}$ falls in R_i. If an individual is selected at random the expected loss resulting from applying this rule is

$$E(L) = \sum_{j=1}^g \sum_{i=1}^g \int_{R_j} \pi_i f_i(\mathbf{x}) r_{ij} \, d\mathbf{x}. \tag{4.24}$$

Finding regions R_j to minimize this expression involves using a generalized version of the *Neyman–Pearson lemma* [see VI, §5.4]. The rule which results from this requires the calculation of the scores

$$S_j = - \sum_{i=1}^g \pi_i f_i(\mathbf{x}) r_{ij} \qquad (j = 1, 2, \ldots, g). \tag{4.25}$$

The individual is then allocated to that population for which S_j is a maximum.

If it is impossible to assign losses r_{ij}—as is likely to be the case in social science applications—we may aim to minimize the proportion of individuals who are mis-classified in the long run. This is proportional to

$$\sum_{i=1}^g \pi_i \sum_{\substack{j=1 \\ j \neq i}}^g \int_{R_j} f_i(\mathbf{x}) \, d\mathbf{x} \tag{4.26}$$

which is a special case of (4.24) obtained by putting $r_{ii} = 0$, $r_{ij} = 1$ ($i \neq j$). Hence the rule in this case is to compute the scores

$$S_j = \pi_j f_j(\mathbf{x}) \tag{4.27}$$

and to allocate to the population for which the score is a maximum.

The application of either set of scores requires an assumption to be made about the form of $f_i(\mathbf{x})$. If we assume multivariate Normality [see II, §13.4] taking

$$f_i(\mathbf{x}) = (2\pi)^{-p/2} \, | \, \mathbf{\Sigma}_i \, |^{-1/2} \exp[-\tfrac{1}{2}(\mathbf{x} - \mathbf{\mu}_i)' \mathbf{\Sigma}_i^{-1}(\mathbf{x} - \mathbf{\mu}_i)] \qquad (i = 1, 2, \ldots, k)$$

the scores in the case of (4.27) can be transformed by taking logarithms to make them quadratic functions of the observations. If we further assume that the dispersion matrices are equal, discrimination depends, essentially, on a linear function of the x's. If, in addition, $g = 2$ the rule coincides with one due to Fisher which also arises as a special case of the second approach now to be described.

This second approach will be described first for the case of two populations. The aim is to find that linear function of the x's which achieves the greatest possible separation between the two populations. Denote any such function by $Y = \Sigma_{i=1}^{p} a_i x_i$ and let $E(x_i) = \mu_{1i}$ for members of the first population and $E(x_i) = \mu_{2i}$ for those of the second. A reasonable measure of separation is

$$\phi = \left\{ \sum_{i=1}^{p} a_i(\mu_{1i} - \mu_{2i}) \right\}^2 \bigg/ \sum_{i=1}^{p} \sum_{j=1}^{p} a_i a_j \sigma_{ij} \qquad (4.28)$$

where $\sigma_{ij}^2 = E(x_i - E(x_i))(x_j - E(x_j))$ it being assumed that variances and covariances are the same for both populations. The quantity ϕ is the square of the difference between the expected values of Y in the two populations expressed in terms of its standard deviation. The mathematical problem is now to maximize ϕ with respect to the coefficients $\{a_i\}$. The standard method gives the maximizing values as the solution of

$$a_1 \sigma_{i1} + a_2 \sigma_{i2} + \ldots + a_p \sigma_{ip} = \mu_{1i} - \mu_{2i}, \qquad (i = 1, 2, \ldots, p)$$

which can be solved in terms of the sample estimates of the σ's and μ's. The allocation rule then consists of choosing a critical value of Y, between its mean values for the two populations; individuals are then allocated to one or other population according as their Y-value lies above or below the critical point. In the absence of information about the costs of mis-classification the point half-way between the means for the two populations is usually chosen as the critical value.

In geometrical terms Y represents a plane which divides the x-space into two regions. This would seem to be a reasonable way of partitioning the space if the populations formed two reasonably compact clusters. With more than two populations a similar kind of partitioning can be obtained by the following generalization of the foregoing method. Again we start with an arbitrary linear function of the x's denoted by Y and suppose that we partition individuals according to their value of Y. The success of such a partitioning can be judged by comparing the between and within groups sums of squares of Y. If $\mathbf{B}$ and $\mathbf{W}$ denote the between and within groups dispersion matrices for the x's then the between groups sum of squares for Y is $\mathbf{a'Ba}$ and the within groups sum of squares is $\mathbf{a'Wa}$. The method is then to maximize the ratio

$$\phi = \mathbf{a'Ba}/\mathbf{a'Wa} \tag{4.29}$$

which is equivalent to (4.28) for $g = 2$. The vector of derivatives of ϕ with respect to $\mathbf{a}$ [see IV, §5.6] is

$$\frac{\partial \phi}{\partial \mathbf{a}} = (\mathbf{a'Wa})(2\mathbf{Ba}) - (\mathbf{a'Ba})(2\mathbf{Wa}) = 0. \tag{4.30}$$

Dividing both sides by $2\mathbf{a'Wa}$ gives

$$\mathbf{Ba} = \phi\mathbf{Wa} \quad \text{or} \quad (\mathbf{B} - \phi\mathbf{W})\mathbf{a} = \mathbf{0}. \tag{4.31}$$

This last equation is satisfied if ϕ is any latent root of $\mathbf{W}^{-1}\mathbf{B}$, $\mathbf{a}$ being its associated latent vector [see I, §7.1]. Hence (4.29) is maximized if we take ϕ as the largest latent root and $\mathbf{a}$ as the corresponding vector. Any new individual can therefore be allocated according to its value of Y in a manner similar to that used for $g = 2$. With more than two populations this method will not be very efficient unless the populations happen to be linearly ordered. An improved partitioning can be obtained by introducing other linear discriminants which are orthogonal to one another. Thus if we form a second linear function Z using the latent vector $\mathbf{a}$ corresponding to the second largest latent root this will be orthogonal to Y. By plotting the population means of Y and Z in two dimensions we could draw boundaries in this plane to produce g regions as a basis for allocation. Taking further latent vectors will provide a more refined basis for partitioning the x-space but the problem of deciding on boundaries in the $Y, Z, \ldots$ space is difficult when the clusters cannot be visualized as in two dimensions.

4.5 Structure and Dimensionality

The group of methods to be described in this section are all concerned with exploring the dimensionality of the data and, in particular, with achieving a representation of them in a small number of dimensions. Of these, principal component analysis is the simplest in the sense that it is concerned only with the geometry of the data points. Factor analysis and latent structure analysis introduce a probability model in which the observed variables are structurally related to a (usually) smaller number of unobservable variables. In multi-dimensional scaling the main problem is to convert ordered information on distances between points into a metric in a space of chosen dimension.

Principal component analysis

We have seen that a data set may be viewed as a set of n points in p-dimensional space. In many multivariate studies it is relevant to ask whether the points lie, exactly or nearly, in a space of fewer dimensions. If this is so the set can be described more economically and, perhaps, meaningfully in terms of those dimensions. The essence of principal component analysis is to choose new axes in turn in such a way that each is in the direction of the greatest variation orthogonal to those already fixed. Thus the first new axis (the first principal component) is chosen to lie along the direction of greatest variability. In algebraic terms it will be the linear function of the original x's which has the greatest variance. We then fix the second axis, at right angles to the first, in the same way and so on. If, to take an extreme case, the variation in all directions but the first was negligible then we would conclude that the data could effectively be represented in one dimension. That is, it would be sufficient to replace the p x-variables by a single linear combination of them. In practice such a drastic reduction is rarely possible but it is often found that the bulk of the variation lies in a space of substantially fewer than p dimensions.

It is convenient to regard each x-variable as measured from its mean, in which case the mathematical problem is to find [see I, Definition 10.2.4] an orthogonal transformation $\mathbf{Y} = \mathbf{XA}$ (where $\mathbf{Y}$ is $n \times p$ and $\mathbf{A}$ is $p \times p$) such that the new variables, y, are uncorrelated [see II, Theorem 13.4.1] and such that they account for as much variation as possible when taken in order as described above. Let $\mathbf{S} = \mathbf{X'X}/n$ be the dispersion matrix of the x's; then it may be shown that the dispersion matrix for the y's is $\mathbf{A'SA}/n$. Let the first column of $\mathbf{Y}$ correspond to the first component; then we require the variance (or sum of squares) of $y_{11}, y_{21}, \ldots, y_{n1}$ to be as large as possible. Their sum of squares is $\mathbf{a_1'Sa_1}$ where $\mathbf{a_1}$ is the first column of $\mathbf{A}$. The point of requiring the transformation to be orthogonal was to ensure that distances between points would be unaffected. This imposes the restriction $\mathbf{A'A} = \mathbf{I}$ on $\mathbf{A}$ [see I, §6.7(vii)] and hence that $\mathbf{a_1'a_1} = 1$. We must therefore maximize $\mathbf{a_1'Sa_1}$ subject to the constraint $\mathbf{a_1'a_1} = 1$. This may be achieved by the standard method using undetermined multipliers by finding the unrestricted maximum of

$$\phi = \mathbf{a_1'Sa_1} + \lambda_1(1 - \mathbf{a_1'a_1}). \tag{4.32}$$

This yields the following equation for the optimum $\mathbf{a_1'}$:

$$\mathbf{Sa_1} = \lambda_1 \mathbf{a_1}. \tag{4.33}$$

The value of $\mathbf{a_1'Sa_1}$ in this case is thus $\mathbf{a_1'}\lambda_1\mathbf{a_1} = \lambda_1$ so that the sum of squares is maximized by taking $\mathbf{a_1}$ as the latent vector associated with the largest latent root of $\mathbf{S}$. This vector is determined uniquely from (4.33) and the normalizing equation $\mathbf{a_1'a_1} = 1$.

We next proceed to the second column of $\mathbf{Y}$ and maximize the variance of $y_{12}, y_{22}, y_{32}, \ldots, y_{n2}$ subject to the additional requirement that this second component is uncorrelated with the first. This requires that $\mathbf{a_2'a_1} = 0$ where $\mathbf{a_2}$ is the second column of $\mathbf{A}$. There are now two restrictions and the function to be maximized can be written as:

$$\phi = \mathbf{a_2'Sa_2} + \lambda_2(1 - \mathbf{a_2'a_2}) - 2\eta\mathbf{a_1'a_2}. \tag{4.34}$$

The second undetermined multiplier [see IV, (5.15.2)] is written as -2η because the vector of derivatives then takes the simple form

$$\mathbf{S}\mathbf{a}_2 = \lambda_2\mathbf{a}_2 + \eta\mathbf{a}_1. \tag{4.35}$$

Pre-multiplying by $\mathbf{a}_2'$ yields

$$\mathbf{a}_2'\mathbf{S}\mathbf{a}_2 = \lambda_2$$

so that λ_2 is the maximum value of the sum of squares. To find λ_2 and $\mathbf{a}_2$ we pre-multiply (4.35) by $\mathbf{a}_1'$ which gives

$$\eta = \mathbf{a}_1'\mathbf{S}\mathbf{a}_2.$$

Transposing both sides of (4.33) [see I, §6.5] gives $\mathbf{a}_1'\mathbf{S} = \lambda_1\mathbf{a}_1'$ so

$$\eta = \lambda_1\mathbf{a}_1'\mathbf{a}_2 = 0$$

and hence $\mathbf{a}_2$ satisfies

$$\mathbf{S}\mathbf{a}_2 = \lambda_2\mathbf{a}_2. \tag{4.36}$$

This shows that $\mathbf{a}_2$ is the latent vector of $\mathbf{S}$ associated with the second largest latent root of $\mathbf{S}$ [see I, §7.1].

The argument proceeds in this fashion to find $\mathbf{a}_3, \mathbf{a}_4, \ldots, \mathbf{a}_p$. At each stage there is the normalizing requirement that $\mathbf{a}_i'\mathbf{a}_i = 1$ and further restrictions of the form $\mathbf{a}_i'\mathbf{a}_j = 0$ to ensure that the component being determined is uncorrelated with its predecessors. The matrix $\mathbf{A}$ is thus determined as the set of normalized latent vectors of the matrix $\mathbf{S}$.

Another way of looking at the same result is to argue that if the p new y-variables are to be uncorrelated then $\mathbf{A}'\mathbf{S}\mathbf{A}$ must have the diagonal form

$$\mathbf{A}'\mathbf{S}\mathbf{A} = \begin{pmatrix} \lambda_1 & 0 & \ldots\ldots & 0 \\ 0 & \lambda_2 & & \vdots \\ \vdots & & \ddots & \vdots \\ 0 & \ldots\ldots\ldots\ldots & \ddots & \lambda_p \end{pmatrix}. \tag{4.37}$$

To find an $\mathbf{A}$ having this property we use the fact [see I, Theorem 7.8.2] that for any square symmetric matrix of rank p, such as $\mathbf{S}$, there is a $p \times p$ diagonal matrix $\mathbf{\Lambda}$ whose elements are the latent roots of $\mathbf{S}$ and a matrix $\mathbf{Z}$ of the same dimensions whose columns are the normalized latent vectors of $\mathbf{S}$ such that

$$\mathbf{S} = \mathbf{Z}\mathbf{\Lambda}\mathbf{Z}' \text{ with } \mathbf{Z}'\mathbf{Z} = \mathbf{I}.$$

Substituting for $\mathbf{S}$ in (4.37) requires that

$$\mathbf{A}'\mathbf{Z}\mathbf{\Lambda}\mathbf{Z}'\mathbf{A} = \begin{pmatrix} \lambda_1 & 0 & \ldots\ldots & 0 \\ 0 & \lambda_2 & & 0 \\ \vdots & & & \vdots \\ 0 & \ldots\ldots\ldots\ldots & & \lambda_p \end{pmatrix}$$

which is achieved by choosing $\mathbf{A} = \mathbf{Z}$.

Yet another way of looking at the problem is to pose it as one of approximating the matrix $\mathbf{S}$, of rank p, by another matrix $\mathbf{S}^*$, say, of smaller rank r. This gives expression to the desire to have a small number of uncorrelated variables which produce, as nearly as possible, the dispersion of the original data set. Finding such an approximation by the method of least squares gives

$$\mathbf{S}^* = \sum_{i=1}^{r} \lambda_i \mathbf{a}_i \mathbf{a}_i'$$

and the closeness of the approximation may be judged from the fact [see III, §6.2.3] that

$$\| \mathbf{S} - \mathbf{S}^* \|^2 = \lambda_{r+1}^2 + \lambda_{r+2}^2 + \ldots + \lambda_p^2.$$

A plot of this quantity as a function of r is a useful way of judging the approximate dimensionality of the data set. The more usual way is to use the fact that λ_i is that part of the total variation attributable to the ith component. The proportion of the total variation accounted for by the first r components is thus $(\lambda_1 + \lambda_2 + \ldots + \lambda_r)/(\lambda_1 + \lambda_2 + \ldots + \lambda_p)$ and one hopes to find that this is close to 1 for small r.

A word of caution is necessary about the application of this method which is especially relevant in the social sciences. The results depend on the scales of measurement used for the x-variables. If the scales used are arbitrary, as they often are, then the conclusions from the analysis will also be arbitrary. Thus, for example, if some variables are times and others lengths or counts a principal component analysis as so far described will be virtually meaningless. To avoid this social scientists often standardize their data by re-scaling to make the standard deviation of each variable unity. The matrix $\mathbf{S}$ then becomes the correlation matrix. This device does not necessarily ease the problem of interpreting the components, but these are not mathematical issues.

Factor analysis

In social science contexts we often speak of quantities such as intelligence, the quality of life, the standard of living, aggressiveness, conservatism and so on. Much social theorizing, as well as popular discussion of current affairs, pre-supposes that it is sensible to conduct rational discussion about such things as if they were capable of measurement on a numerical scale like more familiar variables such as money and time. However, the problem is that there is no simple measuring instrument by which numbers can be assigned to such quantities. Instead, there is usually a whole host of measurable 'indicators' whose values are assumed to reflect the values of the underlying variables in which we are interested. For example, if we are interested in the quality of life the list of possible variables which bear upon the question is almost endless and would include such things as the level of pollutants in the atmosphere and drinking water, density of population, provision of schools, sporting facilities and health care, ease of access to the countryside and so forth. There are several techniques of multivariate analysis which seek to make explicit the relationships between variables which can be observed (called manifest variables) and those unobservable variables in which is our primary interest (called latent variables). Factor analysis and latent structure analysis are the main examples of this kind of technique.

The foregoing account spoke as though we were able to name the latent variables in advance of carrying out the analysis. This will sometimes be the case as it was in the first attempts at factor analysis by psychologists investigating intelligence. More generally, we may wish to approach the data without pre-suppositions about the identity and number of the latent variables. In such cases we shall be asking whether the data matrix $\mathbf{X}$ can be 'explained' in terms of a few basic underlying variables and whether they can be identified with some named latent variables. This is not a mathematical problem though mathematical methods, such as rotation of axes, may help to clarify the position in particular cases.

Factor analysis starts from a simple linear model of the relationship between the manifest and latent variables. Suppose that there are p manifest random variables denoted by $x_1, x_2, \ldots, x_p$ and q latent variables $y_1, y_2, \ldots, y_q$. Usually q is smaller than p and in most applications would be very much smaller. If this were the case we would have 'explained' p variables in terms of q variables and so have effected a considerable reduction in the dimensionality of the problem. The standard model may be written

$$x_i = \lambda_{i1}y_1 + \lambda_{i2}y_2 + \ldots + \lambda_{iq}y_q + e_i \qquad (i = 1, 2, \ldots, p)$$

or

$$\mathbf{x} = \boldsymbol{\Lambda}\mathbf{y} + \mathbf{e} \qquad (4.38)$$

where e_i represents an 'error'.

In factor analysis the y's have been known traditionally as the factors, but we shall continue to use the term latent variables since 'factor' is a somewhat ambiguous term in statistics and the symbol f, often used in place of y, is liable to be confused with its wider use to denote a function. The λ's are called the 'factor loadings' because they determine the weight which each variable carries in determining the x's. For simplicity we suppose that the x's have been located so as to have zero expectation. The error term enters either as an error of measurement or in recognition of the fact that there may be some residual variation in the x's not explained by the y's. In the simplest models the y's are supposed to be independent of one another and of the e_i's. Finally, the y's and e's are assumed to be Normally distributed, the y's with unit variances and e_i with variance ψ_i $(i = 1, 2, \ldots, n)$. The main purpose of the analysis can now be viewed as seeing whether there is a value of q for which the model of (4.38) provides a satisfactory fit to the data. To answer this question estimates are required of the λ's and ψ's.

There is a substantial literature on factor analysis dating back to the beginning of this century. Much of this work has been superseded since the efficient handling of the formidable numerical problems which the model poses had to await the advent of the electronic computer. A full account of the mathematical foundations of the subject is given in Lawley and Maxwell (1971). A useful treatment, including numerical examples, is given by Taylor (1977) who also deals with principal component analysis. A widely used text is Harman (1976). These authors also give references to other work, including fundamental contributions from Joreskog and his co-workers.

The usual starting point of factor analysis is the dispersion matrix of the x's given by

$$\mathbf{\Sigma} = E(\mathbf{x}\mathbf{x}').$$

In practice this matrix would have to be estimated but we shall begin by treating it as if it were known. If the model of (4.38) holds it follows at once that

$$E(\mathbf{x}\mathbf{x}') = \mathbf{\Lambda}\mathbf{\Lambda}' + \mathbf{\psi} \tag{4.39}$$

where $\mathbf{\psi}$ is the diagonal matrix with non-negative elements ψ_i. The first question concerns the identifiability of the model—that is with whether there is a unique $\mathbf{\Lambda}$ and $\mathbf{\psi}$ satisfying (4.39). It is easy to show that this is not so, for suppose that $\mathbf{\Lambda}^*$ is one such $\mathbf{\Lambda}$ and that $\mathbf{M}$ is any orthogonal matrix (i.e. $\mathbf{M}\mathbf{M}' = \mathbf{I}$) of order q. It follows that $\mathbf{\Lambda} = \mathbf{\Lambda}^*\mathbf{M}'$ also satisfies (4.39) since $\mathbf{\Lambda}^*\mathbf{M}'\mathbf{M}\mathbf{\Lambda}^{*'} = \mathbf{\Lambda}^*\mathbf{\Lambda}^{*'}$. Provided that $q > 1$ there are infinitely many $\mathbf{M}$'s and hence infinitely many $\mathbf{\Lambda}$'s which satisfy (4.39). In geometrical terms the orthogonal transformation means a rotation of the axes in the space of the latent variables y. The question of which rotation is most relevant for purposes of interpretation is a substantive matter and will be touched on again later.

It is clear from the foregoing that if one wishes to fit the model having the dispersion matrix $\mathbf{\Sigma}$, uniqueness can only be ensured by imposing further restraints. Once a unique solution has been obtained other solutions satisfying (4.39) (but not these further restraints) can be generated by orthogonal rotation. Lawley and Maxwell (1971) adduce reasons for requiring that $\mathbf{\Lambda}$ should be such that $\mathbf{\Lambda}'\mathbf{\psi}^{-1}\mathbf{\Lambda}$ is diagonal [see I, §6.7(iv)] with elements arranged in decreasing order of magnitude. This requirement imposes $\frac{1}{2}q(q-1)$ restraints upon the λ's and so effectively reduces the number of unknowns on the right-hand side of (4.39) from $pq + p$ to $pq + p - \frac{1}{2}q(q-1)$. If the elements of $\mathbf{\Sigma}$ are given, an element by element comparison of the two sides of (4.39) yields $\frac{1}{2}p(p+1)$ equations for determining the unknowns. If

$$pq + p - \frac{1}{2}q(q-1) = \frac{1}{2}p(p+1)$$

that is if

$$(p - q)^2 = (p + q)$$

then it will be possible to fit a factor model having precisely the same dispersion matrix as that observed for the x's. This is a trivial case because such a model could be fitted perfectly whatever the true structure of the data. If $p + q > (p - q)^2$ there will be more unknowns than equations and hence infinitely many solutions. The non-trivial case is when $p + q < (p - q)^2$ in which case the model cannot be fitted exactly. The question which then arises is whether the fit is within the limits to be expected given the error structure of the model. The foregoing argument is incomplete because it ignores the fact that the ψ_i's must be non-negative so it could happen that, even when $p + q = (p - q)^2$, there is no admissible solution. The detailed investigation of necessary and sufficient conditions required to ensure a unique solution is a complicated matter beyond the scope of this introductory account.

The assumptions of the factor model can be varied. For example, we may suppose that the y's are correlated with one another such that $E(yy') = V$ say. The decomposition of (4.39) then becomes

$$\Sigma = \Lambda V \Lambda' + \psi. \tag{4.40}$$

Any non-singular transformation of a Λ satisfying this equation will also satisfy it, since V is unknown, so further restraints have to be imposed before a unique solution can be found.

The rotation of axes in the factor space is often used as a means of arriving at an interpretation of the latent variables. The question of interpretation is not a mathematical one but the methods by which certain desirable patterns can be achieved in the factor loadings does pose a problem in mathematics. For example, it is sometimes considered desirable to have the loadings for a given manifest variable concentrated on as few latent variables as possible. This helps to 'identify' a latent variable by focussing on those manifest variables on which it is a primary influence. This state of affairs can be produced by making the variability of the λ's in any column of Λ as great as possible. The varimax method, for example, achieves this by maximizing the variance of the squares of the factor loadings. Once more, this leads to the maximization of a function of many variables subject, in this case, to quadratic restrictions on the variables.

Having estimated the parameters of the model we may wish to determine what values of the y's gave rise to the x's. This is not an estimation problem in the usual sense because the y's are random variables and not parameters. (Many texts overlook this point.) That being so our knowledge about them must be expressed in terms of their joint probability density function. Prior to observing the x's the y's were independent normal variables but after x is observed it is the conditional distribution of y given x that is relevant. This is obtained by Bayes' theorem [see II, §16.4, and VI, Chapter 15] and the result is given in a more general context below in (4.46). A joint distribution function is too cumbersome for many purposes but it may be summarized by the conditional expectations $E(y \mid x)$. It may be shown that for the factor model

$$E(y \mid x) = \Lambda' \Sigma^{-1} x. \tag{4.41}$$

Such values are called factor scores and those given by (4.41) are sometimes referred to as 'regression' scores.

In some circumstances it may be reasonable to regard the y's as fixed, in which case they can be treated as parameters and estimated by the method of maximum likelihood. This involves minimizing

$$\sum_{i=1}^{p} (e_i^2/\psi_i) = (x - \Lambda y)' \psi^{-1} (x - \Lambda y) \tag{4.42}$$

with respect to the y's. This determines them in such a way that, in a least squares sense, they leave as little to be explained by the error term as possible. The mathematical problem is again one of minimizing a quadratic form and in this case it yields the solution

$$\hat{y} = (\Lambda' \psi^{-1} \Lambda)^{-1} \Lambda' \psi^{-1} x. \tag{4.43}$$

Many methods have been proposed for estimating the parameters of the factor model from the data matrix. They start with the unbiased estimator of the dispersion matrix

$$S = \hat{\Sigma} = \frac{1}{n-1} \sum_{i=1}^{n} (x_i - \bar{x})(x_i - \bar{x})'.$$

The main obstacle has been the heavy computing necessary, and many methods have been designed to reduce this. Now that these have been largely overcome by the use of computers it is possible to concentrate on methods with a satisfactory theoretical basis. Of these the most satisfying is based on the method of maximum likelihood [see VI, Chapter 6]. The joint distribution of the sample covariances is a function of Σ which in turn is a function of Λ and ψ. It is thus possible to write down the likelihood function and maximize it with respect to the unknown parameters.

Under the Normality assumption the joint distribution of the elements of S has the Wishart form [see VI, §16.2] for which the log-likelihood function for the sample [see VI, §6.13] is, apart from a function of the observations only,

$$\ln L = -\tfrac{1}{2}(n-1)\ln|\Sigma| - \tfrac{1}{2}(n-1) \sum_{i=1}^{p} \sum_{j=1}^{p} s_{ij} \sigma^{ij} \tag{4.44}$$

where σ^{ij} is the (i,j)th element of Σ^{-1}. The function $\ln L$ has to be maximized with respect to Λ and ψ subject to the restrictions. It is a function of some complexity, and methods for its successful maximization have not been easy to devise. The aim is to proceed iteratively, increasing the value of the function at each step. Computer programs for this purpose are available. In the method, based on work of Fletcher and Powell (1963), a second degree approximation to the function is made at each stage using the first and second derivatives of the log-likelihood function. A new approximation is then obtained by maximizing this quadratic function. For this particular problem the procedure generates a sequence of matrices from which the corresponding Λ can be found. This is an example of a maximization procedure in which the maximum may occur on the boundary of the parameter space at a point where not all the first derivatives vanish. If this happens one or more of the variances ψ_i will be estimated as zero and this raises problems about the appropriateness of the model.

The foregoing account of factor analysis is necessarily brief, as a cursory inspection of Lawley and Maxwell (1971) will show. The social scientist who wishes to master the details, especially of the maximum likelihood estimation procedure, will need a thorough grounding in the principles of matrix algebra, including determinants, and techniques for the minimization of functions of many variables. The foundations for this are provided by the core volumes but these must be read in conjunction with a book such as that by Lawley and Maxwell (1971) and the original papers. Such sources will also provide information on other topics, not treated here, such as testing hypotheses about the values of parameters in the model.

Latent structure analysis

Factor analysis may be regarded as a special case of a more general approach to modelling observational data which may be described as follows. Suppose, as before, that there is a set of *manifest* variables, $x_1, x_2, \ldots, x_p$, which are assumed to arise from a smaller set of *latent* variables $y_1, y_2, \ldots, y_q$. The relationship between the two is probabilistic and may be expressed in terms of the conditional distribution of the x's given the y's. If all variables are continuous this may be expressed in terms of the conditional density [see II, Definition 13.1.2]

$$\phi(x_1, x_2, \ldots, x_p \mid y_1, y_2, \ldots, y_q).$$

For ease of presentation we shall treat all variables as continuous but the modifications required to encompass categorical variables are straight-forward. The y's are, themselves, random variables and we denote their joint distribution by $h(y_1, y_2, \ldots, y_q)$. Neither $\phi(\cdot)$ nor $h(\cdot)$ can be observed. All inferences about them must therefore be via the x's whose joint density $f(x_1, x_2, \ldots, x_p)$ can be estimated. The connection between these functions is [see II, Theorem 16.2.2]

$$f(\mathbf{x}) = \int \phi(\mathbf{x} \mid \mathbf{y}) h(\mathbf{y}) \, \mathrm{d}\mathbf{y}. \tag{4.45}$$

The object of the exercise is thus to infer something about the functions $\phi(\cdot)$ and $h(\cdot)$ from what we know about $f(\cdot)$. In practice we are less likely to be interested in $\phi(\cdot)$ and $h(\cdot)$ themselves than in the conditional density of the y's given the x's. This follows directly from Bayes' theorem, which yields

$$g(\mathbf{y} \mid \mathbf{x}) = \phi(\mathbf{x} \mid \mathbf{y})h(\mathbf{y})/f(\mathbf{x}). \tag{4.46}$$

There is no unique solution to the problem as posed because there will, in general, be many functions $\phi(\cdot)$ satisfying (4.45). In other words, the model is not identifiable. Further progress can only be made by injecting sufficient further assumptions to render a solution unique. A common first step is to assume that, given $\mathbf{y}$, the x's are mutually independent. This assumption is justified in social science applications by arguing that if the observed dependence between the x's arises from variation in the y's then when the y's are held fixed the residual variation in the x's should be independent. If this is so

$$\phi(\mathbf{x} \mid \mathbf{y}) = \phi_1(x_1 \mid \mathbf{y}) \, \phi_2(x_2 \mid \mathbf{y}) \ldots \phi_p(x_p \mid \mathbf{y}).$$

In the factor analysis model of the last sub-section this assumption corresponds to treating the e's as independent. As in factor analysis we may also assume that the y's are independent and, further, that the form of the distributions $h(\cdot)$ and $\phi_1(\cdot)$, $\phi_2(\cdot)$, $\ldots$, $\phi_p(\cdot)$ are known. The latter are all taken as Normal in the factor model.

The manifest and latent variables may be either metrical or categorical and it is usually assumed that there is only one latent variable. The statistical problem is first to estimate the joint distribution of the manifest variables and then to use (4.45) to determine the parameters of the latent distributions. The latent variable may be metrical or categorical. In the latter case (4.45) is known as the latent class model and the basic ideas of the approach will be sufficiently illustrated by focusing on that case. The case where the x's are ordered categorical and the y's metrical variables is treated in Bartholomew (1980) where it is called the factor analysis of categorical data.

Basic references on latent structure analysis are the books by Lazarsfeld and Henry (1968) and Goodman (1978). A useful summary account is given by Fielding (1977a). A wider-ranging collection of papers on methods involving latent variables, with special reference to economics, is that edited by Aigner and Goldberger (1977). An interesting extension of the ideas to the analysis of panel data where the object is to estimate a latent Markov chain [see II, Chapter 19] is given in Wiggins (1973).

The latent class model

This model assumes that there is one latent categorical variable with k classes. There are several categorical manifest variables which are all simple dichotomies. In social applications the manifest variables might be the answers given to a series of yes/no questions or the observation of whether some attribute was present or absent in an individual. The general object of the method is thus to see whether the observed pattern of responses on the manifest variables can, apart from random variation, be accounted for by a single underlying variable.

In this case the distribution of the latent variable y may be expressed as a set of probabilities $p_1, p_2, \ldots, p_k$ ($\Sigma_i p_i = 1$), one for each class. An individual in latent class i may make one of two responses, $x_i = 1$ or $x_i = 0$, say. The conditional independence assumption for the x's given y enables us to specify this as

$$\Pr\{x_i = 1 \mid y \text{ is in class } j\} = \pi_i(j) \qquad (i = 1, 2, \ldots, p; j = 1, 2, \ldots, k).$$
(4.47)

The conditional distributions of the manifest variables are therefore binomial.

The joint probability distribution of the x's may now be expressed in terms of the parameters $\{p_i\}$ and $\{\pi_i(j)\}$ and this relationship provides the basis for estimation. We can easily estimate the joint probability distribution of the x's [see II, §13.1.1] from the relevant proportions in the sample. There are 2^p such probabilities corresponding to the cells of the 2^p contingency table [see VI, Chapter 10] in which the data would be set out but since they are constrained to sum to one there are only $2^p - 1$ independent parameters [see VI, §§1.2 and 3.13]. There are $k + kp$ parameters to be estimated subject to one constraint ($\Sigma p_i = 1$). It will not, therefore, be possible to obtain a unique solution if the number of parameters exceeds the number of potential estimating equations. That is, the problem is under-identified if

$$k(p + 1) > 2^p.$$

By having a sufficiently large number of manifest variables it can be ensured that there are at least enough equations to determine the unknowns. If $2^p > k(p + 1)$ there are too many equations and the usual practice has been to select a sub-set just sufficient in number to determine the parameters. The remaining equations can then be used to judge the goodness of fit. A natural way to proceed is to use the marginal probabilities of the x's [see II, §6.3 and §13.1.2]. It is easy to show that the distribution is completely determined by the marginal probabilities

$$\Pr\{x_i = 1\} \quad (i = 1, 2, \ldots, p), \quad \Pr\{x_i = 1, x_j = 1\} \quad (i, j = 1, 2, \ldots, p)$$
$$\Pr\{x_i = 1, x_j = 1, x_h = 1\} \quad (i, j, h = 1, 2, \ldots, p) \ldots$$
$$\Pr\{x_1 = 1, x_2 = 1, \ldots, x_p = 1\}.$$

Note that [see I, (3.10.6)] the number of these probabilities is

$$\binom{p}{1} + \binom{p}{2} + \ldots + \binom{p}{p} = 2^p - 1.$$

By taking these in the order listed one can proceed to the point where there are just sufficient equations to determine the model. The sequence of estimating equations thus obtained is:

$$p_1 + p_2 + \ldots + p_k = 1$$

$$\Pr\{x_i = 1\} = \pi_i(1)p_1 + \pi_i(2)p_2 + \ldots + \pi_i(k)p_k$$
$$(i = 1, 2, \ldots, p)$$

$$\Pr\{x_i = 1, x_j = 1\} = \sum_{l=1}^{k} \pi_i(l)\pi_j(l)p_l$$
$$(i, j = 1, 2, \ldots, p)$$

$$\Pr\{x_i = 1, x_j = 1, x_h = 1\} = \sum_{l=1}^{k} \pi_i(l)\pi_j(l)\pi_h(l)p_l$$
$$(i, j, h = 1, 2, \ldots, p)$$

$$(4.48)$$

etc.

The mathematical problem posed is thus the solution of a set of non-linear simultaneous equations. Lazarsfeld and Henry (1968) and Fielding (1977a) show how this problem may be tackled in certain cases using matrix representations.

In models where the manifest variables are metrical (but the latent variable categorical) one cannot proceed in the above manner. Instead it is usual to work with the moments and product moments of the manifest variables, expressing them in terms of the p_i's and other parameters of the model. The conditions for identifiability and the methods of solution turn out to be essentially the same as for the latent class model.

The somewhat arbitrary selection of equations implied by the method outlined above is rather unsatisfactory in that it will not, in general, be fully efficient. An alternative is provided by the method of maximum likelihood. A fairly simple, iterative, procedure for fitting the model by this method has been given by Goodman (1974).

Non-metric multi-dimensional scaling

Like cluster analysis, non-metric multi-dimensional scaling (MDS) starts from a set of dissimilarities (or similarities) between pairs of individuals. However, instead of merely classifying individuals into groups, MDS aims to go farther and represent the individuals by a configuration of points in p-dimensional space, where p is reasonably small. In other words the aim is to create a 'data-matrix' of points such that the original dissimilarities correspond as closely as possible to the inter-point distances. Once achieved the configuration can be inspected and analysed in the various ways appropriate to such data.

Classical scaling methods, introduced by psychologists (e.g. Torgerson, 1958), treat the dissimilarities as proportional to distance and hence try to re-construct a 'map' of the individual positions from a knowledge of their distances apart. In non-metric scaling, with which social scientists have been largely concerned, the aim is to ensure as far as possible that the inter-point distances are ordered in the same way as the dissimilarities. It turns out that the constraints imposed by the order restrictions are sufficiently strong to be almost as good as metric information.

The pioneering work in MDS was done by Shepard (1962) and Kruskal (1964a, b). The last-mentioned papers still provide one of the clearest accounts of the underlying methodology. A review of more recent developments together with some examples will be found in Coxon and Jones (1977). The mathematics of the method involves the minimization of a function of many variables by a method of steepest descent [see IV, §9.14] and also a restricted minimization of such a function subject to order restraints. The latter problem is a special case of isotonic regression analysis, which is comprehensively covered in Barlow and co-workers (1972).

The starting point of the analysis is an $n \times n$ matrix of dissimilarities $\{\delta_{ij}\}$, δ_{ij} being the value of the measure for the pair of individuals i and j. The aim is to determine a set of coordinates $\mathbf{x}_i = (x_{i1}, x_{i2}, \ldots, x_{ip})$ for the ith individual in p-dimensional space. The choice of p is important but is not a mathematical matter. In practice it is usually desirable to make p as small as possible subject to preserving a reasonable degree of agreement between the dissimilarity matrix and the inter-point distances. This point can be investigated by doing the calculations for different values of p.

The essence of the method is to construct a measure of the success which any configuration of points has in reproducing the pattern of the dissimilarity matrix. It then proceeds by finding that configuration which makes this measure as small as possible. The measure of fit is called the stress, and is defined as

$$S = \sqrt{\sum_i \sum_j (d_{ij} - \hat{d}_{ij})^2 \Big/ \sum_i \sum_j d_{ij}^2}. \tag{4.49}$$

where d_{ij} is the distance between the points $\mathbf{x}_i$ and $\mathbf{x}_j$. This is usually taken to be the Euclidean distance but other metrics are possible [see IV, §11.1], in particular the Minkowski metric given by

$$d_{ij} = \left\{ \sum_{h=1}^{p} |x_{ih} - x_{jh}|^r \right\}^{1/r}. \tag{4.50}$$

The d_{ij}'s will not in general satisfy the same order relations as the δ_{ij}'s. They are therefore 'smoothed' by a procedure outlined below to produce the $\hat{d}_{ij}$'s of (4.49). The role of the denominator in (4.49) is to render S independent of the scale of measurement of the distances. The calculation of the minimum value of S then proceeds as follows:

(i) Choose an initial configuration of points. This can be done in a completely arbitrary fashion, but the speed of convergence to a solution will be increased if the initial distances conform roughly to the dissimilarities.

(ii) Compute the d_{ij}'s from (4.50) with a suitable value of r (usually 2).

(iii) Compute the $\hat{d}_{ij}$'s from the d_{ij}'s. To formulate this as a mathematical problem suppose the similarities are ordered such that

$$\delta_{i_1 j_1} < \delta_{i_2 j_2} < \ldots < \delta_{i_M j_M} \tag{4.51}$$

where $M = \frac{1}{2}n(n-1)$. Then the $\hat{d}_{ij}$'s are those values of D_{ij} which minimize $\Sigma_i \Sigma_j (d_{ij} - D_{ij})^2$ subject to the constraints

$$D_{i_1 j_1} \leq D_{i_2 j_2} \leq \ldots \leq D_{i_M j_M}. \tag{4.52}$$

This is a problem in quadratic programming but is best handled by the special techniques of monotonic regression. It can be viewed as the problem of fitting the best monotonic function, in the least squares sense, to the actual distances $\{d_{ij}\}$ (see Barlow and co-workers, 1972).

(iv) Improve the configuration of points in such a way as to reduce the stress. To do this we note that S is a function of the np variables $x_{11}, x_{12}, \ldots x_{1p}, x_{21}, x_{22}, \ldots, x_{2p}, \ldots, x_{n1}, x_{n2}, \ldots, x_{np}$. The method of steepest descent involves finding the partial derivative of S with respect to each x. These determine the direction in the x-space in which S decreases most rapidly. A new configuration is then selected by moving in that direction.

(v) The foregoing steps are repeated until no further reduction in S is possible.

There are various technical complications which may arise of which the most serious, perhaps, is that the minimum stress achieved may turn out to be a local minimum only. Some protection against this may be obtained by using several different, widely separated, starting points. The method can be modified to deal with missing dissimilarities—a situation which is likely to be very common where there are many individuals to be compared. Asymmetry in the dissimilarities ($\delta_{ij} \neq \delta_{ji}$) and ties in the dissimilarities can likewise be accommodated without affecting the basic mathematical structure. More recent developments (for example, Carroll and Chiang, 1970) involve the introduction of weights into the distance functions d_{ij} but, again, without introducing new mathematical principles.

In practice, of course, a computer is needed to carry out the iterative method described above, and programs exist for this purpose.

References

Aigner, D. J., and Goldberger, A. S. (1977). *Latent Variables in Socio-economic Models*, North-Holland, Amsterdam, New York, Oxford.

Anderson, T. W. (1958). *An Introduction to Multivariate Statistical Analysis*, Wiley, New York.

Bartholomew, D. J. (1980). Factor analysis for categorical data, *J. Roy. Statist. Soc.* B, **42**, 293–321.

Barlow, R. E., Bartholomew, D. J., Bremner, J. M., and Brunk, H. D. (1972). *Statistical Inference under Order Restrictions.* Wiley, London.

Birch, M. W. (1963). Maximum likelihood in three-way contingency tables. *J. Roy. Statist. Soc.*, B, **25**, 220–233.

Bishop, Y. M. M., Fienberg, S. E., and Holland, P. W. (1975). *Discrete Multivariate Analysis*, MIT Press, Cambridge, Massachusetts.

Carroll, J. D., and Chiang, J. J. (1970). Analysis of individual differences in multi-dimensional scaling via an *n*-way generalization of the Eckart–Young decomposition. *Psychometrika*, **35**, 283–319.

Cormack, R. M. (1971). A review of classification. *J. Roy. Statist. Soc.*, A, **134**, 321–367.

Coxon, A. P. M., and Jones, C. L. (1977). Multi-dimensional scaling. In C. A. O'Muircheartaigh and C. Payne (eds), *The Analysis of Survey Data*, Vol. I, Wiley, London.

Draper, N. R., and Smith, H. (1966). *Applied Regression Analysis*, Wiley, New York.

Duncan, O. D. (1975). *Introduction to Structural Equation Models*, Academic Press, New York.

Everitt, B. S. (1974). *Cluster Analysis*, Heinemann, London.

Fielding, A. (1977a). Latent structure models. In C. A. O'Muircheartaigh and C. Payne (eds), *The Analysis of Survey Data,* Vol. I, Wiley, London.

Fielding, A. (1977b). Binary segmentation: the automatic interaction detector and related techniques for exploring data structure. In O'Muircheartaigh C. A., and Payne C. (eds), *The Analysis of Survey Data*, Vol. I, Wiley, London.

Fienberg, S. (1970). An iterative procedure for estimation in contingency tables. *Ann. Math. Statist.*, **41**, 907–917.

Fletcher, R., and Powell, M. J. D. (1963). A rapidly convergent descent method for minimization. *Computer J.*, **2**, 90–97.

Goodman, L. A. (1974). Exploratory latent structure analysis using both identifiable and unidentifiable models, *Biometrika*, **61**, 215–231.

Goodman, L. A. .(1978). *Analysing Qualitative/Categorical Data Log-Linear Models and Latent Structure Analysis*, Addison-Wesley, Reading, Mass.

Gnanadesikan, R. (1977). *Methods for Statistical Data Analysis of Multivariate Observations*, Wiley, New York.

Graybill, F. (1961). *An Introduction to Linear Statistical Models*, McGraw-Hill, New York.

Haberman, S. J. (1973). *The Analysis of Frequency Data*, IMS Monograph Series.

Harman, H. H. (1976). *Modern Factor Analysis* 3rd ed. University of Chicago Press, Chicago and London.

Jardine, N., and Sibson, R. (1971). *Mathematical Taxonomy*, Wiley, London.

Kendall, M. G. (1980). *Multivariate Analysis*, (2nd ed.) Griffin, High Wycombe, Bucks.

Kendall, M. G., and Stuart, A. (1976). *The Advanced Theory of Statistics*, Vol. III, 3rd ed. Griffin, High Wycombe, Bucks.

Kruskal, J. B. (1964a). Multi-dimensional scaling by optimizing goodness of fit to a non-metric hypothesis. *Psychometrika*, **29**, 115–129.

Kruskal, J. B. (1964b). Non-metric multi-dimensional scaling: a numerical method. *Psychometrika*, **29**, 116–129.

Lazarsfeld, P. F., and Henry, N. W. (1968). *Latent Structure Analysis*, Houghton Mifflin, New York.

Lawley, D. N., and Maxwell, A. E. (1971). *Factor Analysis as a Statistical Method*, 2nd ed. Butterworths, London.

Macdonald, K. I. (1977). Path analysis. In O'Muircheartaigh, C. A., and Payne, C. (eds), *The Analysis of Survey Data*, Vol. 2, Wiley, London.

Macdonald, K. I., and Doreian, P. (1977). *Regression and Path Analysis*, Methuen, London.

Maxwell, A. E. (1977). *Multivariate Analysis in Behavioural Research*, Chapman and Hall, London.

Nelder, J. A., and Wedderburn, R. W. M. (1972). Generalized linear models. *J. Roy. Statist. Soc.*, A, **135**, 370–384.

O'Muircheartaigh, C. A., and Payne, C. (1977). *The Analysis of Survey Data:* Vol. I, *Exploring Data Structures*; Vol. II, *Model Fitting*, Wiley, London.

Payne, C. (1977). The log-linear model for contingency tables. In *The Analysis of Survey Data:* Vol. II, *Model Fitting*, Wiley, London.

Plackett, R. L. (1960). *Regression Analysis*, Clarendon Press, Oxford.

Plackett, R. L. (1974). *The Analysis of Categorical Data*, Griffin, London.

Rao, C. R. (1973). *Linear Statistical Inference and Its Applications*, Wiley, New York.

Scheffé, H. (1959). *The Analysis of Variance*, Wiley, New York.

Shepard, R. N. (1962). The analysis of proximities: multi-dimensional scaling with an unknown distance function. *Psychometrika*, **27**, 125–139 and 219–246.

Taylor, C. C. (1977). Principal component and factor analysis. Muircheartaigh, C. A. O., and Payne, C. (eds), *The Analysis of Survey Data*, Vol. I, Wiley, London.

Torgerson, W. S. (1958). *Theory and Methods of Scaling*, Wiley, London.

Upton, G. J. G. (1978). *The Analysis of Cross-Tabulated Data*, Wiley, London.

van der Geer (1971). *Introduction to Multivariate Analysis for the Social Sciences*, Freeman, London.

Wiggins, L. (1973). *Latent Probabilities for Attitude and Behaviour Processes*, Elsevier, Amsterdam.

5

The Dynamics of Social Systems

5.1 Introduction and Literature

Most of the problems of social science with which we have been concerned in previous chapters relate to the state of a system at a particular point in time—or, at least, with things which do not change over an interval of time. There are many other problems, however, where change is of the essence. For example, although the distribution of votes between the political parties at an election is important, the patterns of change in voting behaviour are of greater significance when it comes to predicting the distribution of votes in the future. The concept of 'mobility', whether social, geographical, occupational or in attitudes, is of central interest in the study of human behaviour and is essentially dynamic in character.

A large class of processes in the social sciences may be described in the following terms. At any time, T, a population of individuals (or households, farms, etc.) can be classified into one of k mutually exclusive and exhaustive categories. Let the number in category i at time T be $n_i(T)$ and the set of these numbers be denoted by the row vector $\mathbf{n}(T)$ [see I, §6.2(iv)]. Suppose that $n_{ij}(T)$ is the number of those in i at time T who move to j in the interval $(T, T + 1)$. Assuming there are no losses or gains to the system as a whole the numbers $n_{ij}(T)$ may be set out in a two-way table, known as a mobility table, as follows.

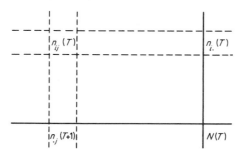

The entry in the (i, j)th cell is the flow from i to j. The ith row total is the number in category i at the beginning of the interval and the column total, $n_{.j}(T + 1)$, is the number in category j at the beginning of the next interval.

Let us first review some examples giving rise to data of this kind in order to motivate the discussion which follows.

We have already mentioned voting behaviour, in which the categories correspond to political parties and the margins to the numbers supporting those parties at two consecutive points in time. Another example is that of geographical mobility. In this case the categories might be towns or regions and the n_{ij}'s the numbers of families moving over some specified interval of time. In studies of buying behaviour the categories might represent different brands of such things as soap powder or petrol. The entries in the cells of the table would then be the numbers who switch from brand i to brand j in successive purchases. In hospital planning the categories may refer to various ways in which patients can be classified, for example medical or surgical, intensive care, private ward, outpatient, etc. One of the most widely studied examples of mobility is that between social or occupational classes. In this case the basic time unit may be the generation if one is looking at inter-generational mobility or calendar time if mobility within an individual's career span is at issue. A closely related application arises in manpower planning where employees are classified according to such things as age, length of service, or grade. Economists have used this approach to study income and size distributions. Income is not something which usually exists at a point in time as do the other attributes discussed above but arrives in a flow over time. However, if a fixed interval, like the tax year, is adopted the population can be classified according to total income on a yearly basis.

In the income example the categories will be ordered according to size of income; political parties may (but not necessarily) be ordered according to their position on a left/right scale. Brands of a commodity and types of hospital treatment will not, in general, be so ordered. Further, the flows in the mobility table may relate to a unit of time like a year or month or they may simply refer to consecutive events in a sequence whose members may be separated by variable intervals of time. These distinctions do not appear explicit in the table but they will affect the way the data are interpreted and analysed.

Social scientists who have studied mobility processes of the kind we have been discussing have had varying objects in view, and these have made differing mathematical demands. In some cases mobility tables have simply been a way of summarizing data which have then been left to speak for themselves. The cell frequencies may be expressed as proportions of their row or column totals or even of the grand total. This requires no mathematics, though it often points the way to more sophisticated analyses such as that of forecasting changes in structure. Forecasting is a recurring theme of mobility studies. The market researcher wishes to know how the market shares of different brands will change and what ultimate division is implied by present patterns of switching. The sociologist may want to forecast changing social structure or, perhaps, see how long it will take before equal opportunity legislation produces the same occupational distribution between the sexes or different races. Scientific prediction of any kind depends on an assumption that regularities occurring in the past will continue into the future. The study of mobility for prediction purposes therefore first involves an analysis of historical data to identify patterns and trends. This is a statistical exercise. The next step is to build a mathematical model of the process and then to use it to forecast the future structure of the system. It is this step which calls for mathematical resources and with which we shall be most concerned in this chapter.

The numbers in the categories are not the only aspect of the mobility process which have practical interest for the social scientist. In manpower planning, for example, the individual employee will be interested in his career pattern as indicated by the probability of reaching a given level and by the length of time spent in different parts of the organization.

Predictions in social science are made with two distinct objects in view. The first is the obvious one of wanting to know what is going to happen. The success of such an operation leans heavily on the assumption that 'present trends' will continue. The second way of viewing predictions is as a way of exhibiting something about the present state of the system. In a certain sense a forecast is a statement about the present direction of the system and this information has value quite apart from the question of whether the system will continue to move along that path.

It often happens that a forecasting exercise raises the question of how to avoid undesirable features which appear to be on the horizon. This is particularly so in the management sciences where, almost by definition, the object is to discover how to control a system. In sociology, politics and geography, on the other hand, the social scientist may neither wish nor be able to affect the course of events, in which case a forecasting exercise is a sufficient end in itself.

In addition to description and prediction, social scientists often wish to construct indices to measure mobility. The motivation usually lies in the desire to be able to compare the levels of mobility between two social groups or within the same group at different times. For example it is often worth asking whether social mobility differs from one country to another or whether it has changed within a single country over a period of time. Indeed, such indices have very little meaning except when compared with one another. In mathematical language the problem is that of finding a mapping from the set of mobility tables onto the real numbers—often the interval $(0,1)$. That is, we wish to place tables on the scale in a way which appears consistent with the intuitive notion which the index is designed to reflect. This is made difficult by the fact that ideas like 'mobility' are not well-defined and it is only by examining the consequences of different mappings that the ambiguities inherent in the everyday use of the word begin to emerge.

Both measurement and prediction depend for their successful execution on having an adequate mathematical model of the process and it is at this stage that the social scientist will find the need for mathematical skills. The mathematical approach to the study of change usually takes one of two forms. If the system is to be viewed deterministically the equations describing the operation of the system will usually be differential or difference equations and the techniques of the calculus will be required to study their behaviour. If, as is often more realistic, the system is to be treated stochastically the theory of stochastic processes will be involved [see II, §18.0]. This may also lead to systems of differential equations but, in addition, draws heavily upon the techniques of linear algebra and especially of non-negative matrices. Time may be treated as continuous or discrete according to considerations of realism or convenience. Continuous time models generally lead to formulations in terms of differential or integral equations while discrete time versions depend on the theory of difference equations and the properties of matrices.

In the body of the chapter we shall review a number of mathematical models (mainly stochastic) which have been employed in the social sciences. The discussion will take a form designed to display the main branches of mathematics employed and it does not, therefore, always do justice to the practical importance of some of the topics covered.

Prior to the 1960's the literature on stochastic processes was very limited and that concerned with applications was almost non-existent. Since then the position has changed rapidly as the theory has found applications in an increasing number of fields. Among the first authors to include accounts of stochastic modelling in books on the mathematical approaches to social science were Kemeny and Snell (1962) followed shortly, on a larger scale, by Coleman (1964a). The first book-length treatment of stochastic modelling of social processes was Bartholomew (1967; 2nd ed. 1973). Several recent volumes in the Elsevier monographs, *Progress in Mathematical Social Science*, especially Doreian and Humman (1976) and Pullum (1975), continue in this tradition. A closely related field is demography, in which there has been an increasing emphasis on stochastic methods exemplified in Keyfitz (1968), Coale (1972), Feichtinger (1971) and Pollard (1973). Education and manpower planning have provided a fruitful area for the application of the theory of stochastic processes. In education a basic reference is Thonstad (1969). Bartholomew (1973) devotes one chapter to models for manpower and education planning and much relevant methodology occurs elsewhere in the book. A number of key papers on manpower planning, some concerned with dynamic aspects, will be found in Bartholomew (1976a) which also contains a bibliography. A fuller and more up-to-date bibliography is given in Bartholomew and Forbes (1979) which is designed as a manual for manpower planning practitioners. A treatment with a slightly different emphasis is in Grinold and Marshall (1977). White (1970) introduced and developed the key idea of a chain of opportunity in his sociological study of manpower systems. Massy and co-workers (1970) describe stochastic models of buying behaviour. There is an extensive literature on time series which we touch on briefly in Section 5.10 and a few references are included at that point.

The serious student will need not only books about applications but accounts of the theory itself. There are now many treatments of varying coverage and difficulty. One of the earliest and most comprehensive accounts is Bartlett (1955) and an elegant exposition is contained in the relevant parts of Feller (1968, 1966). Moran (1968) covers much of the more useful parts of the theory in his introduction to probability. Good general texts are provided by Parzen (1962), Cox and Miller (1965) and Karlin and Taylor (1975). Books with a more applied slant are Bharucha-Reid (1960), Bhat (1972) and Howard (1971). In addition there are books on particular topics—especially Markov processes [see II, §18.0.5]. Of these Kemeny and Snell (1960 and 1976) is still among the most useful; for a more recent treatment see Isaacson and Madsen (1976).

5.2 Discrete Time Markov Models for Closed Systems [see II, §18.0.5]

A closed system is one in which no one leaves or joins. There are very few social systems which meet this requirement in the short term, and in the long term it is impossible because of the inevitability of birth and death. Nevertheless many systems are closed to a good approximation either because gains and losses are very few or because gains and losses roughly balance one another in numbers and in those personal attributes which are relevant for mobility.

The Markov model starts from two assumptions about individual behaviour as follows:

(a) The probability that any individual moves from i to j between one time point and the next is constant over time, is the same for all individuals and depends only on i and j.
(b) Individuals behave independently.

The crucial part of (a) is that the transition probability, denoted by p_{ij}, does not depend on any movements the individual made before his arrival in i. In other words prediction of the future depends only on a knowledge of the current state and not on the past. This is the so-called Markov assumption. The constancy of the p_{ij}'s over time and over individuals can both be relaxed and we shall look at the consequences of doing so. Assumption (b) implies that the aggregate behaviour of the system can be deduced by summing results for the individual processes.

In practice, of course, the social scientist must check whether the assumptions are valid. The p_{ij}'s will not be known but can be estimated from past mobility tables, which also provide the means of checking the constancy assumptions. Mathematical as well as empirical analysis can be useful at this stage by identifying the consequences of departures from assumptions and so showing whether they are of sufficient importance to invalidate the analysis.

Let $p_i(T)$ denote the probability that an individual is in category i at time T. The it is shown in the theory of Markov chains [see II, (19.5.5)] that

$$\mathbf{p}(T + 1) = \mathbf{p}(T)\mathbf{P} = \mathbf{p}(0)\mathbf{P}^T \tag{5.1}$$

where $\mathbf{P}$ is the matrix of transition probabilities and $\mathbf{p}(T) = (p_1(T), p_2(T), \ldots, p_k(T))$.

The reader should notice that, in $p_i(T)$, T does not refer to a random variable, as in the notation used for a probability density, but to the time to which the probability relates. Also $\mathbf{P}^T$ is the Tth power of $\mathbf{P}$ and not the transpose.

If there are N people in the system then, clearly.

$$E\mathbf{n}(T) = N\mathbf{p}(T). \tag{5.2}$$

where $\mathbf{n}(T)$ is the vector of numbers in the categories.

These equations are the basis of most forecasting exercises since they enable the future structure to be predicted in terms of the current structure. It may also be shown that the elements of $\mathbf{P}^r$ are the r-step probabilities, that is $p_{ij}^{(r)}$ is the probability that an individual in i is in j after r time periods. This result is sometimes used to test the applicability of the Markov model. The r-step matrix [see II, §19.4] can be estimated directly from a mobility table constructed for the whole period of r time units. It can then be compared with the rth power of the one-step matrix estimated for a mobility table for a single time period.

The other main result of elementary Markov chain theory which is used in social applications concerns the limiting or stationary behaviour of the model [see II, §19.6]. One may ask what will happen to the structure $\{\mathbf{p}(T)\}$ if the process continues indefinitely into the future. Mathematically we are asking about the limiting behaviour of the sequence $\{\mathbf{p}(T)\}$. The theory shows that provided $\mathbf{P}$ is regular then $\mathbf{p}(T)$ approaches a limit as $T \to \infty$. Roughly speaking the regularity requirement is that any state can be reached from any other state and is almost always met in social applications. To calculate the limiting structure one can use the fact [see II, (19.6.2)] that the limiting structure, $\mathbf{p}$ say, satisfies

$$\mathbf{p} = \mathbf{p}\mathbf{P} \tag{5.3}$$

with

$$\mathbf{p}\mathbf{1}' = 1 \tag{5.4}$$

$\mathbf{1}'$ being a column vector of ones. The system of equations (5.3) is singular but it can be solved by dropping one of the k equations and including (5.4). On a computer it is often more convenient to find the limiting value by repeated use of (5.1) until the value of $\mathbf{p}(T)$ settles down to a stable value.

Equation (5.3) shows that **p** also provides the answer to another question of interest in many applications. This concerns the existence of a stationary structure. In other words, does there exist a **p** which will not change if subjected to movement according to the matrix **P**? The answer is provided by (5.3), from which it is seen to be the same as the structure to which the system will tend if allowed to run on under its own momentum.

Rate of approach to the limit

As well as knowing the ultimate destination of the structure it is also desirable to know something about the rate of approach. This can easily be investigated numerically in particular instances by computation, but a more general treatment is obtained using the spectral resolution of **P**. This enables us to write

$$\mathbf{P} = \sum_{i=1}^{k} \lambda_i \mathbf{A}_i \tag{5.5}$$

where $\{\lambda_i\}$ is the set of eigenvalues or, latent roots of **P** and $\{\mathbf{A}_i\}$ is a set of matrices known as the spectral set [see I, §7.10]. In particular, they have the property that

$$\mathbf{A}_i \mathbf{A}_j = \mathbf{0} \quad \text{if} \quad i \neq j, \quad \mathbf{A}_i^2 = \mathbf{A}_i.$$

These properties imply that $\mathbf{P}^T$ may be written

$$\mathbf{P}^T = \sum_{i=1}^{k} \lambda_i^T \mathbf{A}_i \tag{5.6}$$

and hence that

$$\mathbf{p}(T) = \sum_{i=1}^{k} \lambda_i^T \mathbf{p}(0) \mathbf{A}_i. \tag{5.7}$$

For a regular stochastic matrix **P** [see II, §19.3] the largest eigenvalue(s) is 1 and for the remainder $|\lambda_i| < 1$. Hence, another way of writing the limiting vector is

$$\mathbf{p} = \mathbf{p}(0)\mathbf{A}_1$$

where $\mathbf{A}_1$ is the matrix associated with $\lambda_i = 1$. The sequence $\{\mathbf{p}(T)\}$ will thus approach its limit at a rate governed by the size of the λ_i's and in a manner depending on the signs of the λ_i's and on whether they are real or complex. There may, therefore, be oscillations in the approach to the limit, but the most significant factor will be the size of the second largest eigenvalue. Complications ensue if multiplicities occur among the eigenvalues but these do not affect the broad conclusions.

Sojourn times (durations) [see II, Example 19.4.2 and §18.4]

Another class of quantities of interest in many social applications is sojourn times and passage times [see II, §18.3.2]. In hospital planning the length of time that a bed will be occupied or the length of time before an outpatient can be admitted for surgery are typical random variables of practical interest.

The length of stay (sojourn time) in a particular category has a geometric distribution, as may be deduced by elementary probability arguments. Thus

$$\text{Pr}\{\text{sojourn time in } i = r\} = p_{ii}^{r-1}(1 - p_{ii}) \qquad r = 1, 2, \ldots \qquad (5.8)$$

and hence the mean sojourn time is $(1 - p_{ii})^{-1}$. The length of time taken to reach a particular category is called a passage time. Its distribution can be calculated by using the theory of absorbing Markov chains [see II, §19.7.5]. If one wishes to know the distribution of the time taken to reach state j from i, the technique is to make j into an absorbing state and then study the time to absorption. This is part of a more general problem which arises in connection with open systems so we shall return to the discussion again in that context.

Variances and covariances of category sizes

We have seen how standard Markov chain theory can be used to provide information about the expected sizes of the categories. Often, especially in small systems, it is desirable to know something about the variances and covariances or other distributional properties of the stock numbers. The assumptions of the model amount to saying that the $n_i(T)$ individuals in category i at time T will, over the next time interval, be distributed over the categories according to a multinomial distribution with probabilities $(p_{i1}, p_{i2}, \ldots, p_{ik})$. It is possible to use this fact to deduce the stochastic properties of the changing stock numbers. A method of doing this was given by Pollard (1966) in the context of population mathematics and subsequently adapted for the present context by Bartholomew (1973). The representation used requires the use of the *direct matrix product* (or Kronecker product [see I, §6.15]). If we introduce a vector $\mu(T)$ whose first k elements are $E\mathbf{n}(T)$ and whose remaining k^2 elements are the variances and covariances of the $n_i(T)$'s listed in dictionary order then

$$\mu(T + 1) = \mu(T)\Pi \qquad (5.9)$$

where Π may be partitioned [see I, §6.6] thus:

$$\Pi = \begin{bmatrix} \mathbf{P} & \mathbf{X} \\ \mathbf{0} & \mathbf{P} \times \mathbf{P} \end{bmatrix},$$

$\mathbf{P} \times \mathbf{P}$ denoting the direct product.

The same problem can be approached via the theory of branching processes [see II, §18.1] which gives an alternative representation for the variance–covariance matrix of the $n_i(T)$, $\mathbf{V}(T)$ as follows:

$$\mathbf{V}(T + 1) = \mathbf{P}'\mathbf{V}(T)\mathbf{P} + [E\mathbf{n}(T)\mathbf{P}]_d - \mathbf{P}'[E\mathbf{n}(T)]_d\mathbf{P} \qquad (5.10)$$

where $[\cdot]_d$ indicates a diagonal matrix. This way of viewing a mobility process arises naturally when we consider a generalization of the Markov model which is appropriate for the study of inter-generational mobility.

Measurement of mobility

If mobility is adquately described by a Markov model then it follows that any measure of mobility should be a function of the elements of $\mathbf{P}$. Many such measures have been proposed, most of which rest on simple intuitive notions but some of which involve mathematical methods. Prais (1955), for example, proposed the use of the mean sojourn time in each grade, which we have already discussed in another context. Another approach, used by Bibby (1975) and Shorrocks (1978), is to begin by starting with axioms which embody the properties which one would expect and then trying to find measures which meet the requirements. This kind of reasoning led Shorrocks to a measure depending on the second largest eigenvalue. We have already seen that the magnitude of this eigenvalue governs the rate at which the structure approaches its equilibrium. In a certain sense, therefore, it measures the rate at which the structure is changing.

5.3 Generalizations and Extensions of the Closed Markov Model

In many of the applications which have been described, especially those of occupational and social mobility, the assumptions of the Markov model are a gross simplification of reality. We shall therefore now consider the effects of relaxing the assumptions one at a time.

Transition probabilities changing with time

This is covered by the theory of non-homogeneous Markov chains [see II, §19.3]. In this case (5.1) becomes

$$\mathbf{p}(T + 1) = \mathbf{p}(T)\mathbf{P}(T) = \mathbf{p}(0) \prod_{i=0}^{T} \mathbf{P}(i) \qquad (5.11)$$

where $\mathbf{P}(T)$ is the transition matrix at time T. It is shown in the theory, for example, that under certain conditions the effect of $\mathbf{p}(0)$ on $\mathbf{p}(T)$ diminishes as $T \to \infty$. It is, of course, not possible to speak of a limiting, or stationary, structure unless the sequence $\mathbf{P}(T)$ itself tends to a limit. The examples which the reader will find in texts dealing with non-homogeneous chains (e.g. Isaacson and Madsen, 1976) are usually ones in which the elements of $\mathbf{P}(T)$ are given by some simple functions of T. In applications there may well be doubt about the constancy of **P** and possibly some empirical evidence to suggest that they are changing with time. It is very unlikely, however, that it will be possible to estimate **P**(*T*) as a function of *T* with sufficient accuracy to apply the theory. The latter should be regarded, for practical purposes, as a means of identifying what kinds of behaviour are possible when the transition matrix is not constant.

Transition matrix varying from one individual to another

Perhaps the most vulnerable assumption of the Markov model is that all individuals have the same transition matrix [see II, §19.3]. Individual variation is the norm in social science, and it would be surprising if it did not exist in such areas as buying and voting behaviour. In part it can be dealt with by subdividing the population into more homogeneous groups. For example, if men and women have different **P**'s then it would be sensible to treat each sex separately. However, heterogeneity may well exist without being recognized *a priori*. In such cases we need to have some technique for diagnosing it and for assessing the robustness of the simple model. One method involves the comparison of the *r*-step matrix with the *r*th power of the one-step matrix mentioned above. It has been discovered empirically that heterogeneity produces higher diagonal elements in the *r*-step matrix than would be expected from the *r*th power of the one-step matrix. Singer and Spilerman (1977) have explored the phenomenon from a mathematical point of view and shown that it is not a necessary consequence of heterogeneity. However, as Bartholomew (1973) shows, it is quite difficult to construct examples which fail to produce the effect.

A very simple model incorporating heterogeneity is the mover–stayer model according to which part of the population never moves at all and the remainder moves according to the simple Markov model. Suppose that a proportion S_i in category *i* never move. Then the apparent transition matrix for one time period is

$$(\mathbf{I} - \mathbf{S})\mathbf{P} + \mathbf{S}$$

where **S** is a diagonal matrix with S_i in the (*i*,*i*)th position.

A different way of incorporating heterogeneity which is plausible in applications to occupational mobility is to suppose that some people move more frequently than others. If the process is observed at fixed intervals of time, individuals will then differ in the number of moves they have made since their state was last observed. One such model which has been used is to suppose that moves occur in time according to a Poisson process [see IV, §20.1]. Each individual has the same transition matrix **P** but has a rate λ of making moves which varies from one individual to another. In one version of the model Spilerman (1972) supposes that λ is a random variable with a gamma distribution [see II, §11.3]. This leads to an expression for the transition matrix for moves in an interval of time τ,

$$\mathbf{P}(\tau) = \left(\frac{c}{c + \tau}\right)^v \sum_{m=0}^{\infty} \binom{m + v - 1}{m} \left(\frac{\tau}{c + \tau}\right)^m \mathbf{P}^m \qquad (5.12)$$

where c and v are parameters of the gamma distribution. Series like this can be summed using the fact that $\mathbf{P}^m$ can be written in the form

$$\mathbf{P}^m = \mathbf{H}\mathbf{D}^m\mathbf{H}^{-1} \qquad (5.13)$$

where $\mathbf{D}$ is a diagonal matrix of the eigenvalues of $\mathbf{P}$ [see I, §7.4]. This is, of course, equivalent to the spectral representation of (5.6).

Failure of the Markov assumption

The Markov assumption implies a lack of memory which is often unrealistic in applications. The chance that a person's current state changes may well depend on his previous history. The standard way of incorporating this into the Markovian framework is to incorporate the relevant part of the past history into the description of the present state. Thus if there were 3 states, A, B, C and if the transition probabilities depend on both current and last state we would set up a chain with states AA, AB, AC, BB, BC, BA, CC, CA, CB. Thus the probability of moving out of state B, say, will depend on whether the state preceding B was A, B or C. This poses no new mathematical problems though there may be statistical problems of estimation arising from small numbers in the categories. However, a new feature may arise if the state space is expanded in a different way. It is well established that propensity to move one's residence or job depends on the length of time spent in the present home or job. Mobility is thus not a Markov process but it can be made one by incorporating length of stay into the state description. Thus, for example, all those residing in a particular area would be sub-classified according to their length of residence and these new sub-categories would become the new states of the chain. In practice the number of states will be finite but, possibly, very large. It may be convenient mathematically to treat length of service as having infinitely many categories, in which case we have a chain with a countable state space. To deduce the existence of a limiting structure we then need theorems about such chains.

Branching processes

All of the mobility processes discussed so far can be viewed as branching processes, but it is particularly natural to do so when studying inter-generational mobility. Here we are interested in the development of a family line from one generation to another. In demography, family lines are usually traced through the female line but in social mobility, where class is normally a function of occupation, they are followed through the males. The simple Markov model is unrealistic in that it treats every father as having exactly one son. An obvious generalization is to assume that the number of sons born to each father is a random variable. The development of any family line is thus a branching process or, more exactly, a multi-type branching process since the sons are classified into types according to social class. Pollard (1966) developed his theory of the stochastic properties of the mobility process from this point of view. If we are only interested in expected values the basic Markov model is easily generalized and requires little extra mathematics. Suppose that a father in class i has, on average, v_i sons then the expected number in class j at time $T + 1$ is given by

$$n_j(T + 1) = \sum_{i=1}^{k} n_i(T)v_i p_{ij} \qquad (j = 1, 2, \ldots, k). \tag{5.14}$$

In matrix notation this becomes

$$\mathbf{n}(T + 1) = \mathbf{n}(T)\mathbf{NP} \tag{5.15}$$

where $\mathbf{N}$ is the diagonal matrix formed from the v_i's. If we write $\mathbf{M} = \mathbf{NP}$ then (5.15) is essentially the same as (5.1) except that $\mathbf{M}$ is not a stochastic matrix (i.e. having rows summing to 1.). It is, however, a *positive* matrix and such matrices share many of the properties of stochastic matrices which are a special case [see I, §7.11].

Amalgamation of states (lumpability)

Although not strictly a generalization this is something which has practical implications in many applications of Markov chains. There is often an element of arbitrariness in the definition of the categories in a chain. For example, if we are studying the distribution of city size we may group cities into categories according to size, but the boundaries between categories are bound to be arbitrary. Similarly with incomes or social class the number and the width of classes is at the choice of the investigator. The first practical question which then arises is whether a process which is Markovian using one grouping would also be with any other obtained by the amalgamation of some states. The answer is provided by results on amalgamation which give the conditions under which the Markov property is preserved under the amalgamation of categories. Except in very special circumstances the property is destroyed and this might appear to jeopardize the use of Markov models since the arbitrariness in forming the categories is almost certain to ensure that the process is non-Markovian. However, the successful application of a model does not depend on the assumptions being precisely true. What matters is whether the model is an adequate approximation. We therefore need to know how much effect grouping is likely to have on the predictive value of the model. There appears to be little mathematical theory to guide us here though the matter can always be investigated numerically in particular cases. There is some theory about the properties of functions on a Markov chain (the grouped process is, of course, a mapping from one process to the other) but, so far, this does not appear to have yielded results of practical value.

5.4 Markov Systems with Gains and Losses

Systems with losses but no gains

Systems with loss can be analysed using the theory of absorbing Markov chains [see II, §19.7.5]. The technique is to introduce additional states to cover losses from the system. There may be one such state as when there is no need to classify individuals according to their destination outside the system or there may be several. In multiple decrement analysis the demographer classifies deaths according to cause and in wastage analysis the manpower planner often wishes to distinguish reasons for leaving. The essential characteristic of an absorbing state (corresponding to death, leaving, etc.) is that there is no exit from it. Consequently the only entry in the row of the transition matrix corresponding to such a state is a 1 in the diagonal position. If we arrange to list the absorbing states last the transition matrix has the following canonical form [cf. I, §7.6]

$$\begin{bmatrix} \mathbf{P} & \mathbf{W} \\ \mathbf{0} & \mathbf{I} \end{bmatrix}$$

where $\mathbf{P}$ is the transition matrix for moves within the system, $\mathbf{W}$ contains the probabilities of moving outside the system and $\mathbf{I}$ is the unit matrix.

So far as the stock numbers are concerned their expected numbers can be calculated in the same way as for the closed system. There will not now be a limiting vector because $\mathbf{P}^T \to 0$ as $T \to \infty$ and ultimately there will be no one left in the system. However, there are now two additional kinds of question which did not arise before, viz.

(a) What is the probability that an individual (or, what proportion of individuals) now in the population will be 'absorbed' in a particular category?

(b) How long will it take (on average) for this to happen?

Assuming that movement takes place according to the assumptions of a Markov chain the answers to such questions are provided by the theory of absorbing Markov chains. Much of the theory turns on the so-called *fundamental matrix* $(\mathbf{I} - \mathbf{P})^{-1}$ which always exists for an absorbing chain. Its (i,j)th element gives, directly, the expected time that an entrant to i will spend in j and probabilities of reaching given states can be simply obtained from it. Cohen and Lee (1975) have used a four-state Markov chain with two absorbing states in their study of conflict, conformity and social status. They attempt to model the situation of an Asch-type experiment where a naive subject is placed in a group whose judgements conflict with his own. The typical structure of such an experiment is as follows: the group is presented with, say, three lines of different lengths and asked to choose the one which is equal in length to a standard line. All members of the group, except the subject, give an agreed wrong answer. The purpose of the model is to describe the behaviour of the subject in a sequence of such experiments and hence to relate behaviour to such things as the relative social status of the subject and the group. Cohen and Lee suppose that the subject can be in one of the following states:

S_1: subject has resolved the conflict in favour of non-conformity
S_2: conflict unresolved but temporarily favours non-conformity
S_3: conflict unresolved but temporarily favours conformity
S_4: conflict resolved in favour of conformity

where S_1 and S_4 are absorbing states.

The theory of absorbing Markov chains is then used to compute the probabilities of various sequences of observable responses and these form the basis of the statistical analysis.

Systems with losses and gains

In manpower planning and some other applications it is necessary to allow for both input and output. Two classes of models of this kind are in common use and they are distinguished by the assumptions they make about the input. In one case the inflow is exogenously determined and in the other it is endogenous. In the former case the input is either fixed or determined by a stochastic process independent of the state of the system into which it flows. In the latter, the total size of the system is given and the recruitment flow has to be just sufficient to fill the vacancies created by loss and expansion (if any). For the most part, these models make no mathematical demands beyond those already covered for closed and absorbing Markov chains so we shall treat the subject only briefly.

Because the total size may change we have to work in terms of the expected numbers in the categories rather than proportions. If $\mathbf{R}(T + 1)$ is a row vector of the expected numbers entering the grades the basic prediction equation is

$$\mathbf{n}(T + 1) = \mathbf{n}(T)\mathbf{P} + \mathbf{R}(T + 1). \tag{5.16}$$

A limiting vector exists only if the sequence $\mathbf{R}(T + 1)$ tends to a limit. In that case the limit is given by

$$\mathbf{n}(\infty) = \mathbf{R}(\mathbf{I} - \mathbf{P})^{-1}, \tag{5.17}$$

$\mathbf{R}$ being lim $\mathbf{R}(T)$. This demonstrates another use of the fundamental matrix. Interesting questions arise if $\mathbf{R}(T)$ does not approach a limit. Although $\mathbf{n}(T)$ cannot then approach a limit it may happen that the relative category sizes do. Feichtinger (1976) and Mehlmann (1977) have investigated the subject by showing that the system can be treated as a system with a time-dependent transition matrix and fixed input. This means that questions about limiting behaviour can be answered by reference to standard theory of non-homogeneous Markov chains (see, also, Isaacson and Madsen, 1976).

Young and Almond (1961) first introduced the idea of a Markov model for a system with fixed total size. If there is to be no change in size the inflow must be exactly equal to the outflow. Each gain can be linked with a loss in such a way that the system can be treated as closed. The probability that a move from i results in a gain to j is

$$p_{ij} + w_i r_j = q_{ij},$$

say, where w_i is the probability of a loss from i and r_j the probability that a new entrant goes into j. The transition in question can either happen as a result of an internal move (with probability p_{ij}) or as a loss plus a gain (with probability $w_i r_j$). The matrix $\{q_{ij}\}$ is a transition matrix with row sums equal to 1 and so the system can be treated as if it were closed if one is interested in the changing stock numbers.

If the total size of the system is changing and, in particular, increasing, the model can be modified to take account of the new vacancies created by expansion. In this case the basic difference equation for expected values is

$$\mathbf{n}(T + 1) = \mathbf{n}(T)\{\mathbf{P} + \mathbf{w'r}\} + \mathbf{M}(T + 1)\mathbf{r} \tag{5.18}$$

where $\mathbf{M}(T + 1)$ is the increment in size between T and $T + 1$. The mathematical methods for studying this process are essentially the same as the processes already considered. If the system is contracting so that $\mathbf{M}(T)$ is negative then the model has to be extended to include a specification of how and where individuals will be removed from the system. These ideas have not been developed to the point of requiring new mathematical methods.

5.5 Control and Optimization of Markov Models

The account of Markov models given in the last section was largely concerned with their use as forecasting tools and as a means of gaining insight into the dynamics of the underlying social process. However, they have been increasingly used for planning purposes, especially in education and manpower planning. The aim is then to control some, at least, of the flows in the system so as to achieve some desired management objective such as eliminating age 'bulges' and promotion bottlenecks or the minimization of operating costs. Those flows which are not subject to control are assumed to be governed by constant transition probabilities, which is why we refer to them as Markov chain models [see II, Chapter 19]. Using the terminology of manpower planning, most work has been done on the case where the recruitment flows are subject to control whereas transfer and wastage probabilities are fixed parameters.

Most of the published work on control has appeared in the literature of Management Science and Operational Research. Although there are several distinct lines of development they all have much in common in terms both of their objectives and the mathematical tools which they use. Apart from the basic mathematics of the Markov chain already covered, the main methods are those of mathematical programming. These include the manipulation of systems of linear inequalities, the properties of convex sets and the algorithms of linear programming.

One approach to the control problem is due to Charnes, Cooper and Niehaus and others (see, for example, Charnes, Cooper and Niehaus, 1972 and 1968). The last-mentioned paper is reproduced in Bartholomew (1976a) and provides a useful introduction to the technique of goal programming which is the basis of their approach. The aim is to achieve stock levels as near as possible to a set of goals (or ceilings). The constraints arise, firstly, from the Markovian assumptions [see II, §19.2] about the uncontrolled flows and, secondly, from budgetary limits in each period which place an upper limit on the salary bill at any time. The objective function to be minimized is a linear function of the absolute values of the differences between the desired and attained stock levels. The sequence of recruitment numbers required to solve this problem can then be obtained by the standard methods of linear programming [see I, Chapter 11].

A closely related approach, also using linear programming techniques, dates back to Morgan (1971), Purkiss and Richardson (1971), Purkiss (1974) and, more recently, is found in Grinold and Marshall (1977). These authors differ from Charnes and co-workers in that they do not seek to minimize some measure of the discrepancies between desired and attained stocks. Purkiss emphasizes the exploration of the set of feasible solutions and Grinold and Marshall compute the cost of a given recruitment policy and then seek to minimize that.

A third line of development poses the problems in a slightly different way but draws on the same mathematical ideas and techniques. It seeks first to delineate those sets of stocks (structures) which can be attained and maintained and then to consider classes of strategies which may be used. The fullest account is given in Bartholomew (1973, Chapter 4) and subsequently, in Bartholomew (1975, 1977) and Bartholomew and Forbes (1979). Other authors who have worked in the area include Vajda (1975, 1978), Davies (1973, 1975), Grinold and Stanford (1974) and Grinold and Marshall (1977).

In order to illustrate the kind of mathematical problems which arise in this area we shall now outline some of the main concepts with sufficient of the mathematical background to identify the nature of the techniques which are called into play.

Maintainability

For simplicity we shall assume the system to be of fixed size so that we can work in terms of the vector of proportions in each grade. The basic equation for the Markov model, given in (5.18), may then be written

$$\mathbf{q}(T + 1) = \mathbf{q}(T)\{\mathbf{P} + \mathbf{w}'\mathbf{r}\} \tag{5.19}$$

where the elements of $\mathbf{q}$ are the proportions in the grades. A structure $\mathbf{q}$ is maintainable if there exist values of $\mathbf{P}$, $\mathbf{w}$ and $\mathbf{r}$ such that

$$\mathbf{q} = \mathbf{q}\{\mathbf{P} + \mathbf{w}'\mathbf{r}\} \tag{5.20}$$

which implies, as the term suggests, that no change of structure takes place between one period and the next. The most important, and easiest case, arises when promotion and wastage are uncontrolled so that $\mathbf{P}$ and $\mathbf{w}$ are fixed. In this case control is by recruitment and the maintainability of $\mathbf{q}$ requires there to be an $\mathbf{r}$ such that (5.20) is satisfied. Solving for $\mathbf{r}$ gives

$$\mathbf{r} = \mathbf{q}(\mathbf{I} - \mathbf{P})(\mathbf{q}\mathbf{w}')^{-1} \tag{5.21}$$

which must have non-negative elements if it is to be a solution to the practical problem. This obviously requires that

$$\mathbf{q} \geq \mathbf{q}\mathbf{P}. \tag{5.22}$$

This inequality provides a simple arithmetical means of checking whether or not a given structure is maintainable by recruitment. A broader question which requires further mathematical analysis concerns the characteristics of the set of structures which satisfy (5.22) for any given $\mathbf{P}$. The problem can be visualized and described in geometrical terms as follows. The set of possible structures may be represented by a set of points in k-dimensional Euclidean space [see I, Example 5.2.2]. Each vector $\mathbf{q}$ is then regarded as the coordinates of a point and such points satisfy $\mathbf{q} \geq \mathbf{0}$ and $\mathbf{q}\mathbf{1}' = 1$. (For $k = 3$ this set will be the equilateral triangle with vertices $(0, 0, 1)$, $(0, 1, 0)$, $(1, 0, 0)$.) The inequality (5.22) then determines a region in this space on whose boundary $\mathbf{q} = \mathbf{q}\mathbf{P}$ and which we may call the maintainable region. The mathematical problem is to map out the region and describe its characteristics. Any point in the maintainable region satisfies

$$\mathbf{q} \geq \mathbf{q}\mathbf{P}, \qquad \mathbf{q}\mathbf{1}' = 1, \qquad \mathbf{q} \geq \mathbf{0}. \tag{5.23}$$

The required region is thus the same as the set of feasible solutions of the linear programme [see, I, §11.1.2] with constraints given by (5.23). It is well known that this region is a convex hull [see VI, §4.2.1] whose vertices can be found by solving linear simultaneous equations. Some results and illustrations for this problem are given in Bartholomew (1973, Chapter 4).

A somewhat similar situation arises if $\mathbf{w}$ are $\mathbf{r}$ are fixed and the elements of $\mathbf{P}$ can be controlled. However, in general, there will be more than one $\mathbf{P}$ satisfying (5.20) so there is no longer a unique strategy for maintaining any maintainable structure. In practice, there may well be further restrictions on **P**. For example, if promotion is impossible all elements below the main diagonal of **P** will be zero. If, in addition, promotion is only into the next higher grade all elements other than those on the main diagonal and super-diagonal will be zero and in this case there is a unique strategy which can be obtained by solving (5.20) in a manner similar to that used for recruitment control.

The idea of maintainability has been extended in various directions. Davies (1973, 1975) considers n-step maintainability. A structure is n-step maintainable if one can return to it every n steps. The boundaries of such regions are also convex sets [see VI, Definition 4.2.3] whose geometry can be studied using the methods referred to above. Vajda (1975, 1978) introduced the idea of partial maintainability in which only some of the grade sizes have to be held fixed.

Attainability

This has two aspects. One has to do with whether a given structure can be attained at all and the other with the devising of strategies to attain desired structures. The first aspect leads to the consideration of attainable regions of different kinds. It may be shown, for example, using the theory of the limiting behaviour of Markov chains [see II, §19.6] that the maintainable region is also an attainable region having the property that all points within it can be reached, eventually, from any other structure. Another region of interest is that consisting of all those structures which are attainable from at least one other structure. (Its complement is, perhaps, of greater interest being the set of structures attainable from nowhere—that is the non-attainable region.) The determination of such regions involves similar techniques to those already considered. For example, in the case of recruitment control, a structure **q** is attainable in one step from at least one other point if there exists a **y** with $\mathbf{y} \geq \mathbf{0}$ and $\mathbf{y1}' = 1$ such that $\mathbf{q} \geq \mathbf{yP}$.

Given that a desired structure is attainable the problem of how to attain it can be formulated in a number of ways. All such methods involve the solution of linear equations (or inequalities in non-negative variables). In order to see what mathematics is involved we shall illustrate the control problem in these terms when control is by recruitment and then briefly indicate some variations.

Suppose that there exists a T^* such that the goal $\mathbf{n}^*$, say, can be attained, for the first time, in T^* steps. It then follows that the intermediate stock vectors and the recruitment vectors must satisfy

$$\mathbf{n}(T + 1) = \mathbf{n}(T)\mathbf{P} + \mathbf{R}(T + 1), \quad (T = 0, 1, 2, \ldots, T^* - 2)$$

$$\mathbf{n}^* = \mathbf{n}(T^* - 1)\mathbf{P} + \mathbf{R}(T^*) \tag{5.24}$$

$$\mathbf{n}(T) \geq \mathbf{0}, \quad (T = 1, 2, \ldots, T^* - 1); \quad \mathbf{R}(T) \geq \mathbf{0}, \quad (T = 1, 2, \ldots, T^*)$$

where $\mathbf{R}(T)$ denotes the vector of recruitment numbers at time T. In addition we may wish to add the further requirement that $\mathbf{n}(T)\mathbf{1}' = N(T)$ where $N(T)$ is the desired total size at time T. The test of attainability is made by finding whether there is a T^* for which the equations and inequalities of (5.24) are satisfied. If such a T^* is found there will usually be many solutions and one can then choose among them by optimizing some function such as the total salary cost which will usually be a linear function of the stock vectors. This would be a standard linear programming problem. There may be additional constraints, especially in the form of bounds on the allowable values of $\mathbf{n}(T)$ and/or $\mathbf{R}(T)$. These do not alter the form of the problem though they will usually increase T^*.

One drawback of this formulation is that it requires $\mathbf{n}^*$ to be exactly attained whereas in practice it is often sufficient to get reasonably close to the target. In fact this might be possible in a very few steps even though T^* was large. This could be dealt with by removing the second member of (5.24) and replacing it with a requirement that $\mathbf{n}(T^* - 1)$ should be within an acceptable distance of $\mathbf{n}^*$. Such a restriction would be non-linear and this would destroy the simplicity of the problem.

Another way of handling the situation is to adopt a 'fixed time' formulation in which the aim is to get as close to the target in a prescribed number of steps. Under this interpretation T^* is taken as a given number rather than as an unknown. 'Closeness' has to be measured on a suitable metric [see IV, §11.1] and if this can be agreed the resulting form of the problem is one of mathematical programming with a non-linear objective function [see IV, Chapter 15]. It takes the following form where $D(\mathbf{n}^*, \mathbf{n}(T^*))$ denotes the measure of closeness of $\mathbf{n}^*$ to $\mathbf{n}(T^*)$:

Minimize: $D(\mathbf{n}^*, \mathbf{n}(T^*))$

subject to

$$\left. \begin{array}{l} \mathbf{n}(T + 1) = \mathbf{n}(T)\mathbf{P} + \mathbf{R}(T + 1), \ (T = 0, 1, \ldots, T^* - 1) \\[4pt] \mathbf{n}(T)\mathbf{1}' = N(T), \ (T = 1, 2, \ldots, T^*) \\[4pt] \mathbf{n}(T) \geq \mathbf{0}, \ (T = 1, 2, \ldots, T^*); \quad \mathbf{R}(T + 1) \geq \mathbf{0}, \ (T = 0, 1, \ldots, T^* - 1) \end{array} \right\}.$$

$$(5.25)$$

Other linear constraints can be added as before.

A similar approach can be adopted for control by promotion, but if we were to treat the elements of $\mathbf{P}$ together with the intermediate stock vectors as unknowns the restraints would not be linear because of the products $\mathbf{nP}$. This difficulty can easily be circumvented by expressing the equation in terms of the expected flow numbers between each pair of grades. The details are given in Bartholomew (1973, Chapter 4) but no new mathematical ideas are involved, though the number of equations may be very large.

A practical disadvantage of all these approaches is that they treat the system as deterministic. In reality the uncontrolled flows will be random variables [see II, §4.1] so that the policies prescribed by deterministic theory will not exactly attain the goals aimed for. This fact has prompted two lines of enquiry. One is to develop sequential strategies in which the position is re-considered at the end of each period. These can be derived by solving the fixed time problem with $T^* = 1$. This yields a strategy which is expected to get as near as possible to the goal in one step. Even when judged by deterministic criteria such strategies appear to be almost optimal (see Bartholomew, 1975) but their advantage in a stochastic situation is that they provide the opportunity to take account of past variation in deciding what to do next. When $T^* = 1$ the mathematical programming problem of (5.25) is easily solved for distance functions of the form

$$D = \sum_{i=1}^{k} | n_i^* - n_i(1) |^a \qquad (a = 1 \text{ or } 2)$$

without recourse to special numerical algorithms (see Bartholomew, 1973, Chapter 4).

A second approach has been to investigate the performance of strategies derived by deterministic arguments in a stochastic environment. This requires an extension of the notion of maintainability since any fixed allocation of recruits decided upon before wastage and transfers have taken place is bound to be different from the number actually required. We therefore have to introduce the idea of the probability that a structure can be maintained. The points in the space of possible structures can now no longer be partitioned into those which can and those which cannot be maintained. Instead each point will have a certain probability of being maintained. These matters were investigated in Bartholomew (1977, 1979). A structure **n** can be maintained if $n_j \geq \sum_{i=1}^{k} n_{ij}(T)$ for all j and this probability can be calculated because the $n_{ij}(T)$'s for fixed i have a multinomial distribution. In practice it is simpler and quite adequate to invoke a multivariate Central Limit Theorem to deduce the approximate multivariate normality of the joint distribution of the $n_{ij}(T)$'s. The required probability is then calculated as a volume under a multivariate normal surface.

As far as attainability is concerned it may be shown that the sequential application of the one-step strategies described earlier may be treated as a Markov chain with state space consisting of all possible structures, but here again the dimensions of the problem are such as to make it impracticable to exploit the fact.

A more general and systematic application of control theory ideas to the control of Markovian systems using techniques of dynamic linear programming has been made by Kaplinskii and Propoi (1970, 1972).

5.6 Vacancy Chains

In his book, *Chains of Opportunity*, White (1970) demonstrates a novel way of looking at movement in social structures. He was mainly concerned with studying the movements of clergyman in the Episcopal, Methodist and Presbyterian churches of the U.S.A. with a view to elucidating the sociology of mobility. One of his central ideas is the concept of a vacancy chain. A chain starts when an individual leaves the system (by death or transfer to another occupation). This creates a vacancy which has to be filled by transfer from elsewhere in the system or from outside. The vacancy is then thought of as moving to the place from which the new incumbent comes. As long as vacancies are filled from within the system the chain continues, finally terminating when a vacancy is filled by recruitment. There is thus a dual relationship between the movement of vacancies and people; when a person moves in one direction a vacancy moves in the opposite direction. The length of a vacancy chain is the number of steps it takes before leaving the system. White produced evidence to show that, in his application, the vacancies moved according to a Markov chain and hence it was possible to study the behaviour of vacancy chains using the theory of Markov chains. Stewman (1975) has since found the same to be true of a State Police force.

The mathematical requirements for following White's work are very similar to those needed for the other applications of Markov chains. White was particularly interested in the distribution of the length of chains. This is essentially the distribution of the time to absorption which we mentioned in passing in Section 5.4. The mathematics involved is elementary probability theory and matrix algebra. Suppose there are k 'grades' in the system and that vacancies move from grade to grade according to the $k \times k$ transition matrix V. The row sums of this matrix are strictly less than one because a vacancy may move out of the system. Let $p_i^{(j)}$ be the probability that a vacancy which starts in grade i leaves the system after j steps and let $p^{(j)}$ be the vector with these probabilities as elements. The probability $p_i^{(j)}$ can be expressed as the probability of going from i to h, say, in $j - 1$ steps and then leaving from h, summed over all h. In matrix notation this argument gives

$$p^{(j)} = V^{j-1}[(I - V)1]'. \tag{5.26}$$

The vector in square brackets is the set of leaving probabilities for vacancies and this is given by the complements of the row sums. The vector of expected chain lengths is

$$\mu = \sum_{j=1}^{\infty} j p^{(j)} = (I - V)^{-1} 1'. \tag{5.27}$$

This says that the row sums of the fundamental matrix $(I - V)^{-1}$ give the mean lengths of the chains. The calculation involved in (5.27) is that of summing an arithmetico-geometric progression in which **V** is a matrix rather than a scalar.

5.7 Continuous Time Models

An alternative, and sometimes more realistic, way of modelling process of change is to suppose that time is continuous rather than discrete. Continuous time versions of Markov chain models exist [see II, Chapter 20], and although the results obtained from them are closely parallel to those in discrete time the range of mathematical methods required is different. The main technique required is the solution of systems of ordinary differential equations.

Many of the applications referred to earlier in the chapter have also been treated in continuous time (for examples and references see Bartholomew, 1973). A further area in the study of attitude change has been developed by Coleman (1964b). Here individuals are classified according to the attitude they hold and the object is to model the way in which individuals change their attitudes over time. This requires a continuous time treatment since, presumably, the mental processes and external influences operate on a continuous basis.

A continuous time Markov process may be defined by a set of transition intensities, or rates $\{r_{ij}\}$. Let $r_{ij}\delta T$ be the probability of a transition from i to j in $(T, T + \delta T)$ for all $i \neq j$. These are infinitesimal transition probabilities [see II, §20.6] and they are the continuous analogues of the p_{ij}'s of the discrete theory. Let $p_{ij}(T)$ be the probability that an individual moves from i to j in $(0, T)$; then the theory shows that

$$\frac{\mathrm{d}}{\mathrm{d}T}\mathbf{P}(T) = \mathbf{P}(T)\mathbf{R} \tag{5.28}$$

where $\mathbf{P}(T) = \{p_{ij}(T)\}$ and $\mathbf{R}$ is the matrix with the r_{ij}'s in the off-diagonal positions and diagonal elements

$$r_{ii} = -\sum_{\substack{j=1 \\ j \neq i}}^{k} r_{ij} \qquad (i = 1, 2, \ldots, k).$$

The expected numbers in the categories at time T are given by

$$\bar{\mathbf{n}}(T) = \mathbf{n}(0)\mathbf{P}(T) \tag{5.29}$$

and hence $\bar{\mathbf{n}}(T)$ satisfies

$$\frac{\mathrm{d}}{\mathrm{d}T}\bar{\mathbf{n}}(T) = \bar{\mathbf{n}}(T)\mathbf{R}. \tag{5.30}$$

This equation has often been the starting point of investigations which have adopted a deterministic point of view (e.g. Coleman, 1964a; Herbst, 1963). It expresses the rates of change in each $n_i(T)$ as linear functions of all the $n_i(T)$'s. Such linear equations can be set up directly without any explicit reference to the theory of Markov processes. This is the approach commonly used in the theory of dynamic systems where, of course, the equations need not be linear. Biologists have made use of this approach in the study of morphogenesis but, apart from the examples mentioned above and the work of Hirsch and Smale (1974) in economics, there appears to have been little use of the theory in the social sciences (but see Doreian and Humman (1976).)

There is an extensive theory of equations like (5.30) from which the general form of the solution can be obtained [see IV, §7.9]. However, there are two principal methods of obtaining solutions in particular cases. The direct method makes use of the fact that the solution can be formally written as

$$\bar{n}(T) = n(0) \exp \mathbf{R}T \tag{5.31}$$

where the exponential function of $\mathbf{R}$ is defined by its power series expansion. Using the spectral representation of $\mathbf{R}$ [see I, §7.10] we have

$$\exp \mathbf{R}T = \sum_{i=1}^{k} e^{\lambda_i T} \mathbf{A}_i$$

where $\{\mathbf{A}_i\}$ is the spectral set and the λ_i's are the eigenvalues of $\mathbf{R}$. This means that $\mathbf{n}(T)$ can be expressed as a linear combination of exponential terms. The behaviour of the solution as T becomes large can then easily be deduced from the fact that, in general, at least one eigenvalue is zero and the remainder are negative. Knowing that the solution has the form (if the λ_i's are distinct)

$$\bar{n}_i(T) = c_{i1} + \sum_{j=2}^{k} c_{ij} e^{\lambda_j T} \qquad (i = 1, 2, \ldots, k) \tag{5.32}$$

this can be substituted into (5.30) which then yields a system of linear simultaneous equations for the coefficients. The second method is to take the Laplace transform [see IV, (13.1.3)] of each side of (5.30) to obtain a system of equations whose unknowns are the transforms of the $n_i(T)$'s. For this we require the result [see IV, (13.4.18)] that if

$$f^*(s) = \int_0^\infty f(x) e^{-sx} \, dx$$

is the Laplace transform of $f(x)$ then the transform of the derivative of $f(x)$ is $sf^*(s) - f(0)$. On carrying out this operation on (5.30) we have

$$s\bar{n}^*(s) - \bar{n}(0) = n^*(s)\mathbf{R}$$

from which

$$\bar{n}^*(s) = \bar{n}(0)\{s\mathbf{I} - \mathbf{R}\}^{-1}. \tag{5.33}$$

The right-hand side of (5.33) can then be inverted by the method of partial fractions to yield a solution of the form (5.32).

The methods just described can be used whether or not there are absorbing states in the system. If there are absorbing states then the coefficients c_{i1} of (5.32) will be zero for all transient states [see II, §19.7].

If we move on to consider open systems the mathematical complications are relatively slight. The continuous analogue of (5.16) is

$$\frac{d\bar{\mathbf{n}}(T)}{dT} = \bar{\mathbf{n}}(T)\mathbf{R} + R(T)\mathbf{r}. \tag{5.34}$$

This may be solved to give

$$\bar{n}_j(T) = \sum_{i=1}^{k} \left\{ r_i \int_0^T p_{ij}(T - x)R(x)\,dx + n_i(0)p_{ij}(T) \right\}$$
$$(j = 1, 2, \ldots, k + 1) \tag{5.35}$$

where the $p_{ij}(T)$'s are obtained by solving (5.28) and the case $j = k + 1$ covers those who have left the system.

If the total size is fixed then

$$R(T) = M(T) + \frac{d}{dT}\mathbf{n}(T)\mathbf{r}'_{k+1} \tag{5.36}$$

where $\mathbf{r}_{k+1}$ is the set of loss rates and $M(T)\,\delta T$ is the change in size which occurs between T and $T + \delta T$. The solution in this case is

$$\bar{n}_j(T) = \sum_{i=1}^{k} r_i \left\{ \int_0^T p_{ij}(T - x)M(x)\,dx + \int_0^T p_{ij}(T - x)\frac{d}{dx}\mathbf{n}(x)\mathbf{r}'_{k+1}\,dx \right\}$$
$$(j = 1, 2, \ldots, k + 1). \tag{5.37}$$

The difference between (5.35) and (5.37) is that the latter contains all of the $\bar{n}_j(T)$'s. However, it is shown in Bartholomew (1973) that the system (5.37) can be solved using Laplace transforms. In addition to the result about the Laplace transform of a derivative quoted above this also requires the fact that if

$$h(T) = \int_0^T f(T - x)g(x)\,dx$$

then

$$h^*(s) = f^*(s)g^*(s).$$

The embedding problem

There is an interesting mathematical problem concerning discrete and continuous Markov chains having practical implications which has been discussed in connection with social applications. This is the so-called embedding problem, and its practical relevance may be illustrated as follows. Suppose that a continuous social process involving transitions between states is observed at annual intervals and that this system is modelled by a discrete Markov chain using a year as the time unit. Since the choice of this unit is likely to be an arbitrary one we would clearly be unhappy if the analysis turned out to depend on it in a crucial way. In particular, if the interval had been six months we would want the square of the six-monthly transition matrix to be equal to the annual one. Conversely, for any annual matrix we would want there to be a six-montly matrix which, when squared, gives the annual matrix. In other words, we would expect our **P** to have a square root and, by an extension of the argument, a root of any order. Only if this is so shall we obtain consistent results whatever time interval is chosen. For this to be the case it is sufficient that **P** can be expressed in the form

$$\mathbf{P} = e^{\mathbf{R}T} \tag{5.38}$$

where T is the time interval and **R** is a transition intensity matrix—in other words the underlying process must be a continuous time Markov process. This problem has been discussed in a social context by Singer and Spilerman (1975).

In practice the problem is a little more complicated because we do not know **P** for any interval but will have to rely on an estimate, $\hat{\mathbf{P}}$ say. Thus it can easily happen that $\hat{\mathbf{P}}$ is not embedable even though **P** is, and conversely.

5.8 Statistical Problems of Implementation

The mainproblem of implementing Markov models is that of estimating the parameters. This is a straightforward process if complete data on stocks and flows are available. The method of maximum likelihood [see VI, Chapter 6] leads to the obvious estimators based on proportions for the discrete time model and flow rates for the continuous case (see, for example, Hoem, 1976). The mathematics involved is a straightforward maximization of simple functions of several variables.

If the data are incomplete there are special problems which, although not peculiar to the social sciences, have received most attention from economists and psychologists. The commonest situation is where stock data only are available for estimating the transition probabilities of a discrete time Markov model. This problem seems to have first arisen in psychology but the main extended treatment of the subject is by economists in Lee, Judge and Zellner (1970). Suppose that we have available a sequence of stocks, $\mathbf{n}(T)$, for k years ($T = 0, 1, 2, \ldots, k - 1$). The problem is to estimate **P**, the transition matrix of the Markov chain which it is assumed has generated the data. The idea behind all the methods is to choose that **P** which, in some sense, comes nearest to predicting the observed sequence. This is done by constructing some measure of the discrepancy between the observed set of stocks and those which would be predicted by

P and then minimizing it with respect to the elements of **P**. The minimization should clearly be carried out subject to the constraints that the row sums of **P** are unity and that all the elements of **P** are non-negative [see I, §7.11]. If the measure of closeness is quadratic, the problem can be solved by the techniques of quadratic programming [see IV, Chapter 15]. It may be formulated as:

$$\text{minimize } S = \sum_{T=1}^{k-1} \| \mathbf{n}(T) - \mathbf{n}(T-1)\mathbf{P} \|$$
$$\text{w.r.t. } \mathbf{P}$$

subject to   (5.39)

$$\mathbf{P1'} = 1 \quad \text{and} \quad \mathbf{P} \geq 0,$$

where $\| \cdot \|$ denotes the square of the Euclidean distance [see IV, §11.1].

The success of the method in practice depends on the nature of the function S. The maximum is likely to occur for a **P** with a large number of zeros which might well be implausible on practical grounds. On the other hand if it is known *a priori* which elements are zero then the minimization of (5.39) may be greatly simplified.

5.9 Renewal Theory Models [see II, Chapter 21]

Renewal theory appears to have originated in the study of the age structure of human populations, but it received the major impetus for its modern development in the study of industrial replacement. More recently, however, the theory has been used for investigating wastage in firms and some aspects of social mobility.

In its simplest terms the theory is concerned with processes having the following elements. There is a collection of N items whose lengths of life are independent random variables with a common distribution. As soon as an item fails it is immediately replaced by a similar item, thus keeping the total size fixed. The theory is concerned with finding the stochastic properties of such systems, in particular with the rate of flow of new items into the system and with the age structure. If a group of individuals employed have lengths of completed service which can be described by the same distribution and if the size of the group is fixed, then recruitment, wastage and the seniority structure can be studied using renewal theory. Examples designed to show how crude wastage rates depend on the age of the system are given in Bartholomew (1973). Similar applications arise in situations where there is a fixed capacity of some kind and an unlimited demand on the part of individuals to fill the places. For example, exclusive clubs and societies with limited membership and hospital wards with a fixed number of beds can, under suitable conditions, be regarded in this way.

The kind of mathematics which arises depends to some extent on whether systems are modelled in discrete or continuous time. In the former case the matter can be handled using the theory of Markov chains by the device of defining the states in terms of 'life' or length of service (see, for example, Bartholomew, 1971). We shall therefore concentrate here on the continuous time case in which most of the theory turns on the solution of an integral equation.

Let us consider a system of N individuals whose lifetimes are independent and have the same distribution with density $f(t)$. It turns out that most of the properties of such a system can be expressed in terms of the *renewal function*, $H(T)$, which is the expected number of replacements in $(0, T)$ per place in the system. The derivative of $H(T)$, denoted by $h(T)$, is called the renewal density, and may be thought of as the rate of replacement at time T. Texts on renewal theory (e.g. Cox, 1962) show that $h(T)$ satisfies the following integral equation

$$h(T) = d(T) + \int_0^T h(T - t)f(t) \, dt \tag{5.40}$$

where $d(T)$ is the density of the distribution of time to failure of members of the initial population. (This will be $f(t)$ if all individuals are 'new' at time zero but it can describe any other initial distribution.) The equation (5.40) can be solved numerically by approximating it by a difference equation, but the main practical tool for studying the solution of (5.40) is the Laplace transform [see IV, (13.1.3)]. Using the same notation for the Laplace transform as in Section 5.7, (5.40) becomes

$$h^*(s) = d^*(s) + h^*(s)f^*(s)$$

from which

$$h^*(s) = d^*(s)/\{1 - f^*(s)\}. \tag{5.41}$$

To complete the solution this equation must be inverted. There is a general inversion formula [see IV, §13.4.2] already encountered in (2.28) and tables of commonly occurring transforms are available. If the right-hand side of (5.41) is a rational algebraic fraction (i.e. ratio of two polynomials in s [see I, §14.9]) the inversion can always be effected by first resolving into partial fractions [see I, §14.10]. Typically, $h^*(s)$ will then have the form

$$h^*(s) = \sum_i \frac{a_i}{b_i + s}$$

which may be inverted term by term to give

$$h(T) = \sum_i a_i e^{-b_i T}. \tag{5.42}$$

Some information about the behaviour of $h(T)$ can be deduced without inverting the transform. The most important aspect concerns the limiting behaviour of $h(T)$ as $T \to \infty$. In the theory of Laplace transforms there are what are known as Tauberian theorems which show, for example, that under appropriate conditions

$$\lim_{T \to \infty} h(T) = \lim_{s \to 0} s h^*(s).$$

By this means it can be shown that $\lim h(T) = \mu^{-1}$ where μ is the average lifetime (and hence that one b_i in (5.42) must be zero).

The age distribution of the members of a renewal system is of particular interest in social science applications, but this follows at once from a knowledge of the renewal density. Similarly the variance of the number of renewals and the asymptotic form of its distribution depend for their derivation on the same mathematical techniques.

In the study of human organizations we often find several renewal systems linked together. A simple example is the grade hierarchy in a firm where vacancies at one level are filled by promotion from elsewhere or by direct recruitment. Another example is the kind of system which gives rise to the vacancy chain models of Section 5.6 where incumbencies were divided up into groups. If instead of studying the flow of vacancies we look at the flow of people then we have a multi-stage renewal system. At first sight this may appear to be very similar to the situation discussed in connection with open Markov models for graded systems, but the distinction lies in the fact that here the grade sizes are fixed and movements can only take place to fill vacancies when they arise. Renewal models for the flows of people in multistage renewal models have been discussed in Bartholomew (1963, 1973). Although the mathematical methods used for such models are rather more complicated than those we have mentioned for single systems the solution of integral equations by means of Laplace transforms remains the central technique. In many applications the restraints which have to be imposed on the models destroy their mathematical simplicity and one has to resort to the use of computer algorithms.

5.10 Autoregressive and Simultaneous Equation Models

In all of the models discussed thus far we have been concerned with the movement of individuals among a set of categories. In some of the examples mentioned the categories were formed by grouping a continuous underlying variable, such as income, but no use of this fact was made in the subsequent analysis. There are many applications where it is more natural to work with a continuous state space [see II, Chapter 18] instead of a set of categories. Most of these arise in economics and are thus outside the scope of this book, but some social applications have been made and we therefore give a brief outline of the subject to show what kind of mathematics is involved. Full accounts will be found in the literature of time series and econometrics.

At time T the state of the system will be denoted by x_T. This might be a person's income, the output of a factory, the demand for a social service or any other social variable changing in a random manner in time. The main object is to study the way in which the value of x changes as time passes just as in the earlier part of the chapter we were interested in movement among categories. An obvious kind of model to use is one in which x_T is regarded as composed of a component depending on time and a random error, thus

$$x_T = f(T) + e_T. \tag{5.43}$$

Such models can be handled by the techniques of regression analysis (Chapter 4). If the x's are subject to a trend, $f(T)$ might be a linear or exponential function of T; cyclical effects can be accommodated by including harmonic terms.

An alternative approach is to suppose that future members of the series depend on the present and the past. Such models are called autoregressive models [see VI, §18.8] because they express each member of the sequence as a function of its predecessors and a random error. The direct analogue of the Markov chain is the first-order autoregressive model according to which the next value in the series depends on its predecessors only through the current value. The model is then

$$x_{T+1} = \alpha x_T + e_{T+1} \ (T = 0, 1, 2, \ldots) \tag{5.44}$$

the error terms $\{e_T\}$ being independently distributed with zero mean and variance σ_T^2. The parameter α represents the systematic part of the series and determines the shift in the value of x and e represents a random disturbance. The parameter α and the random variable e together play the same role as the rows in the transition matrix of the Markov chain in that they specify the mechanism of change. The stochastic element of the model enters through the assumptions made about the distribution of the errors. Often it is assumed that they are Normal with constant variance, but more complicated error structures are possible.

Equation (5.44) is a difference equation [see I, (14.2.25] which can be solved for x_T to give

$$x_T = \alpha^T x_0 + \sum_{i=0}^{T-1} \alpha^i e_{T-i}. \tag{5.45}$$

The stochastic behaviour of x_T can then be deduced from the fact that it is a linear combination of random variables with known distribution. The long-run behaviour of the series can also be studied by means of (5.45), and in this connection the magnitude of α is critical. If $|\alpha| > 1$ the x's will tend to grow larger and larger (alternating in sign if $\alpha < 0$) whereas if $|\alpha| < 1$ the first term on the right of (5.45) will tend to zero leaving x_T with expectation zero in the limit.

In order to fit the model to an observed series the method of least squares [see VI, Chapter 11] can be used to estimate α and the sampling distribution of the estimator can then be derived by expressing it as a function of the e_T's and using the mathematics of the distribution theory of linear functions.

The model may be generalized by allowing an x to depend on its two predecessors according to the linear model

$$x_{T+2} = \alpha x_{T+1} + \beta x_T + e_{T+2} \qquad (T = 0, 1, 2, \ldots). \tag{5.46}$$

Here again x_T can be expressed as a function of the errors by solving the difference equation (5.46). The solution depends on the roots of the auxiliary equation

$$\lambda^2 - \alpha\lambda - \beta = 0.$$

The kind of behaviour of x_T, especially in the long run, depends on the roots of this equation—on their size, sign and whether they are real or complex.

More x's can be introduced into the equation so increasing the order of the difference equation to be solved and the complexity of the associated distribution theory.

In many practical situations, especially those arising in economics, there will be several series and members of one series may well be related to those in another. Thus with two series $\{x_T\}$ and $\{y_T\}$ we might postulate equations involving both x and y such as the following:

$$x_{T+2} = \alpha x_{T+1} + \beta y_{T+1} + \gamma x_T + e_{T+2}. \tag{5.47}$$

A typical model might therefore consist of a set of linear simultaneous equations in the values of the various series at different time points and including a variety of random errors. Mathematical methods are called for at two stages of the analysis of such models. The first is in trying to deduce the stochastic behaviour of the individual series and the second is on the inferential side in fitting the model and judging its goodness of fit. An important question which arises here is that of identifiability, which has to do with whether the model is specified in such a way that all of its parameters can be estimated. The methods involved lean heavily on the techniques of linear algebra and least squares theory, but the subject is too large to be developed here in detail.

5.11 The Diffusion of News, Innovations and Rumours

The spread of infectious diseases in human and animal populations is a well-known phenomenon which has been extensively studied by epidemiologists. There is substantial mathematical literature on the subject, beginning with the pioneering study of Kermack and McKendrick (1927); convenient reviews of this work are contained in Dietz (1967) and Bailey (1975). Though less mathematical in its origins there has also been a parallel interest among social scientists in the spread of news, innovations and rumours in human populations. The empirical side of this work can be seen in early papers by Pemberton (1936), Ryan and Gross (1943), Dodd (1955) and Griliches (1957, 1960). Their work was mainly concerned with finding the growth curve of the number of 'knowers' or 'adopters' and in fitting logistic curves [see II, §11.10] to their data. More recently these two streams have merged to some extent: the methods of the mathematical theory of epidemics have been applied to social processes and this has stimulated new developments more appropriate to social applications. It is convenient to use the terminology of epidemiology and, in particular, to use the word 'epidemic' to apply to the spread of such things as rumours as well as diseases. The student who wishes to work in this area will have to consult the literature of epidemic theory where much of the basic methodology is to be found.

Coleman's *Introduction to Mathematical Sociology* (1964a) gives a discussion of the theory of social diffusion. A fuller and more theoretical account is contained in Chapters 9 and 10 of Bartholomew (1973) whose notation we follow here. A more recent paper by Mollison (1977a) deals with the theory of spatial diffusion and contains a substantial bibliography spanning a variety of fields of application. Papers on epidemic theory, in general, often appear in the *Journal of Applied Probability* or *Advances in Applied Probability* and those with particular relevance to social science in the *Journal of Mathematical Sociology*.

Many mathematical methods are involved, but two constantly recur. Some aspects of the stochastic aspects of an epidemic can be described by an absorbing Markov chain. Frequently, the state spaces are large and the transition matrices sparse, so that special techniques may be required, but a basic knowledge of the theory of such chains is indispensable. Secondly, the deterministic approximations to epidemic processes, which are widely used, involve the construction and solution of systems of differential equations, or partial differential equations in the case of spatial spread. The pure birth process [see II, §20.2] is the basis of the simple epidemic processes with which we begin and this also involves the theory of sums of non-identically distributed random variables. In the remainder of this section we shall aim to show how these parts of mathematics are called into play and what kind of equations have to be solved.

Simple epidemic processes are those in which there is no mechanism for the cessation of diffusion. Each person who is in possession of the information will continue to pass it on indefinitely. Provided that no part of the population is completely isolated, this means that the whole population will be informed and the theory is largely directed to charting the path by which this state is achieved. A general epidemic model, on the other hand, incorporates some elements which cause people to cease activity. In such cases we are interested additionally in whether the epidemic can establish itself and, if so, how much of the population will be affected.

Simple epidemic models

The most basic epidemic model is, essentially, a special case of the pure birth process. It assumes a closed population of N people (or farms, families, firms, etc.) into which the information is introduced by an outside source. It continues to spread within the population by person-to-person contact. The model is a set of assumptions about the stochastic nature of source/person and person/person contact and they may be expressed as follows.

(a) Pr{source contacts a given individual in $(T, T + \delta T)$} $= \alpha \delta T + o(\delta T)$
(b) Pr{any given pair communicate in $(T, T + \delta T)$} $= \beta\, \delta T + o(\delta T)$

$$\tag{5.48}$$

It is further assumed that (b) holds for all possible pairs at all times. The parameter α may be termed the intensity of transmission of the source and β the inter-personal intensity of contact. From these postulates it easily follows that, if n is the number of knowers at time T,

$$\Pr\{n \rightarrow n + 1 \quad \text{in} \quad (T, T + \delta T)\} = \lambda_n \delta T + o(\delta T) \tag{5.49}$$

where $\lambda_n = (N - n)(\alpha + \beta n)$. This defines a birth process with birth-rate λ_n when the number of knowers is n. One way of studying the growth of the epidemic is to find the probability distribution of the number of knowers at time T. The theory of the birth process provides a general formula for this purpose, though for our λ_n the result is very cumbersome. The mean value of n for each T can also be obtained and this provides an estimate of the growth curve.

An alternative way of deriving the same kind of information about the process is to study the distribution of the time taken for n people to hear, T_n say, as in Bartholomew (1973, Chapter 9). Let τ_i denote the time interval between receipt of the information by the $(i - 1)$th and ith persons then, clearly,

$$T_n = \sum_{i=1}^{n} \tau_i. \tag{5.50}$$

It follows from (5.49) that the τ_i have independent negative exponential distributions with parameters λ_{i-1} [see II, §11.2]. In principle, then we can find the distribution of T_n by standard methods of distribution theory. In particular, it is easy to obtain the moments or cumulants. For example,

$$E(T_n) = \sum_{i=1}^{n} E(\tau_i) = \sum_{i=1}^{n} \lambda_{i-1}^{-1}. \tag{5.51}$$

The calculation and approximation of this sum when $\lambda_n = (N - n)(\alpha + \beta n)$ requires the use of partial fractions and tables of the digamma function. The higher moments can be similarly represented as sums of powers of reciprocals which turn out to be polygamma functions. It is not true that the distribution of T_n tends to Normality with increasing n because the conditions of the Central Limit Theorem [see II, §11.4.2 and §17.3] do not apply in this case.

By such means it is possible to obtain a good idea of the expected growth of an epidemic proceeding according to the very simple assumptions set out above. These are obviously highly simplified and a good deal of attention has been given to trying to relax them. The most vulnerable assumption is the one of homogeneous mixing which requires that all pairs of individuals are equally likely to make contact. In practice such probabilities will depend on their distance apart (social as well as geographical) and on their degree of mobility. Attempts have therefore been made to introduce 'distance bias' into the models. An extreme case is to suppose that $\beta = 0$, which means that there is no mixing at all and thus diffusion depends entirely on the source. The process then reduces to what is known as the pure death process for which it may easily be shown that the distribution of n at time T is binomial. Another natural step is to suppose that the population is divided into strata such that homogeneous mixing takes place within each stratum but that contact between members of different strata is more difficult. Coleman (1964a) provides a stochastic analysis of such a model for which the strata are of size 2 and there is no contact between strata. In this case the total picture is simply obtained by aggregating the separate results for each stratum. The more general case where there is contact between strata is much more difficult to handle, but progress is easier if we make a deterministic approximation to the stochastic process.

Deterministic approximations

In the simple epidemic model we saw that the probability that the number of knowers will increase by one in $(T, T + \delta T)$ given that its present value is n is $\lambda_n \delta T$. Since δT is infinitesimally small the chance of more than one event in $(T, T + \delta T)$ is negligible so $\lambda_n \delta T$ may also be interpreted as the expected number of new hearers in that interval. The deterministic approximation consists in assuming that n increases by exactly that amount. To do this we introduce a continuous function $n(T)$ to denote the number of knowers at T. Our assumption about growth then implies that

$$n(T + \delta T) = n(T) + \{N - n(T)\}\{\alpha + \beta n(T)\}\, \delta T$$

which as $\delta T \to 0$ gives

$$\frac{\mathrm{d}n}{\mathrm{d}T} = (N - n)(\alpha + \beta n), \tag{5.52}$$

with initial condition $n(0) = 0$. This equation may be integrated in the standard way to give $n(T)$ as a logistic growth function as shown, for example, in Bailey (1975) and Bartholomew (1973). The same kind of approach can be used in more complicated situations as, for example, when the population is stratified.

Let us suppose that there are k strata and that the 'within stratum' contact rate for the ith stratum is β_i. Let γ_{ij} be the inter-stratum contact rate between strata i and j. Then a straightforward extension of the argument leading to (5.52) gives

$$\frac{dn_i}{dT} = (N_i - n_i)(\alpha + \beta n_i) + (N_i - n_i)\sum_{j \neq i} \gamma_{ij} n_i \quad (i = 1, 2, \ldots, k) \quad (5.53)$$

where N_i is the size of stratum i. These equations were first formulated by Rushton and Mautner (1955) who made some progress with their solution. There is now no difficulty in solving the equations numerically using appropriate computer programs. In one very special case when $\beta_i = \beta$ and $\gamma_{ij} = \gamma$ for all i and j the set may be reduced to a single equation having the form of (5.52) (but with a different β) as shown in Bartholomew (1973, Chapter 9).

The numerical solution of differential equations usually involves replacing them by difference equations which are then solved recursively. There may be some situations in which the process itself may be defined in discrete time in which case the derivatives in equations such as (5.52) and (5.53) become first differences. Some possibilities in this direction have been explored by Gray and van Broembsen (1974) and Gani (1978). The last-named author pays particular attention to the simple epidemic process.

The total number of knowers is not the only feature of the epidemic process which is of interest. For example, in the case of such things as rumours it is useful to know the generation distribution. This is concerned with whether the recipient receives the information first hand from the source or second hand from a first hand hearer and so on. A knower belongs to the gth generation of hearers if he first hears the information from a member of the $(g - 1)$th generation. In the case of rumours, which are notoriously liable to distortion as they pass from mouth to mouth, it is of considerable interest to find out what the distribution of knowers by generation is.

A partial solution can be obtained to this problem in the case of the simple epidemic. This tells us what the generation distribution will be when diffusion has ceased; this will usually be the feature of greatest interest. The method exploits the existence of an embedded absorbing Markov chain. Full details of the method are given in Bartholomew (1973, Chapter 9) but the essence of the method is to define a Markov chain with state space [see II, §18.0] consisting of all possible generation distributions. All those distributions with frequencies adding to N will be absorbing states because when everyone knows no further transitions are possible. Each new contact adds one member to the generation with number one greater than that of the person making contact and the probability of such a distribution depends only on the current generation distribution. The number of states is enormous except with very small populations, but the calculation of such things as the mean values of the generation numbers is facilitated by the introduction of probability generating functions. These yield, for example, a recurrence formula [see I, §14.13] for the expected generation sizes as follows:

$$E_N(n_g) = E_{N-1}(n_g) + E_{N-1}(n_{g-1})(N - 1 + \alpha/\beta)$$

$$(g = 2, 3, \ldots, N). \quad (5.54)$$

where the subscript on E denotes the population size. Starting with $E_1(n_1) = 1$ the complete set of expectations can be built up on a computer.

The generation distribution at any stage of the epidemic can be found approximately by using the deterministic approximation as shown by Daley (1967). The system of equations is

$$\left. \begin{aligned} \frac{dn_1}{dT} &= \alpha m \\[2mm] \frac{dn_g}{dT} &= \beta n_{g-1} m \qquad (g = 2, 3, \ldots, N) \\[2mm] \frac{dm}{dT} &= -\alpha m - \beta\{N - m\}m \end{aligned} \right\} . \qquad (5.55)$$

The equations can be solved in a straightforward manner by obtaining $m(T)$ from the last member [see IV, §7.2] and then solving the others, in order, starting with $g = 1$.

Simple epidemics in space

The incorporation of a spatial dimension into a diffusion model is especially necessary in many applications to the social sciences. However, even in the case of a simple epidemic situation the mathematics is liable to become very intractable. Two main approaches to the problem have been made. One is to adopt the stratified model interpreting the strata in spatial terms. Thus the strata become locations and the magnitudes of the γ's reflect the distance between the locations. This is an extremely flexible representation for which methods of solution exist, although the number of equations in (5.53) may be unmanageably large. This kind of approach is likely to be most appropriate where the population consists of widely scattered groups with fairly large numbers of people at each location. Towns, universities, schools and the different branches of a firm would all be examples.

The second approach has been to treat the population through which the information spreads as uniformly distributed over a plane area (or, more simply, along a line). Models of this kind have been investigated by

Kendall (1957, 1965), Bartlett (1956) and, more recently, by Mollison (1972a, b, 1977a, b) and Daniels (1977). They have used simulation methods to study the stochastic aspects of the models, and mathematical analysis has been largely confined to the deterministic approximations. In these the essentially discrete nature of the human population is approximated by a continuous 'layer' of population with the required density. The aim is to find $y(s, T)$, the proportion of knowers at location s at time T. The probability of contact between a pair separated by a distance in $(u, u + \delta u)$ is assumed to be $v(u)\, \delta u$ and then, using arguments similar to those for the simple epidemic, it turns out that $y(s, T)$ satisfies the partial differential equation [c.f. IV, (8.1.1)]

$$\frac{\partial y}{\partial T} = \beta \sigma \bar{y}(1 - y) \tag{5.56}$$

where β is the rate of contact, σ the density of the population and, in the case of a linear population,

$$\bar{y}(s, T) = \int_{-\infty}^{+\infty} y(s - u, T)v(u)\, du.$$

The exact solution of this equation is not known, but it is possible to make some deductions about the nature of the solution. In particular, intuition suggests that if the information is introduced into the population at a particular location it might spread outwards in a wave at a constant velocity. This leads us to ask whether there is a solution of the form $y(s, T) = y(s - cT)$. This is known as a wave-form solution and the search for conditions for such a solution to exist has led to the investigation of differential equations such as;

$$\left.\begin{array}{l}
\beta \sigma K(1 - y)\dfrac{d^2 y}{dx^2} + c\,\dfrac{dy}{dx} + \beta \sigma y(1 - y) = 0 \\[1.5em]
\text{and} \\[1.5em]
K\dfrac{d^2 y}{dx^2} + \left(\dfrac{c}{\beta \sigma}\right)\dfrac{dy}{dx} + y = 0
\end{array}\right\} . \tag{5.57}$$

Unfortunately, the deterministic solutions often provide very poor approximations to the stochastic models.

General epidemic models

General epidemic models are characterized by the fact that spreaders may cease activity. This raises the possibility that an epidemic may die out in its very early stages or, if not, that it will not have reached all members of the population before it dies out. Various models have been proposed but the two principal ones draw on similar mathematical techniques. We shall therefore concentrate on the first general epidemic model introduced in its determininistic form by Kermack and McKendrick (1927) and then mention some of the variations more briefly.

Kermack and McKendrick's model is the same as the pure birth model except that it incorporates an additional assumption about the cessation of activity. In particular it assumes that

$$\Pr\{\text{active spreader ceases in } (T, T + \delta T)\} = \mu\,\delta T + o(\delta T)$$

which implies that the duration of an active spell has a negative exponential distribution with mean μ^{-1}. Once a spreader has ceased activity he cannot be re-activated, though in an alternative model (Bartholomew, 1976b) a spreader who has ceased activity returns to the pool of ignorants. In that case the model is a special case of the birth and death process.

At any time the state of the population can be described by three variables

$m(T)$:   the number of ignorants
$n(T)$:   the number of active spreaders
$l(T)$:   the number of knowers who have ceased activity.

Since $m(T) + n(T) + l(T) = N$ only two of these quantities are needed to specify the state of the system.

A full stochastic treatment is difficult since it requires us to find, for example, the joint probability $P_{m,n}(T) = \Pr\{m(T) = m,\ n(T) = n\}$, say. When a system is in the state (m, n) it can make one of the following two transitions:

$(m, n) \to (m - 1, n + 1)$ with probability $m(\alpha + \beta n)\,\delta T$
$(m, n) \to (m, n - 1)$ with probability $n\mu\delta T$.

It is possible to set up a system of bivariate differential-difference equations which can be solved, in principle at least, by the use of generating functions (see Gani, 1965, and Siskind, 1965). A partial solution can be found by concentrating on the terminal behaviour which corresponds to the state of the system when n becomes zero. This is another example of the use of an embedded Markov chain (or random walk [see II, §18.3]) over the states consisting of all pairs (m, n) satisfying $m, n \geq 0$ and $m + n \leq N$. The absorbing states are those of the form $(m, 0)$ and the probabilities of absorption give the probability distribution of the terminal number of ignorants. The transition probabilities from (m, n) depend only on m and n so the system has the Markov property. Recurrence equations can easily be set up for the state probabilities as shown in Bartholomew (1973, Chapter 10) and they can be solved numerically to give the absorption probabilities.

Adopting the deterministic approximation the differential equations for

$m(T)$, $n(T)$ and $l(T)$ are

$$\frac{dn}{dT} = m\alpha + mn\beta - n\mu$$

$$\frac{dm}{dT} = -m\alpha - mn\beta \qquad\qquad (5.58)$$

$$\frac{dl}{dT} = \mu n$$

with initial conditions $m(0) = N$, $n(0) = 0$, $l(0) = 0$ [see IV, §7.2]. The model is often studied in a version where there is no source ($\alpha = 0$). In this case we cannot have $n(0) = 0$ or the diffusion will not start and so $n(0)$ will have to be given some other non-zero, but possibly very small, value. Dividing the second equation in (5.58) by the third we have, when $\alpha = 0$,

$$\frac{dm}{dl} = -\frac{\beta}{\mu} m \qquad\qquad (5.59)$$

which can be solved to give

$$m = N \exp\left(-\frac{\beta}{\mu} l\right). \qquad\qquad (5.60)$$

Using this equation and $m + n + l = N$, n can be eliminated from the second equation of (5.58) to give

$$-\frac{dm}{dT} = \beta m \{N - m + \mu m \ln(m/N)\} \qquad\qquad (5.61)$$

which can easily be solved by numerical integration [see III, Chapter 7]. Equation (5.60) can also be used to determine the terminal state of the system. Since it always holds, it holds in particular, when $n = 0$ in which case $l = N - m$. Hence at the end of the diffusion the terminal value of m satisfies

$$m = N \exp\left\{-\frac{\beta}{\mu}(N - m)\right\}. \qquad\qquad (5.62)$$

Systems of differential equations can also be constructed for the generation distribution in the same manner as those of the pure birth model of (5.55). The main change is the addition of the term $-\mu n_g(T)$ to the second member of (5.55) giving

$$\frac{dn_g(T)}{dT} = \beta m n_{g-1} - \mu n_g \qquad (g = 1, 2, \ldots).$$

On substituting $w_g(T) = e^{\mu T} n_g(T)$ this becomes

$$\frac{dw_g}{dT} = \beta m w_{g-1} \qquad (g = 1, 2, \ldots)$$

which has the same form as the earlier set and can be solved in a similar fashion (see Bartholomew, 1973, Chapter 10).

In a similar way the extension to spatial diffusion using the deterministic approximation for a uniformly spread population yields the partial differential equations

$$\frac{\partial x}{\partial T} = -\beta \sigma x \bar{y}$$

$$\frac{\partial y}{\partial T} = \beta \sigma x \bar{y} - \mu y \qquad (5.63)$$

$$\frac{\partial z}{\partial T} = \mu y.$$

Some partial results can be obtained from these equations, but nothing approaching a full solution is possible.

Daley and Kendall (1965) proposed an alternative model specifically designed for the spread of rumours. The distinguishing feature of their model is that cessation of activity is caused by what they term 'stifling'. In the simplest version this means that whenever a spreader meets another spreader each forms the opinion that 'everyone knows' and both cease activity; similarly if a spreader meets a former spreader the active member is stifled. In such a model three transitions are possible from the state (m, n) as follows:

$(m, n) \rightarrow (m - 1, n + 1)$, when a spreader meets an ignorant

$(m, n) \rightarrow (m, n - 1)$, when a spreader meets a stifler

$(m, n) \rightarrow (m, n - 2)$, when two spreaders meet.

The analysis of this model proceeds in the same way as with Kermack and McKendrick's model using the same mathematical techniques. The generation distribution and the spatial aspects have not been investigated but should present no difficulty of principle. There are some important qualitative differences in the results obtained by the two models and this is of considerable practical interest. The simple version of the model described here can be generalized in various ways but the mathematical methods involved are similar.

The third kind of general epidemic model is due to Rapoport (e.g. Rapoport 1953a, b; Rapoport and Rebhun, 1952) and others and it arose originally in the theory of the random net as a model for neurological networks. In its simplest version, each spreader passes the information on to exactly d other people chosen at random from the rest of the population. This is in line with the usual assumption of homogeneous mixing but is somewhat weaker in that it treats time only in an ordinal fashion. For this reason it is not possible to work with variables such as $n(T)$ and $m(T)$ but the model lends itself naturally to the determination of the ultimate generation distribution. The initial spreader(s) tells d people who constitute the first generation. Each member of the first generation tells d people of whom those not already in the first generation become the second generation, and so on. The theory of such a process is essentially combinatorial and what we have described is another version of the classical occupancy problem of assigning balls to boxes (see, for example, Barton and David, 1962). Thus if there are n_g people in the gth generation there are $n_g d$ contacts to be made and these will be distributed at random among the N members of the population. Those contacts with ignorants ('empty boxes') make up the $(g + 1)$th generation. The standard theory gives

$$\Pr\{n_{g+1} = i \mid n_g, n_{g-1}, \ldots, n_1\} = \binom{n - N_g}{i} \sum_{j=0}^{i} (-1)^j \binom{i}{j} \left(\frac{i - j + N_g - 1}{N - 1}\right)^{n_g d}$$

$$(i = 0, 1, \ldots, \min(n_g d, N - N_g)) \qquad (5.64)$$

where $N_g = \sum_{i=1}^{g} n_i$. Since the above probability depends on $n_1, n_2, \ldots, n_g$ only through n_g and N_g, we can develop the theory of the process as an absorbing Markov chain defined on the set of states consisting of all pairs (n_g, N_g) as shown in Bartholomew (1973, Chapter 10). The absorbing states are those having the form $(0, N_g)$. This Markov chain has a very large state space ($\frac{1}{2}N(N + 3)$ states) and is therefore difficult to handle unless N is very small. Rapoport devised deterministic methods for finding the expected generation numbers and the ultimate number of knowers using conditional probability arguments.

Several recent papers have made interesting suggestions for extending epidemic models or simplifying their analysis. Conlisk (1976, 1978) has shown that some epidemic models may be regarded as a special case of what he terms an interactive Markov chain. Faddy (1977) has proposed a method of approximating Kermack and McKendrick's model by a time-dependent Markov process and Wang (1977) has made some progress with a generalization of that model which allows, among other things, the duration of spreading to have an arbitrary distribution.

References

Bailey, N. T. J. (1975). *The Mathematical Theory of Infectious Diseases and its Applications*, Griffin, High Wycombe, Bucks.

Bartholomew, D. J. (1963). A multi-stage renewal process. *J. R. Statist. Soc.*, B, **25**, 150–168.

Bartholomew, D. J. (1971). The statistical approach to manpower planning. *Statistician*, **20**, 3–26.

Bartholomew, D. J. (1973). *Stochastic Models for Social Processes*, 2nd Ed. Wiley, Chichester. (1st ed. 1967.) (3rd ed. to appear, 1981)

Bartholomew, D. J. (1975). A stochastic control problem in the social sciences. *Bull. Int. Statist. Inst.*, **46**, 670–680.

Bartholomew, D. J. (1976a). *Manpower Planning*, Penguin Modern Management Readings, Harmondsworth, Middlesex.

Bartholomew, D. J. (1976b). Continuous time diffusion models with random duration of interest. *J. Math. Sociology*, **4**, 187–199.

Bartholomew, D. J. (1977). Maintaining a grade or age structure in a stochastic environment, *Adv. App. Prob.*, **9**, 1–17.

Bartholomew, D. J. (1979). The control of a grade structure in a stochastic environment using promotion control. *Adv. App. Prob.*, **11**, 603–615.

Bartholomew, D. J., and Forbes, A. F. (1979). *Statistical Techniques of Manpower Planning*, Wiley, Chichester.

Bartlett, M. S. (1955). *An Introduction to Stochastic Processes*, Cambridge University Press, London.

Bartlett, M. S. (1956). Deterministic and stochastic models for recurrent epidemics. *Proc. Third. Berkeley Symposium Math. Statist. Prob.*, **4**, 81–109.

Barton, D. E., and David, F. N. (1962). *Combinatorial Chance*, Griffin, High Wycombe, Bucks.

Bhat, U. N. (1972). *Elements of Applied Stochastic Processes*, Wiley, New York.

Bharucha-Reid, A. T. (1960). *Elements of the Theory of Markov Processes and their Applications*, McGraw-Hill, New York.

Bibby, J. (1975). Methods of measuring mobility. *Quality and Quantity*, **9**, 107–136.

Charnes, A., Cooper, W. W., and Niehaus, R. J. (1968). A goal programming model for manpower planning. In J. Blood (Ed.), *Management Science in Planning and Control*, Technical Association of the Pulp and Paper Industry, New York. (Reproduced in Bartholomew, 1976a.)

Charnes, A., Cooper, W. W., and Niehaus, R. J. (1972). *Studies in Manpower Planning*, Office of Civilian Manpower Management, Dept of the Navy, Washington D.C.

Coale, A. J. (1972). *The Growth and Structure of Human Populations: A Mathematical Investigation*, Princeton University Press, Princeton, N. J.

Cohen, B. P., and Lee, H. (1975). *Conflict, Conformity and Social Status*, Elsevier, Amsterdam.

Coleman, J. S. (1964a). *Introduction to Mathematical Sociology*, The Free Press of Glencoe, New York, and Collier-Macmillan, London.

Coleman, J. S. (1964b). *Models of Change and Response Uncertainty*, Prentice-Hall, Englewood Cliffs, New Jersey.

Conlisk, J. (1976). Interactive Markov chains. *J. Math. Sociology*, **4**, 157–185.

Conlisk, J. (1978). A stability theorem for an interactive Markov chain. *J. Math. Sociology*, **6**, 163–168.

Cox, D. R. (1962). *Renewal Theory*, Methuen, London.

Cox, D. R., and Miller, H. D. (1965). *The Theory of Stochastic Processes*, Methuen, London.

Daley, D. J. (1967). Concerning the spread of news in a population of individuals who never forget. *Bull. Math. Biophysics*, **29**, 373–376.

Daley, D. J., and Kendall, D. G. (1965). Stochastic rumours. *J. Inst. Math. Applns.*, **1**, 45–55.

Daniels, H. E. (1977). The advancing wave of a spatial birth process. *J. Appl. Prob.*, **14**, 689–701.

Davies, G. S. (1973). Structural control in a graded manpower system. *Man. Sci.*, **20**, 76–84.

Davies, G. S. (1975). Maintainability of structures in Markov chain models under recruitment control. *J. Appl. Prob.*, **12**, 376–382.

Dietz, K. (1967). Epidemics and rumours: a survey. *J. R. Statist. Soc.*, A, **130**, 505–528.

Dodd, S. C. (1955). Diffusion is predictable: testing probability models for laws of interaction. *Amer. Sociol. Rev.*, **20**, 392–401.

Doreian, P., and Humman, N. P. (1976). *Modelling Social Processes*, Elsevier, New York.

Faddy, M. J. (1977). Stochastic compartmental models as approximations to more general stochastic systems with the general stochastic epidemic as an example. *Adv. App. Prob.*, **9**, 448–461.

Feichtinger, G. (1971). *Stochastische Modelle Demographischer Prozesse*, Springer-Verlag, Berlin.

Feichtinger, G. (1976). On the generalization of stable age distributions to Gani-type person-flow models. *Adv. App. Prob.*, **8**, 433–445.

Feller, W. (1966). *An Introduction to Probability Theory and Its Applications*, Vol. II, Wiley, New York.

Feller, W. (1968). *An Introduction to Probability Theory and Its Applications*, Vol. I, 3rd ed. Wiley, New York.

Gani, J. (1965). On a partial differential equation of epidemic theory: I, *Biometrika*, **52**, 617–622.

Gani, J. (1978). Some problems of epidemic theory, *J.R. Statist. Soc.*, A, **141**, 323–347.

Gray, L. N., and van Broembsen, M. H. (1974). On simple stochastic diffusion models. *J. Math. Sociology*, **3**, 231–244.

Griliches, Z. (1957). Hybrid corn: an exploration in the economics of technical change. *Econometrics*, **25**, 501–522.

Griliches, Z. (1960). Hybrid corn and the economics of innovation. *Science*, **132**, 275–280.

Grinold, R. C., and Marshall, K. T. (1977). *Manpower Planning Models*, North-Holland, New York and Amsterdam.

Grinold, R. C., and Stanford, R. E. (1974). Optimal control of a graded manpower system. *Man. Sci.*, **20**, 1201–1216.

Herbst, P. G. (1963). Organizational commitment: a decision model. *Acta Sociologica*, **7**, 34–45.

Hirsch, M. W., and Smale, S. (1974). *Differential Equations, Dynamical Systems and Linear Algebra*, Academic Press, New York.

Hoem, J. M. (1976). The statistical theory of demographic rates: A review of current developments. *Skandinavian J. Statistics*, **3**, 169–178.

Howard, R. A. (1971). *Dynamic Probabilistic Systems* (2 vols), Wiley, New York.

Isaacson, D. L., and Madsen, R. W. (1976). *Markov Chains*, Wiley, New York.

Kaplinskii, A. I., and Propoi, A. I. (1970). Stochastic approach to non-linear programming problems. *Automation and Remote Control*, **3**, 448–459.

Kaplinskii, A. I., and Propoi, A. I. (1972). Randomization in problems of stochastic control. *Automation and Remote Control*, **12**, 1983–1991.

Karlin, S., and Taylor, H. (1975). *A First Course in Stochastic Processes*, Academic Press, New York.

Kemeny, J. G. and Snell, L. (1962). *Mathematical Models in the Social Sciences*, Ginn, Boston.

Kemeny, J. G., and Snell, L. (1976). *Finite Markov Chains*, Springer-Verlag, Berlin.

Kendall, D. G. (1957). La propagation d'une épidémie au d'un bruit une population limitée. *Publ. de L'Inst de Statistique de l'Université de Paris*, **6**, 307–311.

Kendall, D. G. (1965). Mathematical models in the spread of infection. In *Mathematics and Computer Science in Biology and Medicine*, H.M.S.O., London.

Kermack, W. O., and McKendrick, A. G. (1927). Contributions to the mathematical theory of epidemics. *Proc. Roy. Soc.*, A, **115**, 700–721.

Keyfitz, N. (1968). *Introduction to the Mathematics of Population*, Addison-Wesley, Reading, Mass.

Lee, T. C., Judge, G. C., and Zellner, A. (1970). *Estimating the Parameters of the Markov Probability Model from Aggregate Time Data*, North-Holland, New York and Amsterdam.

Massy, W. F., Montgomery, D. B., and Morrison, D. G. (1970). *Stochastic Models of Buying Behaviour*, M.I.T. Press, Cambridge, Mass.

Mehlman, A. (1977). A note on the limiting behaviour of discrete-time Markovian manpower models with inhomogeneous independent Poisson input'. *J. App. Prob.*, **14**, 611–613.

Mollison, D. (1972a). Possible velocities for a simple epidemic. *Adv. Appl. Prob.*, **4**, 233–257.

Mollison, D. (1972b). The rate of spatial propagation of simple epidemics. *Proc. Sixth. Berkely Symp. Math. Statist. Prob.*, **3**, 579–614.

Mollison, D. (1977a). Spatial contact models for ecological and epidemic spread. *J. Roy. Statist. Soc.*, B, **39**, 283–326.

Mollison, D. (1977b). Markovian contact processes. *Adv. Appl. Prob.*, **10**, 85–108.

Moran, P. A. P. (1968). *An Introduction to Probability Theory*, Clarendon Press, Oxford.

Morgan, R. W. (1971). Manpower planning in the Royal Air Force: an exercise in linear programming. In A. R. Smith (Ed.), *Models of Manpower Systems*, English Universities Press, London.

Parzen, E. (1962). *Stochastic Processes*, Holden-Day, San Francisco.

Pemberton, H. E. (1936). The curve of culture diffusion rate. *Amer. Soc. Review*, **1**, 547–556.

Pollard, J. H. (1966). On the use of the direct matrix product in analysing certain stochastic population models, *Biometrika*, **53**, 397–415.

Pollard, J. H. (1973). *Mathematical Models for the Growth of Human Populations*, Cambridge University Press.

Prais, S. J. (1955). Measuring social mobility. *J. R. Statist. Soc.*, A, **118**, 56–66.

Pullum, T. W. (1975). *Measuring Occupational Inheritance*, Elsevier, New York.

Purkiss, C. J. (1974). *Manpower Planning: a Contribution of Concepts and Practice*, Ph.D. Thesis, University of Lancaster.

Purkiss, C. J., and Richardson, J. Z. (1971). Planning recruitment in the steel industry. In D. J. Bartholomew and B. R. Morris (Eds.), *Aspects of Manpower Planning*, English Universities Press, London, pp. 65–74.

Rapoport, A. (1953a). Spread of information through a population with socio-structural bias: I. Assumption of transitivity. *Bull. Math. Biophysics*, **15**, 523–533.

Rapoport, A. (1953b). Spread of information through a population with socio-structural bias: II. Various models with partial transitivity. *Bull. Math. Biophysics*, **15**, 535–546.

Rapoport, A., and Rehbun, L. I. (1952). On the mathematical theory of rumour spread. *Bull. Math. Biophysics.*, **14**, 375–383.

Rushton, S., and Mautner, A. J. (1955). The deterministic model of a simple epidemic for more than one community. *Biometrika*, **42**, 126–132.

Ryan, B., and Gross, N. C. (1943). The diffusion of hybrid seed corn in two Iowa communities. *Rural Sociology*, **8**, 15–24.

Shorrocks, A. F. (1978). The measurement of mobility. *Econometrica*, **46**, 1013–1024.

Singer, B., and Spilerman, S. (1975). Identifying structural parameters of social processes using fragmentary data. *Bull. Int. Statist. Inst.*, **44**, 681–697.

Singer, B., and Spilerman, S. (1977). Trace inequalities for mixtures of Markov chains. *Adv. Appl. Prob.*, **9**, 747–764.

Siskind, V. (1965). A solution of the general stochastic epidemic. *Biometrika*, 613–616.

Spilerman, S. (1972). Extensions of the mover–stayer model. *Amer. J. Sociol.*, **78**, 599–626.

Stewman, S. (1975). An application of the job vacancy chain model to a Civil Service internal labour market. *J. Math. Soc.*, **4**, 37–59.

148

Thonstad, T. (1969). *Education and Manpower: Theoretical Models and Empirical Applications*, Oliver and Boyd, Edinburgh and London.

Vajda, S. (1975). Mathematical aspects of manpower planning. *Operat. Res. Quart.*, **26**, 527–542.

Vajda, S. (1978). *Mathematics of Manpower Planning*, Wiley, Chichester.

White, H. C. (1970). *Chains of Opportunity*, Harvard University Press, Cambridge, Mass.

Wang, F. J. S. (1977). Gaussian approximation of some closed stochastic epidemic models. *J. Appl. Prob.*, **14**, 221–231.

Young, A., and Almond, G. (1961). Predicting distributions of staff. *Comp. J.*, **3**, 246–250.

Index